TRANSGRESSIVE THEATRICALITY, ROMANTICISM, AND MARY WOLLSTONECRAFT

Transgressive Theatricality, Romanticism, and Mary Wollstonecraft

LISA PLUMMER CRAFTON

University of West Georgia, USA

LONDON AND NEW YORK

First published 2011 by Ashgate Publishing

Published 2016 by Routledge
2 Park Square, Milton Park, Abingdon, Oxon OX14 4RN
711 Third Avenue, New York, NY 10017, USA

Routledge is an imprint of the Taylor & Francis Group, an informa business

British Library Cataloguing in Publication Data
Crafton, Lisa Plummer, 1956–
Transgressive theatricality, Romanticism, and Mary Wollstonecraft.
  1. Wollstonecraft, Mary, 1759–1797 – Criticism and interpretation. 2. Wollstonecraft, Mary, 1759–1797 – Knowledge – Performing arts. 3. Literature and society – Great Britain – History – 18th century. 4. Literature and revolutions – Great Britain – History – 18th century. 5. Romanticism – Great Britain.
  I. Title
  823.7–dc22

Library of Congress Cataloging-in-Publication Data
Crafton, Lisa Plummer.
  Transgressive theatricality, romanticism, and Mary Wollstonecraft / by Lisa Plummer Crafton.
    p. cm.
  Includes index.
  1. Wollstonecraft, Mary, 1759–1797—Criticism and interpretation. 2. Theater and society—Great Britain—History—18th century. 3. Romanticism—England—History—18th century. 4. Performing arts in literature. 5. Theater in literature. 6. Siddons, Sarah, 1755–1831—Criticism and interpretation. I. Title.
  PR5841.W8Z585 2011
  828'.609—dc23

2011025663

ISBN 13: 978-0-7546-6788-9 (hbk)

Contents

List of Figures

Acknowledgments

My thanks to the University of West Georgia, which supported this project in the form of a Faculty Research Travel Grant, and to my wonderful colleagues in the Department of English. Specific thanks are due to Jimmy Worthy, my graduate research assistant, for assistance with research and editing, and to Carol Goodson for assistance with illustrations and copyright.

Finally, this book would not have been possible without the support of my family and friends, who listened patiently and encouraged constantly. My gratitude.

Introduction

While no one will mistake the moody, intelligent face of Bette Davis for Mary Wollstonecraft, the character of Margo Channing (whom Davis portrays in this book's cover illustration) in Joseph Mankiewicz's 1950 film *All About Eve* is, in fact, a good double for the Wollstonecraft that this study seeks to convey. Although it might not surprise anyone that Bette Davis adorns a book cover of a study about theatricality and transgression—nor even a book about Romanticism since recent scholarship has convincingly argued that the Romantic era witnessed the emergence of a recognizably modern celebrity culture—Wollstonecraft has rarely been featured as a central figure in critical debates about Romanticism and (anti)theatricality. The invisible mediating figure between Bette Davis and Wollstonecraft is the famous eighteenth-century actress Sarah Siddons, who features significantly in Mankiewicz's film. At least a *representation* of her appears in the film: the opening scene occurs at an awards ceremony where the Siddons Award (an equivalent of the Oscar) is being given out, and Sir Joshua Reynolds's famous painting of *Mrs. Siddons as the Tragic Muse* (Fig. I.1) looms visually over the final scene. Seven years after the film, Bette Davis participated in the Laguna Beach Festival of the Arts featuring a tableau-vivant of Reynolds's painting, thus figuring Sarah Siddons literally. It is Siddons then whose celebrity is indubitably tied to that of Davis through the lasting visual impression of Reynolds's painting. Siddons had an incredible theatrical afterlife, her performances tending to stay in the memories of audiences and affecting each new interpretation, as McPherson and others have argued.[1] In Chapter 5 I argue that Siddons's performance style, theories, and stage preparations offer a compelling new lens through which to view Wollstonecraft and theatricality, and, as played by Bette Davis, Margo Channing's explorations of the blurred lines between performed and personal identity enrich that discussion.

Godwin's Advertisement to *Maria, or The Wrongs of Woman* labels it a "performance," and Wollstonecraft, in that novel's Preface, juxtaposes her fiction to "what may justly be termed '*stage-effect*.'" No substantive critical studies have explored theatricality—as both a key historical and figurative site—in her works, which consistently interrogate the connected network of theater, culture, and self-representation. While feminist criticism, including my own, has overwhelmingly focused on Wollstonecraft's exposure and critique of the theatrical construction of gender roles, my argument is that a conscious appropriation of theater (in its literal,

---

[1]   Heather McPherson, "Siddons Rediviva: Death, Memory, and Theatrical Afterlife," in Mole, *Romanticism and Celebrity Culture*, 120–40. See Tom Mole's edited collection *Romanticism and Celebrity Culture, 1750–1850* (Cambridge: Cambridge University Press, 2009) and Martin Postle's *Joshua Reynolds: The Creation of Celebrity Culture* (London: Tate, 2005).

Fig. I.1   *The Tragic Muse*, 1783–1784, Joshua Reynolds. Courtesy of the
Huntington Art Collections, San Marino, California.

cultural, and figurative dimensions) figures prominently in all of Wollstonecraft's work.[2] Contributing to recent work on Romanticism and theater—especially Pascoe, Backscheider, Burroughs, Hadley, Bolton, and Carlson—I explore Wollstonecraft's appropriation of, immersion in, and contributions to debates about theatricality. Considering all of Wollstonecraft's many permutations of "self"—reviewer, translator, novelist, polemicist, correspondent, moral philosopher, lover, wife, and mother (a trajectory of roles that Barbara Taylor labels a "prissy moralist," a "bluntspoken philosophic radical," a "lyrical romantic," a "satirist, teacher, melancholy solitaire")—allows us to see competing notions of "theatrical."[3] Ultimately, I argue that Wollstonecraft's persistent use of the trope reveals theatricality's transgressive potential for self-invention, instead of simply its negative connotations with regard to gender roles and the display of state power, thus representing both the limitations of and inherent potential in "stage-effect." My study engages the contexts of five intersecting theoretical prisms which I discuss in Chapter 1—Romantic theatricality, the politicization of theater and the theatricalization of politics, theories of masquerade, theories of mimicry, and the divide between theater and performance critics.

Initially following the Oxford English Dictionary's three definitions of "theatrical," as does Judith Pascoe in *Romantic Theatricality*, I situate my interest in Wollstonecraft's texts as they intersect with the three dimensions of the term: 1) pertaining to the stage/theater; 2) representing in the manner of an actor; and 3) calculated for display, spectacular. Of the first denotation, "pertaining to the stage/theater," I argue the function of Wollstonecraft's explicit references to Shakespearean and contemporary plays (especially Rowe's *The Fair Penitent*, treated in Chapter 1), theaters, and actresses in the works. I focus specifically on Sarah Siddons, whom Hazlitt called "tragedy personified" and whom Backscheider astutely calls a "Foucauldian site for the representation of warring sexualities and powers."

Of the second meaning of "theatricality"—"representing in the manner of an actor"—I consider how the trope of theatricality functions in cultural commentary and in fictional frameworks to represent the performative nature of self-representation and subjectivity. I situate, in Chapter 1, my position on the polymorphously variable term "performative" by using Jonathon Culler on the distinction between Austin's and Butler's discussion of performative utterances, Catherine Burrough's helpful, succinct distinction between performances (on both theater and social stages) and performativity as a metaphor that interrogates the "ways that identities are

---

[2]   My earlier discussion of Wollstonecraft's attack on the hypocrisy of modesty in *A Vindication of the Rights of Woman* does not use the trope of theatricality but clearly foregrounds her exposure of gender roles as constructed and artificial; see "'Insipid Decency': Modesty and Female Sexuality in Wollstonecraft," *European Romantic Review* 31.1 (2000): 55–88.

[3]   Barbara Taylor, *Wollstonecraft and the Radical Imagination* (Cambridge: Cambridge University Press, 2002), 31.

constructed iteratively through complex citational processes" (17),[4] and Jill Dolan's thorough discussion of and disagreement with the legacy of Butler's theories in terms of their emphasis on the constraints on (as opposed to the potential for) human agency as a consequence of citational gender identity.

While Wollstonecraft does use the contextual/theoretical framework of the theater to indict what she calls, in *A Vindication of the Rights of Woman*, the "insipid decency" of her culture, whose definitions of sexual deviance are markedly gendered, my study exposes her exploration of the inherently subversive potential of theatricality, especially for women. As Litvak's study of theatricality in the nineteenth-century novel neatly articulates, critics have to be aware of the functionally ambiguous boundary line between "theatricality-as-conventionality" and "theatricality-as-subversion" (42). Extending this concern to the broader context of feminist performance theory and its appropriation of linguistic and philosophical theories of performativity, I argue that Wollstonecraft's appropriation of acting theory (deduced from notes, correspondence, and performances of Sarah Siddons) can be understood in terms of Luce Irigaray's philosophical model of female mimicry. Drawing attention to the theatricality of all systems, Irigaray, in *This Sex Which Is Not One*, urges consideration of "*the conditions under which systematicity is possible*" (75, original italics). Applying this premise to women's finding a place within philosophical disciplines, Irigaray suggests that mimicry may be the only option, but, significantly, that mimicry can be subversively affirmative: "One must assume the feminine role deliberately. Which means already to convert a form of subordination into an affirmation, and thus to begin to thwart it" (76). I argue that Wollstonecraft's persistent reflections on and manipulations of theatricality expose a similar thwarting of conventional sexual, social, and generic systems. A final scholarly context for discussion of this second definition of "theatrical" is current critical studies of masquerade, including the arguments of Terry Castle on masquerade's subversive potential, Craft-Fairchild on the inevitable objectification of woman as spectacle, and Hoeveler on the gothic heroine's deliberate masquerade of femininity as both subverting and reifying postures of complacency.

Of the third definition of the term, "calculated for display, showy," I focus on how Wollstonecraft engages the question of the moral utility of theater/spectacle, theater tropes used in French Revolutionary political discourse, theatricality in juridical discourses, and acting/theater theory as constructed in Siddons's notes and articles, contemporary reviews, and women playwright's "theater theory," to use Burroughs's phrase. Overall, the cohesive guiding question is whether theatricality *enables* or *subverts* various cultural mechanisms of power.

While no critic has offered a reading of Wollstonecraft and theatricality, Burroughs, whose work significantly offers a new domain for and redefinition of "theater theory," suggests briefly but persuasively that critical attention should

---

[4]   *Closet Stages: Joanna Baillie and the Theater Theory of British Romantic Women Writers* (Philadelphia: University of Pennsylvania Press, 1997).

be paid to Wollstonecraft, who she asserts must have drawn upon "theater history and her knowledge of late eighteenth-century stage for metaphors with which she could formulate her critical readings of women's cultural position" (19). Using Burroughs' broadening of theater theory to include "a variety of theoretical moments that occur in a wide range of texts and performance situations" (2), we see that for Wollstonecraft, theatricality is not simply a trope with which to represent "women's cultural position," but also the performative nature of all human self-representation as well as national and cultural identity formation.

While Chapter 1 offers the theoretical foundation for the intersecting premises outlined here, Chapter 2 examines both the intertextual relationship between Wollstonecraft's *Maria, or The Wrongs of Woman* and Nicolas Rowe's play *The Fair Penitent* and how the theater trope functions in the novel, suggesting ways in which notions of performativity direct individual, national, and cultural identity formation. Chapter 3 situates Wollstonecraft within two philosophical debates circulating in the late eighteenth century: the issue of the moral utility of public spectacle (including state pageantry, public executions, and public addresses) and the effects of sympathy, exploring Wollstonecraft's divided, often ambiguous conclusions on this issue as found in her *Thoughts on the Education of Daughters* and *Letters Written During A Short Residence*.

Chapter 4 uses the juridical contexts of both treason and divorce trials, the transcripts of which became wildly popular in the 1780s and 1790s as both amusement for spectators and as dramatic roles for attorneys and which mirror the culture's ambivalence toward theatricality. I consider the influence on Wollstonecraft of the treason trials, using Pascoe's analysis of them as a foundation, and then explore the influence of the published transcripts of the very popular civil divorce trials for adultery. Wollstonecraft's methodical representation of Maria's arrest by George, indictment for adultery with Darnford, and plea before a judge (in *Maria, or The Wrongs of Woman*) was, I argue, influenced by these transcripts. I further interrogate how Wollstonecraft's portrait of the suffering mother Maria intersects with the cultural legacy of Marie Antoinette's 1793 trial, particular her deployment of a maternal identity to bring a hostile crowd over to her side, thus creatively manipulating the most "authentic" of female roles. Further theorizing Wollstonecraft's manipulation of juridical discourse, I consider her representations of authoritative speech (judicial, legal, theological, and royal pronouncements) as binding performatives to be resisted and rewritten. Chapter 5 explores Wollstonecraft's immersion in French Revolutionary political discourse from her defense of Richard Price and rebuttal to Burke in her *A Vindication of the Rights of Men* (1790) to her little-known text *An Historical and Moral View of the French Revolution* (1794) in which she analyzes the false theatricality (both in drama and in the workings of the *ancien regime*), of the French king and queen (whom Wollstonecraft branded as having a "criminal insincerity"), and of the "profane theater" of the National Assembly. I specifically treat her critique of Burke's famous, eroticized, melodramatic staging of Marie Antoinette in his

Reflections on the French Revolution. As she rebukes, in *VRM*,[5] Burke's aristocratic defense of the "decent drapery of life," Wollstonecraft exposes his theatricality—how his famous paean to the drapery, the curtain behind which any "lovely" country ought to hide its degradations, occurs in the *Reflections* immediately after his staged rendition of the October Days episode in which the queen is taken from her palace and marched to Paris by an angry mob. While she challenges his axiom that the "pleasing illusion" of drapery allows "vice itself [to lose] half its evil by losing all its grossness," her later analysis of that same mob scene suggests a rethinking of the politics of performance and begs us to consider how her own representations attempt a portrait of authenticity and sincerity that is itself a performative act. Finally, Chapter 6 considers the relationship between Wollstonecraft and Sarah Siddons, including the nature of the spectacle of the female actress and her body on stage, specifically the potential for theatricality as transgressive mechanism. I explore the paradox—so typified by Sarah Siddons— of women on stage being objects of allure, of the gaze, and yet disrupting codes of female behavior at the same time. Perhaps the most original and exciting proposition here is that Siddons, in her acting theory which we surmise through notes and letters, and in performance (as documented in reviews), offers an enabling model for Wollstonecraft's manipulation of the theater trope.

Wollstonecraft's texts as a whole—from earliest literary reviews, translations, through histories and correspondence, nonfiction, and the two fictional novels— display a trajectory of Wollstonecraft's seemingly ambiguous thinking on these issues. My study consistently argues that Wollstonecraft works out in fiction the connections she had argued in political discourse between theatricality, politics, and social practice and suggests an important new direction for understanding Wollstonecraft's works, for current reconsiderations of assumed Romantic anti-theatricality, for historicist revisions of performance and theory of Sarah Siddons, and for theories of spectacle and gender.

---

[5]   Throughout this study I use *VRM* to refer to *A Vindication of the Rights of Men*; *VRW* to refer to *A Vindication of the Rights of Woman*; and *HMV* to refer to *An Historical and Moral View of the French Revolution.*

Chapter 1
Wollstonecraft and Romantic (Anti)Theatricality

While a new understanding of Wollstonecraft is the primary intention of my work—I want to take up the gauntlet offered by Virginia Woolf's remark that Wollstonecraft was "no cold-blooded theorist"—this study owes its genesis to five theoretical prisms: 1) recent revisionary criticism on Romantic theatricality; 2) cultural and literary studies of the politicization of theater and the theatricalization of politics; 3) theories of masquerade; 4) theories of mimicry; and 5) a conceptual crisis in drama studies, resulting in the divide between theater and performance critics. The first critical lens has revised traditional assumptions regarding Romanticism and theater both in terms of theoretically informed studies of male and female-authored dramatic texts and of reading cultural and non-dramatic literary productions as informed by theater. Most important to my study are Judith Pascoe's *Romantic Theatricality*, Catherine Burroughs's *Closet Stages: Joanna Baillie and the Theater Theory of British Romantic Women Writers*, and Julie Carlson's *In The Theater of Romanticism: Coleridge, Nationalism, Women*.[1] All of these works continue a line of New Historicist critique of the traditional idea of a Romantic, constructed (Wordsworthian) self that is sincere and spontaneous, and, thus, overtly anti-theatrical.[2] Burroughs summarizes how the assumed anti-theatricality of the Romantic period is linked to three factors: the material facts of

---

[1] Pascoe, *Romantic Theatricality: Gender, Poetry, and Spectatorship* (Ithaca: Cornell University Press, 1977); Catherine Burroughs, *Closet Stages: Joanna Baillie and the Theater Theory of British Romantic Women Writers* (Philadelphia: University of Pennsylvania Press, 1997) and her edited collection *Women in British Romantic Theatre: Drama, Performance, and Society, 1790–1840* (Cambridge: Cambridge University Press, 2000); Julie Carlson, *In The Theatre of Romanticism: Coleridge, Nationalism, Women* (Cambridge: Cambridge University Press, 1994).

[2] Most significant to my study, Liu, McGann, Levinson and Litvak definitively rewrite notions of Romantic "authenticity," just as Jacobus, Gaull, and Carlson have revised understandings of the achievements of the Romantic stage. Alan Liu, *Wordsworth: The Sense of History* (Stanford: Stanford University Press, 1989); Jerome McGann, *The Romantic Ideology* (Chicago: University of Chicago Press, 1985); Marjorie Levinson, *Wordsworth: The Great Period Poems* (Cambridge: Cambridge University Press, 1986); Joseph Litvak, *Caught in the Act: Theatricality in the Nineteenth-Century English Novel* (Berkeley: University of California Press, 1992); Mary Jacobus, "'That Great Stage Where Senators Perform': *Macbeth* and the Politics of Romantic Theatre," *Romanticism, Writing, and Sexual Difference* (Oxford: Clarendon Press, 1989), 33–68; Marilyn Gaull, "Romantic Theater," *Wordsworth Circle* 14 (1983): 255–63; and Carlson.

the eighteenth-century London theater scene, especially the consequences of the 1737 Stage Licensing Act; a bias against the stage as a feminine space; and the male Romantic poets' elevation of the imagination over the corporeal. The Stage Licensing Act of 1737, in authorizing only the two official theaters at Covent Garden and Drury Lane, effectively produced, for more than one hundred years, a large-house theatrical monopoly in London more fitted to opera and spectacle than drama, thus relegating minor drama immediately to non-canonical status and deterring serious critics from dramatic productions since it was hard to see and hear what was being played on the stage. Another explanation for a Romantic anti-theatricality suggests that the male poets were biased against the stage because of, as Jacobus has argued, a distrust of the "inherent theatricality of the imagination itself" (387) linked to the feminine and the histrionic. Carlson, as well as Galperin and Bruhm, suggest a third factor in this bias, the male poets' dislike of the elevation of the corporeal over the imaginative on stage.[3] Charles Lamb's famous diatribe against the acting of King Lear is most often cited:

> So to see Lear acted,—to see an old man tottering about the stage with a walking-stick, turned out of doors by his daughters in a rainy night, has nothing in it but what is painful and disgusting ... the Lear of Shakespeare cannot be acted. ... On the stage we see nothing but corporeal infirmities and weakness, the impotence of rage; while we read it, we see not Lear, but we are Lear,—we are in his mind. (107)

Lamb is not, as Burroughs points out, opposed to stage representation per se but adamant about the changes in meaning that such embodiment effects with regard to a prioritizing of body over mind. As Carlson puts it,

> On the one hand, the stage's dependence on physical "reality" makes its investigations of even the most abstract subjects more accessible. ... On the other hand, the stage's special relationship to body is also its chief danger, since the body's appeal can block out the less palpable and immediate workings of mind ... subvert[ing] the chief end of drama.[4]

All of these factors help to explain the critical assumption of Romanticism's anti-theatricality. Revising that history by turning attention to construction of a Romantic women's theater theory, to use Burrough's phrase, opens up an

---

[3]   Bruhm posits this in political terms, saying that Byron, Coleridge, and Shelley "preferred the sentiments of Burke's disembodied, aesthetic drama [while] their political allegiance to Paine's representational government continually drew them toward the presentation of the aesthetic in its physical, empirical sense." Steven Bruhm, *Gothic Bodies: The Politics of Pain in Romantic Fiction* (Philadelphia: University of Pennsylvania Press, 1994), 69; William Galperin, *The Return of the Visible in British Romanticism* (Baltimore and London: Johns Hopkins University Press, 1993).

[4]   Julie Carlson, "A New Stage for Romantic Drama," *Studies in Romanticism* 27.3 (1988): 419–27, 426.

important new direction for seeing women writers of all genres, not just female dramatists, as contributing to a new understanding of Romantic theatricality. My study of Wollstonecraft is, in a sense, heeding Burroughs's caution not to neglect "a variety of theoretical moments that occur in a wide range of texts and performance situations" (2) and her passing suggestion that Wollstonecraft must have drawn on her knowledge of the stage to formulate her critical readings of women's cultural position.

A second critical context that informs my study is eighteenth- and nineteenth-century cultural literary criticism that has exposed and theorized the relationship between theater venues, actors/actresses, and social and political displays of power, especially Elaine Hadley's *Melodramatic Tactics: Theatricalized Dissent in the English Marketplace*, Paula Backscheider's *Spectacular Politics: Theatrical Power and Mass Culture in Early Modern England*, and Kristina Straub's *Sexual Suspects: Eighteenth-Century Players and Sexual Ideology*.[5] Hadley's work on melodrama uncovers the debates about the effects of large-scale spectacular shows at the licensed theater houses. Some critics believed melodrama's staging of special effects functioned as an instrument of power, a medium for oppression by rendering audiences passive. Others argued that theatrical displays did not function like state pageantry, awing its spectators, but rather effected a catharsis of sorts, exposing powerful emotions while creating a collective, unified sense among spectators. Hadley's study also offers solid discussions of the OP wars and rioting over ticket prices, where spectators themselves became performers in an off-stage melodrama.[6] In a broad sense, it is vital to see the interconnectedness of theatricality, politics, and social practices and to keep clearly in mind that metaphors of theater would be very polyvalent in a Revolutionary culture; as Gillian Russell, in her study of theatricality of the military, asserts, such metaphors were prevalent in "a world where performance, display, and spectatorship were essential components of the social mechanism."[7] While the theatricality of social

---

[5]   Paula Backscheider's study of eighteenth-century culture is enormously important in arguing the function of theatricality in sustaining/challenging social practice; see Backscheider, *Spectacular Politics: Theatrical Power and Mass Culture in Early Modern England* (Baltimore: Johns Hopkins University Press, 1993). Hadley's study of the theater marketplace and cultural effects of melodrama as a genre emphasizes that theatricality includes the visual, public, and performative quality of social interactions; see *Melodramatic Tactics: Theatricalized Dissent in the English Marketplace* (Stanford: Stanford University Press, 1995). Although focused on the Victorian novel primarily, Joseph Litvak's work very much parallels my own questioning of the positive and negative consequences of theatricality in terms of a potentially transgressive, subversive relation to state and cultural institution of power; see *Caught in the Act*.

[6]   See also Marc Baer, *Theater and Disorder in Late Georgian London* (Oxford: Clarendon, 1992), 33–4. My Chapter 4 discusses the way audience members at courtroom trials acted in similar performances.

[7]   Gillian Russell, *The Theatres of War: Performance, Politics, and Society, 1793–1815* (Oxford: Oxford University Press, 1995), 124–5.

order is always a background in my discussions of Wollstonecraft, I particularly draw on this critical legacy in considering Wollstonecraft's political and travel writing, especially *Letters Written During a Short Residence* and *An Historical and Moral View of the French Revolution* in which she overtly turns to the consequences of theater or spectacle as both coercive and subversive.

Also contributing to my analysis are critical debates about masquerade which have instrumentally connected cultural, linguistic, and performance theories. Like the critics discussed above who focus on the theater of social mechanisms, scholars of masquerade examine its subversive as well as conservative tendencies; that is, the female in disguise may be seen as submissive to dominant social norms or disruptively resistant to them. Terry Castle's seminal work on eighteenth-century carnivalesque, in tracing the history of the masked assembly, suggests masquerade's subversive potential in challenging patriarchal structures. Although Castle does admit the possibility that the masked assemblies might act as a kind of safety-valve that ultimately reaffirms the status quo by exorcising social tension, masquerade is primarily subversion, a "World Upside Down" that offers a "realm pervaded by female desire, authority, and influence" and a mask that provides "an abrupt exit from the system of sexual domination."[8] Craft-Fairchild, on the other hand, interrogates the nature of masquerade as spectacle, raising questions like the following—Who is displayed? Who is the subject who takes pleasure in looking? Who is the object of the gaze?—and argues the inevitable objectification of woman as spectacle. Masquerade, then, for Craft-Fairchild is a gesture which theatrically stages gender roles, quoting Irigaray from *This Sex Which Is Not One*: "What do I mean by masquerade … a woman … has to enter into the masquerade of *femininity* … into a system of values that is not hers and in which she can 'appear' and circulate."[9] Hoeveler's work on the gothic heroine's deliberate masquerade of femininity offers a fruitful complication. Gothic writers who create heroines who "cannot bare their teeth in other than a smile" construct a "set of literary masquerades and poses" that allow their heroines, and by extension their female readers, a fictitious mastery, a pose she calls "professional femininity."[10] Arguing to some extent against Kate Ellis's influential study of gothic as subversive, Hoeveler posits the genre as more problematic, as both subverting and at the same time reifying postures of complaisancy within the dominant economy, and in so doing, suggests a broader premise, that the pose of femininity is born out of the juridical systems of the culture (prison, school, asylum, bourgeois family,

---

[8]   Terry Castle, *Masquerade and Civilization: The Carnivalesque in Eighteenth-Century English Culture and Fiction* (Stanford: Stanford University Press, 1986), 254, 255.

[9]   Elizabeth Craft-Fairchild, *Masquerade and Gender: Disguise and Female Identity in Eighteenth-Century Fictions by Women* (University Park: Pennsylvania State University Press, 1993), 54.

[10] Diane Hoeveler, *Gothic Feminism: The Professionalization of Gender from Charlotte Smith to the Brontës* (University Park: Pennsylvania State University Press, 1998), xiii.

confessional) as well as the literary discourse systems of melodrama, sentimental fiction, and gothic. I argue similarly in chapter two that Wollstonecraft's adept manipulation of sentimental and gothic conventions in her use of theatrical tropes throughout *Maria, or The Wrongs of Woman* suggests that "performance" can be empowering and liberating and not just coercive, which brings us to the fourth and most contentious critical context: performance.

From theories of masquerade, it is a *short* step to theories of performativity in general. Gender studies have, of course, made performance a touchstone, gender itself the ultimate theater. As Cixous summarizes,

> [M]en and women are caught in a network of millennial cultural determinations of complexity that is practically unanalyzable: we can no more talk about "woman" than about "man" without being caught within an ideological theater where the multiplication of representations, images, reflections, myths, identifications, constantly transforms, deforms, alters each person's imaginary order and in advance, renders all conceptualization null and void.

Culler, in his synthetic study of the fate of the term "performative," offers a most concise and helpful overview of the genesis of performance studies, helpful for understanding the contexts for my use of the terms "performative" and "theatrical." Beginning with a simple definition of performative as an utterance that accomplishes the act that it designates, Culler traces its use in literary criticism, from deconstruction to gender studies. The performative utterance, as developed by J.L. Austin in *How To Do Things With Words*, is that which performs the act to which it refers as opposed to constative utterance, which makes a true or false statement. While Austin's focus on the performative is primarily of social situations—getting married, christening a baby, for example—literary critics found it useful for describing the literary utterance. Literature's being performative contributes to a defense of literature itself as made up of acts of language that can change the world by bringing new orders into being. The heavy theorizing of performance, its key moment, was inaugurated by Derrida's "Signature event context." Derrida relates the performative to the problem of iterability, analogous to both democracy and to literature: literature is a "system of performative possibilities that accompanied the modern form of democracy." As Culler words it, "an act of constitution like that of literature, depends on a complex and paradoxical combination of the performative and the constative" (510). The statement in the Declaration of Independence, for example, that the colonies are free looks like a constative but is a performative that creates the reality to which it refers. This notion of the power of authoritative utterance and the possibilities that emerge from it (instead of just the obviously coercive and repressive effects of such discursive forms) greatly informs my specific readings of Wollstonecraft's use of juridical discourse, primarily in Chapter 4.

Finally, the question of positive and negative registers of meaning for the term informs what Culler calls the "singular turn in the fate of performative": its emergence in contemporary feminist and queer theory. The key figure here is, of course, Judith Butler, and my interest is in how, post-Butler, we define our terms. *Gender Trouble* takes issue with notions of essentialism; it is commonplace in gender studies now to say that identity categories are social constructions and productions. Gender is the cultural interpretation of biological difference and is performative, achieved by repeated acts formed by social conventions.[11] This premise spurred some critics to interpret Butler as implying that gender was something one could choose freely and led to charges that she was slighting the real weight of gender identities. *Bodies That Matter* refuted that interpretation of her theory, a reading that was based on the misplaced notion that

> gender is a role or that gender is a construction that one puts on, as one puts on clothes in the morning, that there is a 'one' who is prior to this gender, a one who goes into the wardrobe of gender and decides with deliberation what gender it will be today. ... [T]his presumes a subject, intact, prior to its gendering ... [rather] performativity is a matter of repeating the norms by which one is constituted: it is not a radical fabrication of a gendered self. It is a compulsory repetition of a priori norms, ones which cannot be thrown off at will but which work, animate, and constrain the gendered subject, and which are also resources from which resistance, subversion, displacement are forged.[12]

As Culler says, Butler leaves a gap, an opening, in which "lie possibilities for resistance and change."[13] Although some critics of Butler continue to stress her larger emphases on the strict limits placed on performance by the regulatory discourses governing social intelligibility, I agree with Culler and Henstra that even the term "subjection" in Butler's *Psychic Life of Power* insists, as Henstra puts it, on a "sustaining tension between the inauguration of one's 'self' through the recitation of norms and the way one is 'made subject' to those norms as a condition of cultural viability."[14] The contemporary positioning of performance theorists is a far cry from Austin's concerns about language and how it should be studied; for Butler at stake are the nature of identity, the function of social norms, problems of agency, and the relationship between individual and social change. This book will argue that Wollstonecraft saw the applicability of the theatrical trope to engage all of those ideas.

---

[11]   Judith Butler, *Gender Trouble: Feminism and the Subversion of Identity* (New York: Routledge, 1999).

[12]   Judith Butler, *Bodies That Matter: On the Discursive Limits of Sex* (New York: Routledge, 1993), 22–3.

[13]   Jonathon Culler, "The Fortunes of the Performative in Literary and Cultural Theory," *Literature and Psychology* 45.1–2 (1999): 7–28. See 12.

[14]   Sarah Henstra offers a helpful discussion of Butler in "Looking the Part: Performative Narration in Djuna Barnes's *Nightwood* and Katherine Mansfield's 'Je Ne Parle Pas Français,'" *Twentieth-Century Literature* 46.2 (Summer 2000), 125–49. For Butler, see *Psychic Life of Power: Theories in Subjection* (Stanford: Stanford University Press, 1997), 2.

Another term that I use, mimicry, also offers a provocative if problematic register of meaning. Mimicry is originally a theatrical term but has become laden with political connotations primarily through the postcolonial theory of Homi Bhabha.[15] Bolton's *Women, Nationalism, and the Romantic Stage: Theatre and Politics in Britain 1780–1800* is helpful in parsing the term. Bolton points out that in the theater, mimicry involves three parties, a mimic parodying a public figure for a canny audience. In Bhabha's theory, these three parties are blurred. His essay on mimicry begins with a compelling quotation from Lacan's *Of the Gaze*:

> Mimicry reveals something in so far as it is distinct from what might be called an itself that is behind. The effect of mimicry is camouflage. … It is not a question of harmonizing with the background, but against a mottled background, of becoming mottled—exactly like the technique of camouflage practised in human warfare.[16]

Lacan's distinction of self/other as not a harmonized but a mottled background is useful in understanding my argument about Siddons's and Wollstonecraft's beliefs in the potentially enabling power of acting, but Bhabha uses Lacan's comparison to warfare to project mimicry as the dominant power relationship in colonialist discourse:

> Mimicry emerges as one of the most elusive and effective strategies of colonial power and knowledge. … Within that conflictual economy of colonial discourse which Edward Said describes as the tension between the synchronic panoptical vision of domination—the demand for identity, stasis—and the counterpressure of the diachrony of history—change, difference—mimicry represents an *ironic* compromise. … [T]he discourse of mimicry is constructed around an ambivalence. (85–6)

Bolton's discussion of farce takes issue with Bhabha's eliding the theatrical contexts of the term, saying that in doing so he "obscures questions of agency" (165), and suggests Luce Irigaray's model of feminine mimicry as a useful alternative. Irigaray's *This Sex Which Is Not One* precedes Bhabha's theory and retains a theatrical perspective. Beginning with the pure philosophical and linguistic standpoint, Irigaray set out to "reopen" the figures of discourse and make them "render up" what they owe to "the feminine."[17] Drawing attention to the theatricality of all systems, she urges an interrogation of "*the conditions under which systematicity itself is possible*" and attention to the "scenography that makes representation feasible … the architectonics of its theatre … its props, its actors …" (75). But if she is skeptical of the specular economy, she is also adamant about women's choices within it. When it comes to the issue of women's actual

---

[15] Homi Bhabha, *The Location of Culture* (New York: Routledge, 1994).

[16] Quoted in Bhabha, 85.

[17] Luce Irigaray, *This Sex Which Is Not One*, trans. Catherine Porter with Carolyn Burke (Ithaca: Cornell University Press, 1985), 74.

agency, she suggests mimicry as a significant choice, one that may be subversively affirmative: "One must assume the feminine role deliberately. Which means already to convert a form of subordination into an affirmation, and thus to begin to thwart it" (76). I agree with Bolton that Irigaray's mimicry means entering into existing systems, but preserving the differences that those systems erase, which returns us to Lacan's phrase about a specular relation with an "other" that is behind, in the mottled background. All of these permutations are important in my argument in Chapter 6 about how Siddons's performances and her theorizing of the very act of performance serve as models for, if not an influence on, Wollstonecraft's representations of theatricality. Like Irigaray's suggestion that mimicry can convert and thwart subordinating discourses, Wollstonecraft's persistent reflections on and manipulations of theatricality expose a similar thwarting of conventional sexual, social, and generic systems.

The slippage between the terms theatricality and performance, and my decided preference in this study for the term "transgressive theatricality" rather than the term "performance," brings me to the final theoretical context which informs this study, the divide between "theater theory" and "performance theory." My use of Burroughs and Pascoe as models for my own work on Wollstonecraft suggests my bias: Pascoe's title *Romantic Theatricality: Gender, Poetry, and Spectatorship* includes in its subtitle the nod to performance theory in "spectatorship," but her introduction asserts that she will use "the world of the theater as a contextual and theoretical framework" (2) and that "in [her] staging of romanticism the female actors assume their rightful place at center stage, and there are no bit parts" (11). As my introduction explains, I employ Pascoe's paradigm of a tertiary definition of the term "theatrical" throughout my study. Burroughs's very project to construct a "women's theater theory" based on a "variety of 'theoretical moments' that occur in a wide range of texts and performance situations" (2) has to no small extent encouraged my opening Wollstonecraft's texts to this theoretical prism. The critical divide between theater/performance studies is, however, much larger than arguments about Romantic theatricality; Worthen, in fact, labels it a "conceptual crisis" and a rupture that needs attention. Elin Diamond, in *Performance and Cultural Politics*, offers a helpful summary of how the binary developed, suggesting that as a consequence of 1960s experimental theater, and poststructural theory, performance came to be defined in opposition to theater conventions.[18] Leaving behind "theater," which was charged with being subject to a playwright's authority and actors who were subject to fictional representations of characters, performance studies offered a challenging and vivid hermeneutics to study nondramatic, nonscripted, ceremonial, and everyday-life performances, becoming particularly central in gender studies. A negative consequence of this theoretical drift, however, is that performance studies began to misrepresent its own ontological source.

---

[18]   Elin Diamond, ed., *Performance and Cultural Politics* (New York: Routledge, 1996). See also the excellent anthology edited by Janelle G. Reinelt and Joseph R. Roach, *Critical Theory and Performance* (Ann Arbor: University of Michigan Press, 1992).

As Worthen puts it, performance critics carry a sense of superiority because their field has been so honored with dismantling textual authority, illusionism, and the canonical actor that now there is an all-too-easy "derision of theater as the string quartet of the twenty-first century!"[19] The premise, however, that "theater" is fully inscribed within a discourse of textual and cultural authority whereas "performance" engages in more resistant, oppositional ways fails to acknowledge the multiplicities, complexities, and ambiguities that occur in any embodiment of character on stage, and we need to rethink the relations of authority in these terms. Worthen especially faults Sedgwick and Parker for reducing theater studies to some narrow model in order to negate its effectiveness and for thinking they have invented the idea of the performative aspects of rituals and ceremonies, an idea which is, of course, quite old.[20] Rather than casting theater as an "incapacitating notion of performance as a version of the text, a version emptied of multiplicity and ambiguity through the process of (authorized) embodiment," Worthen asks how "the performance *of* a text ... might be conceived to investigate or retheorize the problematics of performance" and rethinks "the relations of authority that inform texts and performances" (1095).

This revisionist project—rethinking relations of authority as well as understanding, if not bridging, the divide between theater/performance critics—strongly informs my own interrogation of Wollstonecraft and theatricality, especially in my Chapter 5 on Siddons. What paradigm of authority comes to play, for instance, in the case of Wollstonecraft, a famous female author, friends with a famous female actress and frequent audience member at theatrical performances, who uses a dramatic character's dialogue as spoken by that specific actress to offer, in her own novel, a nuanced representation of a female heroine thinly disguised as herself? The context certainly involves theater (a fixed site) and theatricality in all three of the *OED*'s definitions—of or pertaining to theater; representing in the manner of an actor, affected; or calculated for display, showy—but the example also involves broader philosophical questions about the implications of these theatrical facts and registers of meaning, like "performance" (actual actions by individuals either on stage or in social venues) and "performativity" (a concept Parker and Sedgwick define as "ways that identities are constructed iteratively through complex citational processes" and that Butler describes as "a matter of repeating the norms by which one is constituted ... a compulsory repetition of a priori norms, ones which cannot be thrown off at will but which work, animate,

---

[19]   Worthen, W.B. "Drama, Performativity, and Performance," *PMLA* 113.5 (Oct. 1998): 1093–107. The quote is from 1094.

[20]   Worthen's characterization of Sedgwick and Parker's collection may itself use a bit of a straw man argument, but I think his reading of the introduction to that volume is on target. See Andrew Parker and Eve Kosofsky Sedgwick, eds., *Performativity and Performance* (New York and London: Routledge, 1995).

and constrain the gendered subject, and which are also resources from which resistance, subversion, displacement are forged."[21]

Finally, the chapters following seek to bring together these warring terms; if at times I use the word "performance" when it may seem to some readers that "theatrical" makes the point more precisely, I urge patience with the (conscious) slippage, and more importantly, foresee that very different usages will arise as the debate continues. Jill Dolan's careful, revisionist assertions calm the contentious waves, urging theater critics to use the questions that the metaphors of performativity offer and performance critics to acknowledge and revisit rather than "rai[d] and discar[d]" concepts and terms originary to theater. In a review of one of Siddons's Lady Macbeth performances, a critic marvels that she "combines more than ever existed at once in the same person." Whether we call it performance, mimicry, or transgressive theatricality, such acts serve as "retaliatory self-invention" and offer a powerful trope with which to read all of Wollstonecraft's texts as anything but (anti)theatrical.

---

[21]   Parker and Sedwick 2; Butler, *Bodies* 23.

Chapter 2
"Stage Effect":
Transgressive Theatricality in Wollstonecraft's *Maria, or The Wrongs of Woman*

We censure and with justice the corruption of morals in Paris. But in no public space in that metropolis is vice permitted to bear so open and so audacious a front as in the theatres of London.

—Sir Walter Scott, "Essay on the Drama"

I knew I should be the Mrs. Brown, the *shameful incendiary* in this shocking affair of a woman's leaving her bedfellow.

—Mary Wollstonecraft, "Letter to Everina Wollstonecraft"[1]

Casting herself in the role of a "shameful incendiary," in the dramatic narrative of helping her sister escape an abusive husband, Wollstonecraft reveals a keen awareness of the theatricality of social praxis; not surprisingly, her fictional depictions of wronged women both rely on and creatively manipulate the trope of theatricality. Much of Wollstonecraft's nonfiction, especially the most well-known *A Vindication of the Rights of Woman*, unveils the ideological theater of gender in which women participate with false and formulaic poses, thus undermining their status as moral beings. Less obvious and yet foundational to understanding Wollstonecraft's contribution to the discourse of theatricality are the ways in which her work appropriates theatrical tropes to dramatize the possibility of meaningful moral choice and action. This complex negotiation of competing interpretations of "theatrical" serves, in fact, as the most significant paradigm in her novel fragment *Maria, or The Wrongs of Woman*, which dramatizes the plot of a woman who is labeled deviant by patriarchal systems (marriage, medicine, the court) and who exposes her culture as a theater in which both virtue and vice are staged constructions. Whether physically incarcerated in an asylum, which will itself become something of a closet stage for her, or metaphorically captive to her

---

[1]   The first epigraph is from Scott's 1819 "Essay on the Drama" and is quoted in Julie Carlson. Wollstonecraft's first quotation is from a 1784 letter that refers to a "Mrs. Brown," possibly a reference to a carping wife in Robert Lloyd's *Chit-Chat*, according to Wardle. See Carlson, *In The Theatre of Romanticism: Coleridge, Nationalism, Women* (Cambridge: Cambridge University Press, 1994), 155; Ralph M. Wardle, ed., *Collected Letters of Mary Wollstonecraft* (Ithaca: Cornell University Press, 1979), 86.

husband, Maria attains a performative status on the world's stage, marking the potential inherent in a kind of "acting."

Godwin's Advertisement labels Wollstonecraft's novel a "performance." Wollstonecraft's Preface, moreover, foregrounds its theatrical aspects, ironically, by implying that "stage effect" is *not* the most significant characteristic. Asserting that she could have made the "incidents more dramatic," Wollstonecraft maintains that her purpose is to "exhibit the misery and oppression, peculiar to women, that arises out of the partial laws and customs and society."[2] Furthering her attention to the dramatic quality of the text, she claims a special status for her female character as what I will call "embodied":

> In many works of this species, the hero is allowed to be mortal, and to become wise and virtuous as well as happy, by a train of events and circumstances. The heroines, on the other hand, are to be born immaculate and to act like goddesses of wisdom just come forth, highly finished Minervas from the head of Jove. (5)

Intent on depicting a female heroine who, like her male counterpart, is allowed to "become" wise through a train of events, Wollstonecraft promises an essentially dramatic unfolding of character, in effect suggesting a need for her audience to redefine their proclivities for the judgment of female heroines. In a complicated sentence that first appears to read as a rejection of theatricality, Wollstonecraft de-emphasizes the novel's emphasis on situational "misfortunes":

> What are termed great misfortunes, may more forcibly impress the mind of common readers; they have more of what may justly be called *stage-effect*; but it is the delineation of finer sensations, which ... constitutes the merit of our best novels. (6)

Employing the phrase "stage effect," echoing an earlier statement in her *An Historical and Moral View of the French Revolution,* in which she disparages French theater where "almost everything is said and done for stage-effect," Wollstonecraft judgmentally critiques a kind of theatrical presentation of suffering.[3] Her rejection of strategies of "stage-effect" allies her work to the redefinitions being drawn by Wordsworth and Coleridge at roughly the same time (Wollstonecraft worked on the draft of the novel in 1797, leaving it unfinished when she died in August 1797). In her important revisionary study of Coleridge and Romantic theatricality, Julie Carlson persuasively argues how Wordsworth and Coleridge consciously debated the function of theatricality in the experiment of the

---

[2]   Preface," *Maria, or the Wrongs of Woman,* ed. Anne K. Mellor (New York: Norton, 1975), 5.

[3]   *An Historical and Moral View of the French Revolution. The Works of Mary Wollstonecraft,* ed. Janet Todd and Marilyn Butler, 7 vols (New York: New York University Press, 1989), 6: 25. The specific phrase "stage-effect" is also used by Burke and informs, of course, much of the French Revolutionary pamphlet wars; Chapter 4 synthesizes the scholarship on this issue, argues for the ambivalence undergirding the use of theatrical metaphors by both radical and conservative activists, and offers a thorough reading of *HMV.*

1798 *Lyrical Ballads*. While Wordsworth at times overtly distances his work from frenetic scenes—avowing in "Hart-Leap Well" that "The moving accident is not my trade"—his own Preface, like Wollstonecraft's, foregrounds the very dramatic properties that he appears to reject, offering a redefinition of them, as in his formulation of a paradoxical "lyrical ballad" where "the feelings give importance to the action and situations, and not the action and situation to the feelings." Coleridge's correspondence with Wordsworth in 1798 reveals a similar concern with how to combine "stage effect" (produced through admirable "situations") with the "permanent and closest beauties of style, passion, and character."[4] This conscious revaluation in the 1780s and 1790s of the registers of meaning in the term suggests the necessity of contextualizing Wollstonecraft's use of the trope.

Using Burroughs's definition of theater theory to include "a variety of theoretical moments that occur in a wide range of texts and performance situations" (2), we see that in *Maria, or The Wrongs of Woman*, theatricality is not simply a trope with which to represent "women's cultural position" but also the performative nature of all human self-representation as well as national and cultural identity formation. Wollstonecraft's consistent metaphor for the theatrical dimensions of social mechanisms is a cloak. The cloak of decency, of manners, is also the cloak of pageantry and patriotism that enables state and national power. On the other hand, the novel suggests that playing a part does not always make one complicit in such hypocritical concealment, but can offer, through a kind of functional mimicry, a potent path for independent self-staging; thus, we must recognize both the limitations of and inherent potential in "stage-effect."

Emphasizing the interconnectedness of theatricality and political and social practices, this chapter investigates the novel's representation of theatricality in terms of both characters and contexts, exploring two of the most significant manifestations of the trope in the novel. First, pertaining to the material stage and theater, I argue the significance of Wollstonecraft's intertextual appropriation of Nicolas Rowe's play *The Fair Penitent*.[5] Second, I discuss figurative, theoretical, and political dimensions of theatricality, including the following:

1. how the novel consciously invokes the metaphor of acting and how the theater functions, literally and figuratively, in the characterization of Darnford (who has a past with theater women), George (who denounces Maria's "theatrical flourishes" when she denies him sexually but then offers himself as a "convenient cloke" when he tries to prostitute her to his friend), female theatergoers at Ranelagh who reject Maria for not

---

⁴ See Carlson, 421. For the letter from Coleridge, see *Collected Letters of Samuel Taylor Coleridge*, ed. E.L. Griggs, 6 vols (Oxford, Clarendon, 1956) 1: 379. For the Wordsworth quote, see *Lyrical Ballads*, ed. W.J.B. Owen, 2nd edition (Oxford: Oxford University Press, 1970), 159.

⁵ Much of this section is reprinted from my article "'A Shameful Tale to Tell for Public Sport': Wollstonecraft's Revision of Rowe's *The Fair Penitent*," *New Perspectives on the Eighteenth Century* 4.1 (2007): 28–37. The author thanks *NPEC* for permission to reprint.

posturing as a happy wife in "the cloak of fashionable women," the "mad" prisoners in the asylum whose mental aberrations allow for an unmediated and unpoliced playing of roles, and of Maria, whose growth from reader of sentimental fiction to active theatergoer to a kind of actress (depicted as a criminal on a "WANTED" poster and delivering a scripted performance in the final trial scene) reveals recognition of both the boundaries and possibilities of theatrical social context, and, more theoretically, of the potential empowerment of mimicry; and

2. how the novel represents cultural displays of power in terms of their reliance upon theatricality, especially in the final trial scene.[6]

The cohesive guiding question is whether theatricality (in all of these senses) *enables* or *subverts* various cultural mechanisms of power.

* * *

Tis fixed to die, rather than bear the insolence
Of each affected she that tells my story,
And blesses her good stars that she is virtuous.
To be a tale for fools! (Calista, *The Fair Penitent*)

Had she remained with her husband, practicing insincerity, and neglecting her child to manage an intrigue, she would still have been visited and respected. If, instead of living openly with her lover, she had called into play a thousand arts which ... might have allowed people who were not deceived to pretend to be so, she would have been caressed and treated like an honourable woman. (Maria, *Maria, or The Wrongs of Woman*)

In the first epigraph, Calista, a suffering heroine from Nicholas Rowe's 1703 *The Fair Penitent*, a play which had a continuous production history of over one hundred years, appears to accept death rather than living a life of scandal. With a closer look, however, Calista sounds far from "the penitent" of Rowe's title, as she here sarcastically refers to the virtuous crowd of women, "each affected she," who will enjoy telling a story of sexual seduction and betrayal in order to congratulate herself on her own virtue. In this reading, her closing line "To be a tale for fools!" marks Calista as decidedly non-penitent and, in fact, knowing herself to be above the level of "fools" who will enjoy "a shameful tale to tell for public sport."[7] Sarah Siddons performed the role of Calista in 1796, and in

---

[6]   Some of this discussion comes from my article "'Stage Effect': Transgressive Theatricality in Wollstonecraft's *Maria, or the Wrongs of Woman*," *Women's Writing* 14.3 (2007): 367–81.

[7]   Calista speaks these lines in III.119 of the play; all quotations are taken from Rowe, *The Fair Penitent*, ed. Malcolm Goldstein (Lincoln: University of Nebraska Press, 1969). Subsequent quotations from the play are referenced parenthetically by act and line number.

the audience was Mary Wollstonecraft, at that time still going by the name of Mary Imlay, all the while confessing publicly that she was not nor ever had been officially Mrs. Gilbert Imlay, engaging in an intimate relationship with William Godwin, and working on a draft of what would become her novel fragment *Maria, or The Wrongs of Woman*.[8] Having explicitly critiqued the "insipid decency" of those whom Calista calls the "affected she[s]," Wollstonecraft (engaging a multiplication of identities in the audience) would certainly have paid attention to these lines. Her heroine Maria, in the second epigraph, has a similar outburst against those who no longer speak to her once she stops play-acting—"practicing insincerity"—and decides to live "openly with her lover."[9] In a novel permeated with ideas about theatricality, Wollstonecraft includes explicit allusions to two popular female dramatic heroines, characters whom she saw interpreted on stage by Sarah Siddons in the 1790s: Roxana, from Nathaniel Lee's *The Rival Queens, or the Death of Alexander the Great*, and, more significantly, Rowe's Calista. General editors of Wollstonecraft's novel gloss the references to Calista and Roxana, but no significant studies have explored the questions that these intertextual references raise and the ways in which Wollstonecraft may be manipulating the conventions and heroines of contemporary stage melodrama and "she-tragedies," in much the same ways that she appropriates and then inverts patterns from gothic and sentimental novels.[10] Given the fact that Sarah Siddons's performances of Roxana

---

[8]   Wollstonecraft had registered as Gilbert Imlay's wife while in France for safety and to be allowed to stay there and retained the name in England, but as Godwin points out, never tried to keep secret the fact that she was not ever his wife. Wollstonecraft must have been working on the manuscript of the novel in November 1796 since Godwin says that she was involved in writing it "more than twelve months before her decease" in September 1797. See William Godwin, *Memoirs of the Author of A Vindication of the Rights of Woman* in *The Wrongs of Woman and Godwin's Memoirs*, ed. Cynthia Richards (Glen Allen, VA: College Publishing, 2004), 283–4.

[9]   All quotations from Wollstonecraft's novel are taken from Wollstonecraft, *Maria, or the Wrongs of Woman*, ed. Anne K. Mellor (New York: Norton, 1975). The quoted lines are from 127. Subsequent quotations from the novel are cited parenthetically by page number.

[10]   In his 1976 edition of *Mary and The Wrongs of Woman*, Kelly endnotes the reference to Calista as "the heroine of Nicholas Rowe's popular 'she-tragedy' *The Fair Penitent* who is seduced by the original Lothario." He further adds that Wollstonecraft would have seen Sarah Siddons play the part of Calista in November 1796 and that Wollstonecraft had supper with Siddons in August 1796. See Kelly, Gary, ed. *Mary and the Wrongs of Woman*, by Mary Wollstonecraft (Oxford: Oxford University Press, 1976), 225. The reference to Roxana, Kelly simply notes as "one of the heroines of Nathaniel Lee's *The Rival Queens, or the Death of Alexander the Great*" and also points out that Siddons performed in the role in April 1796. See 227. In her 2004 edition, Cynthia Richards calls Calista "one of the great, but controversial roles for eighteenth-century actresses" and summarizes that she is "seduced and abandoned by her lover, then dutifully marries a man against her inclinations, all the while continuing to protest her fate." She offers a kernel of controversy herself by pointing out that Siddons abandoned her friendship to Wollstonecraft after her marriage to Godwin and pregnancy became known. See Richards, *Memoirs of the Author of A Vindication of the*

and Calista (and other Rowe heroines) were well-known during the time that Godwin and Wollstonecraft were active London theatergoers, Wollstonecraft has not only the plays themselves but the contemporary performances of them from which to draw. While Wollstonecraft plays upon Roxana's negative role in Lee's play, more significant is her use of Calista from Rowe's play to underscore the issue of women's self-staging and role as spectacle.[11] *The Fair Penitent* is the first of Rowe's three "she-tragedies," preceding by a decade *The Tragedy of Jane Shore* and *The Tragedy of Lady Jane Grey*; all of these were in circulation in London theaters at the same time and dramatize issues of concern to Wollstonecraft's novel by suggesting the extent to which state politics could be represented through the spectacle of the suffering female. *The Fair Penitent*, however, is an indisputably fascinating and key intertext for Wollstonecraft's novel in the following ways: 1) the play's thematic concerns (especially the tyranny of marriage); 2) the female heroine used as a central spectacle of suffering; 3) the play's history in terms of the politicization of theater in the eighteenth century; and 4) the specific interpretations of Calista on stage by Sarah Siddons, as referenced in Wollstonecraft's novel, and the implications of those performances.

Wollstonecraft criticism has more often than not simply and briefly referenced the novel's allusions to Rowe's play as though they functioned to point out Maria's lapses into a stereotypical sentimentality, a posture of sensibility; the novel, of course, has been highly debated in terms of whether we should read the narrative as a critique of Maria's "romantic expectations," or whether the author herself succumbed to this very weakness. Most influentially, Mary Poovey argues that Wollstonecraft's "repeated lapses back into sentimental jargon and romantic idealism" demonstrate that the generic expectations of the novel of sensibility overwhelm the political potential of the novel, as both Maria and Wollstonecraft herself ultimately lose their voices.[12] If we take a more positive attitude toward Wollstonecraft's narrative control, however, as Claudia Johnson has done, and consider the novel in terms of a trajectory of Maria's growth as an autonomous female, then the allusions to Rowe deserve much more attention. Anne McWhir briefly suggested, in her 1992 "Revising Rowe's *The Fair Penitent*: Goldsmith, Holcroft, Wollstonecraft," that Wollstonecraft's novel resists penitence as a response to an existing structure of power. In a four-page article focusing most on Goldsmith's *The Vicar of Wakefield* and Holcroft's *The Adventures of Hugh Trevor*,

---

Rights of Woman, by William Godwin (Glen Allen, VA: College Publishing, 2004), 129. Of Roxana, she refers to her as the "murderess" in Lee's play; see 159.

[11]   The reference to Roxana comes as George angrily demands that Maria stop the "theatrical flourishes" like a "fair Roxana," 100. While my study focuses on the Rowe/Wollstonecraft relationship, more work needs to be done on Wollstonecraft's use of the Lee heroine.

[12]   Mary Poovey, *The Proper Lady and the Woman Writer: Ideology as Style in the Works of Mary Wollstonecraft, Mary Shelley, and Jane Austen* (Chicago: University of Chicago Press, 1984), 105.

McWhir importantly asserts that Siddons's performances would have been subversive representations of the Calista character:

> Yet while Rowe's text allows [Goldsmith's] reading of Calista as justly condemned rebel against patriarchy, it also allows Holcroft and Wollstonecraft … to read her as a defiant champion of the oppressed. Sarah Siddons seems to have encouraged such a reading, for both Mary Wollstonecraft and Thomas Holcroft describe her playing Calista, both reading Calista as a radical, feminist heroine. Holcroft's *Hugh Trevor* refers to Calista's disregard of the "world's scorn" … and to the right of women to an "equal empire o'er the world."[13]

While McWhir does not develop her assertion that Wollstonecraft read Calista as a "radical, feminist heroine," she does, in a short paragraph focusing on Jemima, assert that the novel's purpose is to show how repressive systems and corrupt institutions breed tyrants and victims.

I contend that Wollstonecraft uses the play's thematic representation of the tyranny of marriage and its suffering but strong female heroine as part of a full-scale manipulation of the theater trope throughout the novel—an appropriation of a complex dramatic character whose interpretations on the contemporary London stage revealed a subversive female voice, critiquing both the oppression of the female body and the body politic. While it is clear that in *The Fair Penitent*, the heroine comes in conflict with a normative hierarchy of values, suffers extreme moral and emotional anguish, and dies at the play's end, Calista herself has been read as somehow outside the space of this containment. Some contemporary critics, like Elizabeth Howe, continue the argument that Calista is reduced to the status of passive victim whose punishment provides the play with its clear moral, but others note that Calista's final repentance and supposed conversion do not sound convincing. Harris argues that even eighteenth-century critics found it hard to reconcile the Calista of Acts I–IV with the repentant Calista of Act V. By the time Rowe has enacted the necessary punishment, she has, in Harris' words, "already transcended it."[14] Given the play's ambiguous critical reputation, the guiding question becomes, does Rowe create a fairly formulaic portrait of a tragically flawed heroine or depict a subversive female character whose ultimate death, nonetheless, critiques the apparatus of cultural power? Many of Calista's contemporary critics who felt a disjunction between the strong-minded Calista and the repentant heroine of Act V did so in judgment of Rowe, arguing that what ought to be a moral message was muddled by Calista's lack of authentic penitence, despite the title. As Johnson observes in his *Life of Rowe*, "… the title

---

[13]   Anne McWhir, "Revising Rowe's *The Fair Penitent*: Goldsmith, Holcroft, and Wollstonecraft," *Women's Studies* 304 (1992): 827–30. The quotation is from 828.

[14]   Harris, Susan Cannon, "Outside the Box: The Female Spectator, *The Fair Penitent*, and the Kelly Riots of 1747," *Theatre Journal* 57.1 (2005): 33–55. Also see Elizabeth Howe, *The First English Actresses: Women and Drama 1660–1700* (Cambridge: Cambridge University Press, 1992).

of the play does not sufficiently correspond with the behavior of Calista who ... expresses more shame than sorrow, more rage than shame." Even more pointedly, an anonymous writer wrote a poem called "Prologue Sent to Mr. Rowe ... but refus'd" in which he labels Calista a whore:

> He from the Sock the PROSTITUTE transplants
> And swells the humble whore with Buskin rants,
> His whore, indeed, repents the slippery Fault
> But, like the rest, it is not 'til she's caught.
> She is not sorry she has Plaid the whore,
> But that, discover'd, she can do't no more.[15]

The multiple readings suggest to McWhir that

> *The Fair Penitent*, like Blake's version of the war in heaven, can be—and has been—adopted by both parties, a fact which perhaps accounts for its continued popularity throughout the eighteenth century. Emphasis shifts from acceptance of social duty in Goldsmith to individual challenge of social institutions in Holcroft and Wollstonecraft, and readings of Calista mark this shift. (828)

McWhir's suggestion that appropriations of the play shift markedly in the late eighteenth century legitimates the question of how Wollstonecraft interpreted the play, and Rajan's study of Godwin's political novels provides a useful paradigm. In "Reading the Secrets," Rajan uses Godwin's distinction between the moral and the tendency of the text—moral being the authorial intention, tendency, the "intersubjective and historically developing significance" (229).[16] Thus, as Rajan points out, authors can be ignorant of the tendencies of their own texts. Godwin, in "A Choice of Reading," says that Rowe's *The Fair Penitent* may have been written as a critique of illicit love and ultimately a condemnation of the sinful heroine, pitiable and tragic though she may be, but, despite itself, the play exposes limitations of patriarchal attitudes toward women. Godwin's reading of Rowe, then, goes beyond the moral to, in Rajan's words, the tendency "that becomes evident through the enlightened reading that historical progress makes possible" (229). It is significant that Godwin would see Rowe as potentially subversive despite the outcome of the text, its formulaic rendering of the inevitable confession and death of the fair penitent, and suggests how radical theatergoers in 1796 (through readings that only "historical progress" makes possible) might have been responding to Siddons's performances of Calista, as my Chapter 4 analyzes in detail. Certainly, Wollstonecraft's manipulation of the character suggests a subversive potential to Calista, just as recent reconsiderations of Rowe (and the genre of "she-tragedy") reveal a similar debate within critical studies of the play.

---

[15]   Johnson's, the anonymous poet's, and other responses to the play are summarized by Annabel Jenkins in *Nicholas Rowe* (Boston: Twayne, 1977), especially 66–7.

[16]   See Tilottama Rajan, "Wollstonecraft and Godwin: Reading the Secrets of the Political Novel," *Studies in Romanticism* 27.2 (Summer 1988): 221–51.

Representing much more than just a female victim, in fact, Calista is quite a good model for Wollstonecraft's portrait of Maria. Calista's story comments on many of the same substantive obstacles as Maria's. As Tumir notes, Calista "calls into question Sciolto's dominating rule, Horatio's sanctimonious demand for self-abnegation, Lothario's libertine self-regard, and in her famous speech at the beginning of Act III, even the very notion of patriarchal authority itself."[17] What Tumir identifies as Calista's four targets of critique are also Wollstonecraft's: parental tyranny, hypocritical self-denial in the name of decency, male libertinism, and the very notion of patriarchal authority. Like Maria, Calista is a victim of a loveless marriage, and thus when Maria quotes from *The Fair Penitent*, she reveals an identification with the unhappy, unsatisfying marital status of Calista. On this simple level, Calista's suffering fulfills Rowe's promise in the Prologue to introduce a tale of woe in which "you shall meet with sorrows like your own" (Prologue 18). The fiery verbal exchanges, however, between Calista and the figures who represent or obey tyrannical authority in the play demonstrate that Calista's resistance would have been a more significant model for Wollstonecraft's shaping of Maria.

The passage in which Wollstonecraft invokes Rowe's play and its performance by Siddons occurs in Maria's narration of her marriage, and the context of Rowe's dialogue provides a good example of how Calista is an unstable sign in the novel. On a basic level, her first introduction as an analogy obviously foreshadows the impending disaster of Maria's marriage. The narrator tells us that early in their union, George and Maria frequent literary and artistic social groups in London, and Maria very specifically invokes one theatrical moment:

> … the theaters were a never-failing source of amusement. My delighted eye
> followed Mrs. Siddons, when, with dignified delicacy, she played Calista; and
> I involuntarily repeated after her, in the same tone, and with a long-drawn sigh,
> "Hearts like our's were pair'd—not match'd." (76)

While the "long-drawn sigh" and mention of "delicacy" at first suggest a rhapsody characteristic of a sentimental heroine, a performative role which Maria certainly adopts during various moments of the novel, especially in her romanticizing of Darnford, the quoted line itself in the context of Rowe's play is quite the opposite. Spoken in the context of Calista's recognition that she has been "pair'd" with a husband she does not love instead of being "match'd" with one she does, the line is a sharp realization of woman's lack of autonomy in the marriage transaction of the play, and in this way calls attention not to Maria's illusions but to the gradual but irrevocable unmasking of them.[18]

---

[17]   Vaska Tumir, "She-Tragedy and Its Men: Conflict and Form in *The Orphan* and *The Fair Penitent*," *Studies in English Literature* 30.0 (1990): 411–29. See 418.

[18]   Kelly points out that Mary Robinson, who had herself acted Calista and was friends to both Wollstonecraft and Godwin, also quoted these lines in her partly autobiographical novel *Vancenza*. See Kelly, 225.

While this nuanced allusion suggests the double-sided valence of Calista as an interpretable sign in the novel, a clear and direct example of Calista's strength, and the similarity of her rhetoric to Wollstonecraft's feminist discourse, occurs as Calista uses the vocabulary of conquest to describe her impending forced marriage. While critics debate the issue of Calista's position (assertion versus subordination, strength versus weakness), which is quite understandable given her ultimate end in suicide, all of them identify Calista's powerful rhetoric in Act III. Speaking to her father Sciolto, she asks, "Has not your daughter ... yielded the native freedom of her will/To an imperious husband's lordly rule?" (III.14–15). Her insinuation that marriage is imperialism, conquering the "native freedom" of her will, sets up her metaphorical assertion that women are "slaves" who are "born with high souls" and who must "shake off this vile obedience [men] exact"(III.50–52). Wollstonecraft, of course, persistently refers to the slavery of marriage in the *VRW* and combines slavery and imprisonment in the novel, as Maria ponders: "Was not the world a vast prison and women born slaves?" (11).[19] While these obvious echoes from the third act demonstrate how the heroine's discourse in the play would have paralleled Wollstonecraft's own, the entire scene deserves much more attention. Pitting Calista against three representatives of arbitrary power (father, husband, and social norms), the scene stages her in conversation with all three. The often-quoted lines from above occur in a speech where Calista bemoans woman's continuous dependance upon tyrants—from the "rigid father who dictates" to a "tyrant husband's reign" to a cultural system which "shuts us/ Like cloistered idiots, from the world's acquaintance" (III.42, 44, 47–8). Much of Wollstonecraft's discourse against tyranny in the *VRW* follows a similar argument; devoting two separate chapters to "Parental Affection" and "Duty to Parents," Wollstonecraft argues that it is forced obedience to parents that sets a foundation for subordination in all forms: "... the absurd duty, too often inculcated, of obeying a parent only on account of being a parent, shackles the mind, and prepares it for a slavish submission to any power but reason" (153). Like Calista, however, Wollstonecraft exposes the unique consequences of the tyranny of obedience for women who "thus taught slavishly to submit to their parents ... are prepared for the slavery of marriage" (155). Not surprisingly, then, in the novel, Maria is raised by two familial tyrants who expect her obedience: her father, whose "orders were not to be disputed," and who was "to be instantaneously obeyed, especially by [her] mother" and her eldest brother who "became in due form the deputy-tyrant of the house" (59).

Yet, it is not just Calista's liaisons with Lothario and her exposure of the sexual vulnerability that is "the state of our sex" which liken her to Wollstonecraft, but also her pointed, bold rejection of external definitions of honor or purity. Recognizing that honor cannot be granted or taken away but comes from a woman's own internal moral monitor, Wollstonecraft, in the *VRW*, comments explicitly on

---

[19]   *A Vindication of the Rights of Woman*, 2nd edition, ed. Carol Poston (New York: Norton, 1985), esp. 155.

Samuel Richardson's notoriously famous, seduced beauty Clarissa and blasts Richardson for asserting that the rake Lovelace had stolen Clarissa's honor:

> When Richardson makes Clarissa tell Lovelace that he had robbed her of her honour, he must have had strange notions of honour and virtue. For miserable beyond all names of misery is the condition of a being who could be degraded without its own consent! (72)

In Rowe's play, Horatio, the sanctimonious friend, reveals to her that her affair with Lothario has become a "shameful tale for public sport" and warns her that she will be "shunned/By all your virtuous maids and nobler matrons" (III.52–3). It is this "insipid decency," as Wollstonecraft calls it, that spurs Calista into even stronger rhetoric than her speech about the fate of woman. Rejecting Horatio's offer of "help," she vows, "I am myself the guardian of my honor/And wo' not bear so insolent a monitor" (III.179–80).[20] At this point in the scene, the third representative of tyrannical power enters, and having sparred with her father (Sciolto) and the voice of social normativity (Horatio), Calista turns her full indictment to her husband. Calista conjectures that he will listen to Horatio's tale and then "treat me like a common prostitute" (III.211) and boldly refuses him sexually: "No force shall drag me to thy hated bed" (III.213). The fact that Calista confronts three men in the scene and rejects penitence in her exchanges with all of them underscores her autonomy at this point in the narrative, an independence that is mirrored in Maria's similar drama. The pinnacle of Maria's growth, in the narrative of her marriage, occurs after she refuses to participate in the prostitution of her body to George's friend, then refuses to share her husband's bed, and finally leaves the house in search of hiding places, acts dangerous enough to get her hunted down through "WANTED" ads in the newspapers and imprisoned for insanity.[21]

---

[20] The full quote for Wollstonecraft's phrase is "Weak minds are always fond of resting in the ceremonials of duty, but morality offers much simpler motives; and it were to be wished that superficial moralists had said less respecting behavior and outward observances ... a kind of insipid decency." See *VRW*, 133.

[21] This element of the plot links the novel to another of Rowe's she-tragedies, *The Tragedy of Jane Shore*. One of the greatest examples of tyranny in that play comes when the state declares it treason to harbor Jane in any way, on pain of death. This act officially turns sympathy into a capital crime and marks the tyrants as outside the community of mutual sympathy that the play posits as an alternative to tyranny. Rowe's representation is an apt analogue to Wollstonecraft's having Maria turned out from her lodgings and hunted like a felon. The "WANTED" ad in the newspaper criminalizes any help offered to Maria in just the way the state defined as treasonous any aid to Jane Shore. The novel, thus, depicts the law, both in the "WANTED" advertisement and more specifically in the trial scene, as itself outside the communal interchange of mutual sympathy which the novels' characters have created. As in Rowe's play, tyranny and oppression are challenged by the text's evocation of this potential mutuality.

While Calista provides Wollstonecraft a significant model for issues of female agency, she operates beyond the level of gender critique. Wollstonecraft also uses this character (Calista-as-Maria) to comment on political tyranny and Revolutionary events, just as Rowe did. Brett Wilson argues that Rowe used "she-tragedy" as vehicle for promoting a cultural politics of sympathy with *The Fair Penitent* in 1703, a nuanced kind of political critique, yet the play invokes very explicitly the connection between cultural and political revolution. Not just privately sexual wantons, both Calista and Maria are connected with potential anarchy in the state. The link between Calista's private actions and the public sphere occurs not only in her impassioned rhetoric of Act III, but also in Act V when she is at her weakest, near suicide, and mad with grief and despair. Sciolto, entering the cell where both he and Calista will die, explains that the chaos of their private lives is echoed by the "wreck" of the state. Whereas the judge in Wollstonecraft's novel firmly rejects any foreign principles in his court, his defensiveness demonstrating the fear he has of such revolutionary change occurring in England, Sciolto in this scene confirms that it has already happened:

> And yet distraction and tumultuous jars
> Keep all our frighted citizens awake;
> The senate weak, divided, and irresolute
> Want pow'r to succor the afflicted state.
> Vainly in words and long debates they're wise
> While the fierce factions scorn their peaceful orders,
> And drown the voice of law in noise and anarchy. (V.45–52)

Leaving no doubt of the link between Calista's sexual rebellion and this anarchy, Sciolto points to Calista, saying, "Like Helen in the night when Troy was sacked, / Spectatress of the mischief which she made" (V.1.53–4). After Calista's and Sciolto's deaths, Horatio, the public face of communal morality in the play, addresses the audience with the formulaic moral, admonishing, "By such examples are we taught to prove / The sorrows that attend unlawful love" (V.288–9). Even without an epilogue, audiences are left with the disjunction between the strong-willed Calista and the tragic suicidal one; however, with the epilogue, designated to be spoken by Lavinia, Calista's maid, the questions, not the moral, get the last word. With the play's last reference to the disorder in the state, the female epilogue speaker suggests that the disorder is not caused by the sexual wantonness, and the breakdown of moral system that such implies, but rather it is caused by the absolute tyranny of the system itself, by wives' obedience to "the force of laws which for themselves [husbands] made" (Epilogue 7). Allying husbands to tyrants, and more specifically, arbitrary monarchs, the speaker aggressively identifies the agent of blame: "With tales of old prescriptions they confine / The right of marriage-rule to their male line, / And huff and domineer by right divine" (8–10). The play's epilogue ends with a challenge for men to "begin the reformation" (28), if they want to bring constancy in fashion, just as Wollstonecraft instructs in the *VRW*. Then and only then could men rest assured that "no foreign charms shall cause domestic strife" (31). Calista's story clearly requires audiences to reflect on the consequences not only of sexual wantonness, but also of regulatory forms of power over individual actions.[22]

Wollstonecraft's interrogation of the link between "foreign charms" and "domestic strife" in the body politic is most significant in Maria's final confrontation with the judge in the adultery trial, an authority figure like Sciolto who also fears "foreign" charms, in his words "French principles" (133). Maria's "madness" is not only her resistance to the sexual and legal entanglements of marriage, but also her championing of the rights of the lower-class women burdened by economic as well as sexual and legal enslavement and, further, her implicit support of the French Revolution, an analogy she herself spotlights with the phrase, "Marriage had Bastilled me for life" (87). Thus, when the judge concludes against her in the chancery scene, it is not only for her rebellion to her husband and marriage vows; the judge connects her "being allowed to plead openly her feelings" to an "opening [of the] flood-gate for immorality," specifically the premises of the French

---

[22] The epilogue's acknowledgment of a "fear of foreign charms" encourages reading the play for more subversive themes than has been suggested, and it also allies this play with the more explicitly topical politics of the other two plays in the cycle, both of which were performed by Siddons during the season of Wollstonecraft's active theatergoing; *The Tragedy of Jane Shore* in particular confronts the threat of Jacobitism and the issue of threatened Protestant succession. A dramatization of the political succession crisis of Edward IV and Richard III, Rowe's play debuted at Drury Lane in February 1714 during fears about Protestant succession; more significantly for this study, it was performed (over 18 times in one month) in the 1790s during French Revolution debates. Thus, both productions occurred at a time of pamphlet wars which advertised the risks of a Popish successor and an arbitrary government, and which exalted principles of the Glorious Revolution in their agendas. Political censors forced Rowe to strike specific lines in the play about succession because of fear of their incendiary potential. The play evokes very specific fears which crystallize in the person of Jane Shore, whose victimization at the hands of an oppressive state apparatus is acknowledged in a highly pathetic register and makes her a resistant martyr character, and, thus, as Wilson notes, Rowe distills this large-scale politics of Civil War, the constitution, and the succession crisis in concentration on the deprivations of one helpless, private woman. Wollstonecraft's novel attempts a similar agenda: it highlights the sufferings of one woman, Maria, but uses this figure as a vehicle for critique of marriage and property laws, the regulation of asylums that allowed them to be prisons for wives who transgressed boundaries defined by husbands, revolutionary politics in favor of the laboring poor, and legal procedures that allowed betrayed husbands to sue for damages but not wives. In sum, Wollstonecraft's distillation of all these agendas in the spectacle of a suffering female reveals a similarity to the popular dramatic genre of she-tragedy, with an important difference. Where Rowe could not allow for his heroines to be both virtuous and sexually autonomous, even to the point of his rewriting historically sexual female characters as non-sexual, Wollstonecraft defiantly does just this. Maria's day in court condemns all the tyrannical systems of power while maintaining her right to autonomous choice of partner and expression of desire. See Brett Wilson, "Jane Shore and the Jacobites: Nicholas Rowe, The Pretender, and the National She-Tragedy," *ELH* 72.4 (2005): 823–42.

Revolution on English soil. He concludes, "We [do] not want French principles in public or private life" (133).

The fact that Wollstonecraft's narrative proper ends here with Maria defiant against this juridical body of men is telling, especially when we consider again one of the questions with which this study began—that is, how Wollstonecraft not only appropriates the stage heroine Calista but also manipulates the conventions of staged melodrama as genre. Wollstonecraft's conscious echoes and distortions of structural patterns from gothic and sentimental fictions demonstrate the extent to which she comments upon popular literary paradigms; her similar inversions of the conventions of stage melodrama are evident in her patterns of introduction and closure. The narrative of Maria's life encompasses Chapters 7 through 14 as a retrospective memoir written to her daughter, but the novel opens, of course, as Maria finds herself imprisoned in the asylum. The book, thus, begins with the heroine's having lived through the horror of marriage and now being placed in a physical site of horror. Rowe's play begins with the talk of an arranged marriage and ends, appropriately for a "she-tragedy," with Calista incarcerated and ultimately dead in a gloomy cell. Wollstonecraft's novel, then, inverts the beginning and end of Rowe's play in interesting ways. Where Rowe's play begins with what Tumir has called a "little parliament of men" discussing arrangements for Calista's marriage to Altamont and ends with a gothic scene of nightmarish intensity, Wollstonecraft opens the narrative with a gothic scene—full of shrieks, groans, madmen, and a dark cell—but ends the narrative proper with a courtroom full of a juridical parliament of men.[23] Substantially rewriting Calista's fate, Wollstonecraft's revisionary portrait begins with an echo of the gothic machinery with which Rowe ends; Act V of *The Fair Penitent* opens with a conventional nightmarish scene: "SCENE is a room hung with black: on one side Lothario's body on a bier; on the other a table with skull and bones, a book, and a lamp on it. Calista is discovered on a couch in black, her hair hanging loose and disordered." Wollstonecraft's story begins with such a gothic scenario, or more appropriately a comment on such tableaux: "Abodes of horror have frequently been described, and castles, filled with specters and chimera, conjured up by the magic spell of genius to harrow the soul … but what were they to the mansion of despair, in one corner of which Maria sat" (7). Even in this opening line, Wollstonecraft signals readers that she will not be presenting a simple gothic story, and her heroine ends, in the finished narrative, in defiance, "claim[ing] a divorce" (133). Wollstonecraft fulfills this hint to the reader—that the "mansion of despair" is a more horrible site than

---

[23]   To the complex question of where this fragment novel can be said to "end," and to what extent the sketchy notes for potential conclusions may be counted as part of an "ending," I concur with Rajan that the text proper ends with what she calls the chancery scene, despite all of Godwin's apparatus (the "detached sentences," "scattered heads," and "passage [that] appears in some respects to deviate from the preceding hints"). Rajan astutely reflects on the problematics of reading that that apparatus causes, including a blurring of boundaries between Wollstonecraft and Godwin, text and notes, author and editor.

tangible, material "abodes of horror"—by rejecting a gothic suicidal ending for the heroine. Rowe's final scene, however, reveals a parallel instability in its use of gothic scenarios in a similar metanarrative move. In the overtly gothic setting of skull and bones at the opening of Act V, Calista picks up a book teaching "contrition / And penitence" (V.1.25–6) and tosses it aside, scornful of those who would turn genuine sorrow into a "trick," saying, "I have more real anguish in my heart / Than all their pedant discipline e'er knew" (V.1.29–30). Like Maria, whose real suffering in the opening scene of the novel is contrasted to "specters and chimeras, conjured up by the magic spell of genius to harrow the soul" (7), Calista recognizes the artifice of the gothic scene around her, concluding, "Fie! This is pageantry" (V.1.33). Thus, even as she goes to her death having begged forgiveness, she does not cease to recognize and comment on the artificial machinery of artistic, cultural, and political norms. Finally, then, the intertextual play between Wollstonecraft's text and Rowe's, far more significant than has been claimed, foregrounds issues of tyranny on many levels and plays with the limits of popular genres (gothic, sentimental fiction, melodrama) even while existing within them.[24]

Issues within the production history of this play also emphasize its pivotal role in the politicization of theater. Susan Harris's fine study solidly links the play to the Kelly Riots of 1747, the pamphlet wars regarding the proper role of actresses, and to the political turmoil that emerged after the play was restaged at a benefit

---

[24] A revisionary critical look at Rowe's achievements within popular genres has been in progress for a decade now. Restoration scholars had been reluctant to investigate the she-tragedy, a form which they had dismissed as an unfortunate lapse in taste, as Tumir points out. Rowe's achievements (and failures) within the genre provide a complex look at how political themes and popular audiences had uneasy alignments, in particular, how difficult it was to achieve public sympathy for a female victim who is both innocent and sexual, a feat which Wollstonecraft attempts in the person of Maria. The she-tragedy most often required suffering for sexual sin, where heroines were tragic, in distress, pitiable, but not innocent. According to Jean Marsden, for instance, Rowe's play *Lady Jane Grey* never achieved a consistent status in theatrical repertoire because Rowe's aims were at odds with the template of the genre; that is, the "problems inherent in Rowe's representation arise from the collision of his political propaganda with a dramatic tradition in which the female figures suffer not for their virtue but for their sins. These female figures are spectacles with one specific and noninterchangeable function: either model of virtue or fallen heroine." Thus, Rowe's attempt to have Lady Jane Grey both virtuous and suffering meant he had to repudiate her sexuality, which Marsden sees as a difficulty for the audience: "Here, no longer a fallen woman, the title figure has become a symbol of virtue whose own desires are sublimated to a higher political good. His play presents a new heroine, as political propaganda requires the erasure of female desire and overt ... qualities which until then had been hallmarks of the she-tragedy." So in Jane Grey, Rowe creates a heroine who is both icon of political virtue and a spectacle of female suffering. The play suggests that Rowe felt that only when made virtually asexual, when recreated as a saint, could a woman be placed in the public sphere and used as a vessel for political ideology. See Jean Marsden, "Sex, Politics, and the She-Tragedy: Reconfiguring *Lady Jane Grey*," *Studies in English Literature* 42.3 (2002): 501–22.

for the Hospital for Incurables, more a tool for social control of the poor than a real hospital. Harris argues that the performances of the play became a stage for power relations of all kinds, offering a specific example from Rowe of Hadley's cultural arguments about melodrama and the marketplace. These juxtapositions of social and theatrical arenas were a part of the intellectual conversation of the Godwin/Wollstonecraft circle; as Karr's historical study of the plays of Holcroft reveals, Godwin was intrigued by radical "counterperformances," seditious audience events, in that they revealed that "meaning was something that was produced through performance and reception: supposedly hegemonic displays were open to alternative readings."[25] Just as Sheridan's restaging of Rowe's play during theater riots at a benefit for a state-run hospital that was more like a prison, in effect, politicized all three—the play, the theater riots, and the issue of the incarceration of the poor and the role of the asylum—Wollstonecraft's staging of Maria's suffering and critique of tyranny in the 1790s during an age of political turmoil politicized the position of woman not just within marriage, but also in cultural institutions of the court and medicine. Her foregrounding of the asylum, for example, draws attention to the regulatory and misguided premises about madness, particularly the ways in which husbands could easily imprison disobedient wives. As Wollstonecraft says in the *VRW*, "Asylums and Magdalens are not the proper remedies" for betrayed women: "It is justice, not charity ... that is wanting in the world" (71).[26]

Finally, we should mention here a final layer in this reconsideration of Wollstonecraft's manipulation of Rowe, that of contemporary London productions of the play, especially Sarah Siddons's performances of Rowe's heroines. In a letter to Godwin on August 7, 1796, Wollstonecraft teasingly writes, "I supped in company with Mrs. Siddons last night. When shall I tell you what I think of her?"[27] Siddons's preparation for her performance as Calista would have been in process by then; she acted in *The Fair Penitent* in the fall season of 1796. My Chapter 5 takes up at length the argument of the crucial significance of Siddons on Wollstonecraft as well as theoretical implications regarding theatricality that we can infer from her acting theory (surmised both through Siddons's stage notes, through letters, and through contemporary reviews of her performances), but here I will just note that what Wollstonecraft would have seen in 1796 is Siddons's

---

[25]   See David Karr, "'Thoughts That Flash like Lightning': Thomas Holcroft, Radical Theater, and the Production of Meaning in 1790s London," *Journal of British Studies* 40 (July 2001): 324–56, esp. 326.

[26]   Even a cursory reflection on the other minor characters in the asylum suggests the misunderstanding of suffering and madness, especially for women, as is evident in the case of the "lovely maniac" who had been "married against her inclination to a rich old man" and who "in consequence of his treatment, or something which hung on her mind, ... during her first lying-in, lost her senses" (21).

[27]   Mary Wollstonecraft, *The Collected Letters of Mary Wollstonecraft*, ed. Ralph Wardle (Ithaca: Cornell University Press, 1979). See 335.

complex interpretation of this historically ambiguous (in terms of passivity vs. subversion) female character. As Ellen Donkin summarizes,

> Although audiences demanded from the text the comfort and familiarity of the norms of Womanhood, what in fact they responded to in performance was something that potentially ruptured that comfort and familiarity.[28]

Thus the staged performances emphasize the instability of boundaries and draw attention to how the play itself destabilizes boundaries by revealing the tenuous cultural logic upon which they are based.

Finally, the connections between Wollstonecraft's novel and Rowe's play are substantive: female characters shunned for sexual indiscretions, sexual seduction and betrayal by a lover, an acknowledgement of marriage as slavery and imperialism (link of public/private tyranny), a redefinition of honor versus insipid decency, and a conflation of sexual, economic, and national identity conflicts. More importantly, the novel explicitly invokes Rowe's plays—not only to revise his spectacle of the fallen woman and to do what he could not—offer a portrait of a sexual and innocent female—but also to suggest how the figure of the suffering woman could be used to offer both a critique of tyrannical power in all its forms and to suggest the potential power of imaginative sympathy, a quality necessary for good "acting," in the process of self-invention, and to define morality in terms other than those in the "shameful tale to tell for public sport."

* * *

"I claim then a divorce." (Maria, *Maria, or The Wrongs of Woman*)

While Rowe's Calista is an important dramatic character with which Wollstonecraft's Maria is in dialogue, the novel itself is permeated by the trope of theatricality. Again, the cohesive guiding question is whether theatricality *enables* or *subverts* various cultural mechanisms of power, a question which the text explores from multiple perspectives. First, the characterizations of Darnford, George, and Maria all reveal recognition of both the limitations of and possibilities within theatrical social contexts; second, the novel exposes the extent to which the cultural institutions of marriage and of the judicial system repress their inherent artificiality and thus normalize a kind of theatricality; and third, the narrative dramatizes a potential for women to gain a kind of power of self-fashioning by moving from spectator to active dramatic agent.

The first male romantic lead, Darnford is linked materially and metaphorically with theater. Becoming known to Maria through his handwritten, marginal notes

---

[28]   Ellen Donkin, "Mrs. Siddons Looks Back in Anger: Feminist Historiography for Eighteenth-Century British Theater" in *Critical Theory and Performance*, ed. Janelle G. Reinelt and Joseph R. Roach (Ann Arbor: University of Michigan Press, 1992). See 278.

in the books Jemima procures for her, Darnford is introduced in the novel as a sentimental hero; once he meets Maria, however, he confesses to a depraved life, characterizing his relations with women as one that could "scarcely be comprehended by female delicacy," admitting that he "formed [an] acquaintance with them at the theaters" (28). Darnford's position then in the novel is twofold: 1) he, as sentimental hero, is a stimulus for Maria's sensibility, and 2) his material connections with theater invoke the novel's network of competing meanings of theatricality. Both dimensions of Darnford signal Maria's educational trajectory with regard to the dramatic. My earlier discussion of Wollstonecraft's manipulations of genre of sentimental fiction (Poovey's judgment against and Johnson's argument for Wollstonecraft's narrative achievement) pertain, of course, most directly to Maria's relationship with Darnford. Anne Mellor has argued that Maria's excessive sensibility with regard to men is a form of psychological madness, and, more recently, Anna Wilson asserts that "the body of the text enacts the failure of its theory, rendering visible the consequences of the attempt to speak the female text in the theater of rationality."[29] It is, however, through the *material* world of theater that the text speaks most powerfully. Wollstonecraft uses these early associations of Darnford and theater to introduce cultural presumptions regarding the sexual immorality of the theater scene. Those culture wars have been well theorized by Straub and Hadley: Straub's work on spectatorship in the eighteenth century demonstrates that "actresses' inherent challenge to the gendered opposing spheres of public and private becomes increasingly the object of rhetorical containment and erasure," and Hadley's work on melodrama points out that not only were pimps and prostitutes a well-known part of the theatrical dynamic, but also their concealed illicit affiliations with aristocracy were presumed, the kind of concealment that Wollstonecraft persistently labels as perversion.[30] Another culturally resonant fact about Wollstonecraft's use of the sign of theater in her agendas is that London theater was likened to French politics in the 1790s, as my Chapter 4 discusses at length. As Carlson notes, "London theater is the cultural domain of England that most nearly embodies the sexual politics associated with France" (20). Darnford, then, is a sign for both the culture's presumptions about the sexual immorality of theaters and the theatrical "posing" which Wollstonecraft overtly critiques in all three main characters.

Maria's excessively sentimental and hasty obsession with Darnford is at first an "error of cognition" (xiv) to use Mellor's words, a misreading of him as the hero of the romances she reads in the asylum. Wollstonecraft's portrayal, however, of this part of Maria's growth stresses not just her sensibility and his arrogance,

---

[29]   Anna Wilson,. *Persuasive Fictions: Feminist Narrative and Critical Myth* (Lewisburg, PA: Bucknell University Press, 2001), 49.

[30]   See Kristina Straub, *Sexual Suspects: Eighteenth-Century Players and Sexual Ideology* (Princeton: Princeton University Press, 1992), 89 and Elaine Hadley, *Melodramatic Tactics: Theatricalized Dissent in the English Marketplace* (Stanford: Stanford University Press, 1995).

as critics have claimed, but also theatrical gestures—both positive and negative—that Maria's complex character adopts in the relationship. Beginning the fourth chapter, Wollstonecraft as narrator contemplates the "native soundness of [Maria's] constitution" (32). Underscoring the "struggles of the understanding to trace or govern the strong emotions of the heart" (32), Wollstonecraft asserts that Maria's feminine sensibility made her "appear" like a weak heroine (32), but then explains this as a pose regulated by society, the first use of a cloak metaphor that dominates the book (as well as her nonfiction). She uses this trope consistently in *VRW*, for example, arguing aggressively that modesty is a "pharisaical cloak of weakness," and that conduct book writers actually support a perverse ideology that denies the sexuality of the female body while stimulating the cultural production of a gaze that pins women in vulnerable sexual postures, a discussion I take up at length in Chapter 5. Here in this moment, the narrator allies Maria to such products of proper education for women: "… nay such was the sensibility that often mantled over [her brow] that she frequently appeared, like a large proportion of her sex, only born to feel" (32). Appearing, thus, through the mantle or cloak of sensibility to be one of the "yielding mass" (32), Maria is, nevertheless, presented as having from her first days in the asylum a complex relation to theatricality, a stance Wollstonecraft unfolds subtly and persuasively. First asserting that Maria's simplicity of manner often struck some as "infantine ingenuousness that led people of common discernment to underrate her talents" (32), Wollstonecraft then attaches this simplicity, misread as lack of maturity, to her "unfailing sympathy" which made her "beloved by characters of very different descriptions" (33). Maria's ability to affect diverse constituencies would seem to embody what Wollstonecraft had argued as one important potential in theater, especially as education for young people. In the 1786 courtesy book *Thoughts on the Education of Daughters*, for example, she devotes a chapter to the theater in which she argues for its moral utility (an important issue I take up at length in Chapter 3): "Young people who are happily situated should do well to enter into fictitious distress," especially if they then have a "judicious" person to direct their judgment. Wollstonecraft highlights the effect of Maria's character on diverse people, stressing the potential inherent in Maria's dramatic propensities. Specifically, she charts the beneficent effects of Maria and Darnford's closet drama on their one and only audience member, Jemima.

During the course of their encounters, staged by Jemima who stands guard at the door, the asylum becomes transformed into a theater: "A magic lamp now seemed to be suspended in Maria's prison" (33). Wollstonecraft's description of this projection of images as a magic lamp recalls the performances popular in Paris in the 1790s as phantasmagoria, a public dramatic spectacle that linked gothic imagery to political revolution, as shadows and light were manipulated to project horrifying images around the walls. Wollstonecraft's first use of the image of a magic lamp, in fact, occurs in the overtly gothic opening chapter as Maria imaginatively reflects on the train of events which led her to the asylum: "The retreating shadows of former sorrows rushed back in a gloomy train, and seemed to be pictured on the walls of the prison" (8). The transformation of the phantasmagoric image of pictures of sorrow reflected in a "gloomy train," to a "magic lamp" from which "fairy landscapes flitted around the gloomy walls" (33) underscores Maria's imaginative displacement of her grief into joy and also metaphorizes her and Darnford's illicit encounters as a performance, consistently attended by Jemima, who "ever watched on the tip-toe of fear" (33).

While Maria is at times a gullible reader of romance, passively imagining herself cast in a variety of object roles, Wollstonecraft suggests that she, at other times, plays a role as actress in full awareness of why and how she does so. Fearful of showing Darnford too much love too early, the effects of which she knows through her marriage to George, Maria consciously adopts a mask in her early encounters with Darnford in order to "assume a coldness and indifference foreign from her character" (33). How is this posturing different from the kind of hypocritical dissembling urged by male conduct book writers and so persistently critiqued by Wollstonecraft in *VRW*?[31] While Fordyce, Gregory, and Rousseau all encourage pretense as part of the ritual performance of courtship, Maria here adopts it as self-preservation and uses it only until she is ready to confess herself as an experienced woman. Her yielding to Darnford, for example, comes as a result of her honest admission that she has been a wife and therefore will not physically resist him any longer: "'I must open my whole heart to you; you must be told who I am, why I am here, and why, telling you I am a wife, I blush not to'—." Played out with Jemima as audience, this love scene causes Jemima to cry as she watches in a vicarious participation which frees her to shed her first tear of "social enjoyment," as a spectator to "enter into fictional distress," as we saw in the earlier quote from Wollstonecraft's *Thoughts on the Education of Daughters*. Importantly, it is this first experience with a dramatic portrayal of emotions that allows Jemima to "voluntarily" begin "an account of herself," a narration that comprises the fifth chapter of the novel and which juxtaposes the horrid melodrama and gothic scenarios of Jemima's tortured life to these tender scenes in the asylum-theater.

Having moved from passive reader to actress within her budding relationship with Darnforth and then to active listener of Jemima's life narrative, Maria shifts to a new role as writer, again adopting a performative stance as Chapters 7 through 14 function as memoirs to her daughter, to be read at a later date. Significantly, Maria very self-consciously presents her early vulnerability to staged performances, especially to male "heroes" in her past, but also reveals her steadily growing awareness to and ultimate appropriation of theatrical gestures. Within the staging of her marriage to George, Maria moves from an explicit acknowledgment of binding theatricalized social norms, especially gendered ones, to a sense of the potential inherent in a conscious self-staging. Early in their relationship, Maria acknowledges George's superior manners to be no more than acting: "The mask he wore was so complete a covering of his real visage … . In short, I fancied myself

---

[31]   For Wollstonecraft's attack on hypocrisy of modesty, see my article "'Insipid Decency': Modesty and Female Sexuality in Wollstonecraft," *European Romantic Review* 31.1 (Summer 2000): 55–88.

in love— ... with the hero I had dubbed" (64). Wollstonecraft shows remarkably similar awareness of her selective acknowledgement of her lover Gilbert Imlay's theatrical behavior in a letter of 1795: "I shall judge more coolly of your mode of acting, some time hence.[32] In this quotation, Wollstonecraft's acceptance of her own trajectory of judgment, her self-consciousness about her vulnerable tendency to project dramatic roles for her lovers to play, brings into focus how Maria can both admit in her memoirs how she fancifully "dubbed" George a "hero" while, ironically, at the same time reproducing this error in the asylum with Darnford (using the analogy of Pygmalian, she says she formed a heroic character in her mind and then accepted Darnford as a "statue in which she might enshrine them" [33]). Given her consistent playing with Maria's inconsistent awareness of her own illusions, it is not surprising that Wollstonecraft, as we have seen, emphasizes Maria and George's participation in theater circles in London:

> ... the theaters were a never-failing source of amusement. My delighted eye followed Mrs. Siddons, when, with dignified delicacy, she played Califta; and I involuntarily repeated after her, in the same tone, and with a long-drawn sigh, "Hearts like our's were pair'd—not match'd." (76)

Wollstonecraft's allusion to Calista, as we have seen, explicitly invokes Rowe's play to offer a portrait of a female who is both sexual *and* innocent and to dramatize how the figure of the suffering woman could both critique tyranny and suggest the potential growth within imaginative sympathy.

The trajectory of Maria's growth can, in fact, be read as a progression from spectator to actress, suggesting the potential for redefinition in the theatricalized arenas of social, legal, and national power. Such a move constitutes nothing less than a profound shift in potential, from compliance and complicity to confrontation. As I treat at length in Chapter 5, the most significant premises of acting theory (both contemporary eighteenth-century discussions and recent feminist performance theory) direct our critical attention to questions of how "acting," in Litvak's words, "frustrates the attempt to define—let alone to patrol—the border between the safely domestic and the menacingly foreign, between the private and the public, between the inside and the outside."[33] While Maria begins as a theater *spectator* by empathizing with Calista (the "long-drawn sigh") in the passage quoted above, she shifts dramatically when George attempts to sell her to prostitution with Mr. S. Again, the cultural links between prostitution and actresses highlight the force of Wollstonecraft's narrative interplay here. While Straub has argued that it was the actresses' "challenge to the gendered opposing spheres of public and private" (89) that threatened both male and female audiences, Hadley points out that actresses were likened to prostitutes not only for rejecting the domestic sphere in favor of the public, and not only for the public display of their bodies, but "because

---

[32] See *Collected Letters*, 321.

[33] Joseph Litvak, *Caught in the Act: Theatricality in the Nineteenth-Century English Novel* (Berkeley: University of California Press, 1992), 8.

they feigned emotion in the execution of their trade" (149). For Maria to reject prostitution as planned by her husband underscores not only the issue of a wife's compliance but also a conscious appropriation of a role as actress that her culture defined as threatening. Wollstonecraft strikingly has Maria perform her freedom, with Mr. S as her first audience:

> Then turning to Mr. S, I added, "I call on you Sir to witness" [and I lifted up my hands and eyes to heaven] "that as solemnly as I took his name, I now abjure it" [and I pulled off my ring and put it on the table] "and that I mean immediately to quit his house never to enter it more … I leave him as free as I am determined to be myself." (95)

In her narration, complete with stage directions, Maria literally performs the separation without institutional or legal intervention. A narration of a performance that underscores her physical gestures in tandem with her performative utterances, this scene functions as a turning point in Maria's awareness and manipulation of her own theatrical potential. Butler would suggest that the body figures importantly in the text precisely because of its performative language, since for her "the 'force' of the performative is never fully separable from bodily force."[34] This physicality of signification, to use Butler's term, provokes George's coercive orders for her to invoke "prudence and propriety," qualities he mistakenly characterizes as natural rather than constructed. When she refuses, he orders her to pretend at least for a while so as "not to expose [yourself] to the servants," a request Maria rightly rejects as "subterfuge" (97), a form of acting, dissimulation, to which she will no longer concede. Again, Wollstonecraft provides this network of competing interpretations of theatrical, which climaxes when Maria firmly rejects her husband's sexual advances. Entering her bedroom at midnight, George calmly argues for sex as the best way for "husbands and wives to end their differences," and when she refuses her body, he asks how long she intends to "continue this pretty farce" (99). Persistently building on the theatrical trope, Wollstonecraft has Maria explain his final outburst:

> … conquering his anger … he exclaimed, "very pretty, theatrical flourishes! Pray Fair Roxana, stoop from your altitude, and remember that you are playing a part in real life. (100)

Suggesting a specific part to play, he counsels her to "act like a prudent woman," and to take a lover while using him as a cloak: "'I was not,' he laid a stress on his words, 'without my passions; and a husband was a convenient cloke'" (101). As this instrumental scene climaxes, Wollstonecraft conflates her image of the cloak of sexual hypocrisy with that of the cloak or spectacle of state power. After her refusal of his sexual advances, when George returns to her bedroom

---

[34]   Judith Butler, *Excitable Speech: Politics of the Performative* (London and New York: Routledge, 1997), 141.

in the morning, Maria reports that he says he "came as my gentleman usher to hand me down to breakfast" to which Maria retorts, "Of the black rod?" (102). Maria's allusion to the historical figure of the "usher of the black rod" invokes a public symbol of state authority whose label overtly ascribes to state power a phallic quality. In her edition of the novel, Richards notes that this figure was "an officer of the House of Lord who summoned defendants to trial" (159), a figure whose title is derived from his staff of office, an ebony stick surmounted with a gold lion. Certainly, insofar as this figure is a summoner, Maria's casting George as this character exposes his attempts both to command authority over Maria and to assign guilt to her. The actions of the black rod, however, are more than simply summonings; in fact, this character has a rich cultural resonance with regard to state power and pageantry. Originally set up in 1361 by Edward III to provide an usher for the Most Noble Order of The Garter, the Black Rod's primary job was to lead the knights in procession to their assembly in St.George's Chapel and stand guard over the door during their deliberations, thus both performing a role in state spectacle and working to ensure discipline. The figure's role in British parliamentary proceedings adds a further dimension to Wollstonecraft's appropriation of it; during the ceremonial opening of parliament, the Gentleman Usher of the Black Rod, as chief security officer of the Lords, proceeds to the lower chamber to summon the Commons. Knocking on the door three times, he waits to have it opened and shut in his face, a ceremonial act that commemorates the unsuccessful attempt of King Charles I to personally arrest revolutionary members of the Commons in 1641. Since then, no member of the Royal Court has been allowed to enter the Commons without that body's permission. The spectacle then both conveys the power of the Lords in summoning the Commons and at the same time underscores British resolve against any tyrannical abuse of power by the sovereign. Maria's referencing the black rod, then, invokes questions about how George perceives his authority and clearly has an effect upon him: "this question, and the tone in which I asked it, a little disconcerted him" (102). Her interrogative statement— "of the black rod?"—flatly accuses him of likening a husband's authority over his wife to that of state power, and, more significantly, simultaneously undermines that authority by highlighting not a real figure of state power, but a spectatorial *symbol* of it.

Maria's conflation of domestic and sexual power struggles with the mechanisms of state government in this scene and her refusal of George's "convenient cloke" lead to her becoming victim to the very theatrical cultural mechanisms of power. First, she is literally rejected by the social posse at the opera, the female theatergoers who ostracize her *not* because she has a lover but because she *openly* has a lover:

> She ... was refused admittance ... at the opera or Ranelagh, ... these ladies [availed] themselves of the cloke of marriage to conceal a mode of conduct that would have damned their fame. ... Had [Maria] remained with her husband practicing insincerity, she would have been respected. If instead of openly living with her lover, she could called into play a thousand arts to allow those not deceived to pretend to be so, she would have been caressed and treated like an honorable woman. And Brutus is an honorable man. (127)

In this extraordinary passage which suggests another specific stage for Maria's growth, Wollstonecraft refers to both contemporary material theatrical sites, the opera and Ranelagh gardens—defining these spaces in terms of the cloak of concealment, to pretense—and to Shakespeare's *Julius Caesar*. First, the echo of Antony's speech in *Julius Caesar* invokes the public performative power of speech, and the analogy similarly works to discredit the publicly iterated definition of "honorable" behavior by sarcastically praising the Brutus that these ladies at the opera represent. With regard to the public spaces, Ranelagh, in particular, encodes a cultural phenomenon in that, by the late eighteenth century, it was a social site for entertainment only nominally, being well-known as a place for prostitution and other illicit assignations. Wollstonecraft's passage exposes a cultural hypocrisy not only through specific references to these contemporary sites, but also by allusions to the hypocritical and self-conscious "practicing [of] insincerity" within Wollstonecraft's own circle, the acquaintances who insisted on calling her Mrs. Imlay even though, as Godwin points out, Wollstonecraft never tried to keep secret the fact that she was not ever his wife. It was the "polite circles" who refused to accept that truth—who as Godwin says "persisted in shutting their eyes, and pretending they took her for a married woman"—that rejected Wollstonecraft after her marriage to Godwin publicly negated what they had chosen to believe.[35] Thus, as Wollstonecraft narrates Maria's rejection by these theater-goers, she indicts the cultural mechanisms of power based on normative, insincere acting out of definitions of decency.

More drastically even than the forces of cultural hypocrisy, Maria becomes victim to coercive powers of state theater as well. The cloak which serves as a hypocritical repression of human knowledge, and which functions in polite society for fashionable women to hide sexual immorality is, therefore, the same cloak, manipulated by the state apparatus in its manipulation of power. The novel has consistently chronicled the abuses of women within the cultural institution of marriage, leading Maria at one point to doubt whether women are in fact national citizens since "… the laws of her country—if women have a country—afford her not protection or redress from her oppressor" (92). George's posturings, in fact, are linked to his public character as a British citizen, his shows of patriotism as fake as his pretense at affection for her:

> He at one time professed patriotism, but he knew not what it was to feel honest indignation; and pretended to be an advocate for liberty, when with as little affection for the human race as for individuals, he thought of nothing but his own gratification. He was just such a citizen as a father. (93)[36]

---

[35]   See William Godwin, *Memoirs of the Author of A Vindication of the Rights of Woman* in *The Wrongs of Woman and Godwin's Memoirs*, ed. Cynthia Richards (Glen Allen, VA: College Publishing, 2004), 283–4.

[36]   It is unclear whether Darnford's marginal notes where he, in Maria's interpretation, "warmly alludes to the enslaved state of suffering humanity," are insincere or genuine validations of some judicial aspect of his character. Given the sketches for the fragmented

The conclusion of the novel dramatizes both Wollstonecraft's sense of the tension between political theater as a dangerous seduction, an ornamental gilding over the abuse of government power to which the trajectory of the narrative leads Maria, and her belief that individuals can fight back by subverting or manipulating the very theatrical apparatus that threatens them. Maria becomes a sexually independent female understudy who has the "hounds of law" unleashed upon her, becoming public theater herself in both the media and the judicial system. Burroughs, in *Closet Stages: Joanna Baillie and the Theater Theory of British Romantic Women Writers*, quotes Anna Jameson's 1838 metaphoric description of the ways women were made public theater, a passage which highlights both of Maria's experiences: "a woman may be libelled and pilloried in an audacious newspaper; or dragged from private life into a court of justice ... exposed ... in shame and despair. ... If such a scene CAN by possibility take place, one stage is not worse than another."[37] Maria finds herself on both these stages. She at first is branded as a public criminal once she is indeed, in Jameson's words, libeled "in an audacious newspaper," as George takes out a "WANTED" ad in the newspaper: "An advertisement quickly met my eye, purporting that 'Maria Venables had, without any assignable cause, absconded from her husband; and any person harbouring her, was menaced with the utmost severity of the law'" (105). It is this advertisement, this spectatorial use of her, that ultimately undermines her as her female friends can no longer protect her once she is criminalized, and this train of events concludes with her imprisonment in the asylum, the final scene in the written narrative of memoirs to her daughter. This point in the narrative—the conclusion of the memoirs—is not, however, the closure of the novel but rather opens up Maria's active pursuit of independence, actions which assure that she will become public theater in a courtroom. Just as the wildly popular trials of the late eighteenth century can be seen as a "mirror of [the] culture's ambivalent attitude toward theater," Maria's navigating of the judicial system—her move from prisoner in the asylum to defendant, judge, and jury in her own case—offers a compelling representation of competing notions of the theatrical; Maria, in fact, invokes a subversive act of self-fashioning which, as Litvak says about acting, is difficult to patrol and which achieves what Wayne Koestenbaum calls a "retaliatory self-invention," one that, I argue, is achieved in a courtroom independent of judge, jury, or verdict.

Wollstonecraft's representation of the marital laws and the final courtroom scene would have been influenced by her knowledge of both treason trials and civil trials for adultery, both of which were popular entertainment in the late

---

ending, none of which validate Darnford's worth as a lover, it is likely that these too may be posturings of a different kind of "patriotism."

[37]   In her chapter on celebrity narratives, Burroughs uses Anna Jameson's 1838 *Winter Studies and Summer Rambles in Canada* from which this quotation is taken (1: 60–61). See Catherine Burroughs, *Closet Stages: Joannie Baillie and the Theater Theory of British Romantic Women Writers* (Philadelphia: University of Pennsylvania Press, 1997), 17.

1790s and which I take up at length in Chapter 4. Wollstonecraft's version of an adultery trial, Maria's courtroom experience, concludes the narrative proper, as it is the last completed scene before the fragmented sketches for an ending. My reading of Maria's presence in the scene emphasizes her understanding of the spectator-spectacle dynamic and Wollstonecraft's conscious manipulation of it. Insisting on arguing Darnford's defense against the charge of seduction herself, Maria does not flinch from facing "the condemnation of a mistaken world" (130). Her decision to write her defense is shaped by her rejection of the overtly theatrical position allotted her as courtroom defendant. Seeking a potential at least for a sincere performance, she rejects the possibility of "acting contrary to those feelings which were the foundation of her principles" (130); thus, she decides on an original mode of performance: "Convinced that the subterfuges of law were disgraceful, she wrote a paper, which she expressly desired might be read in court" (130). I analyze the courtroom scene very closely in Chapter 4 within the discursive contexts of trial discourse, but here I will simply assert that the scene masterfully concludes the novel proper in that her statement of defense rejects all notions of state-coerced definitions of morality and uses performative speech (e.g., I declare, I protest) to avow her own (and Darnford's) innocence. The judge's inflammatory response suggests the power of this performance as he equates her "newfangled ideas" with "French principles," thus demonstrating the cultural anxiety about role-playing as that which, as Litvak says, frustrates the attempts to define—let alone to patrol—the border between the domestic and the foreign, the private and public. Thus while Wollstonecraft critiques the coercive power of public spectacle and the subterfuge of law, she also sees performance as a subversive, transgressive mechanism. Although the fragmented sketches for an ending reveal Wollstonecraft's indecision about whether Maria's performance would lead to success or failure, the body of the novel stages the possibilities for those women who refuse to "play their part by rote," as Wollstonecraft says in *Letters Written During a Short Residence*, and instead act up and act out as "signposts" in creative and empowering ways.

Chapter 3
Becoming a "Sign-post":
Ethics and Theater

All the world is a stage, thought I; and few there are in it who do not play the part
that they have learned by rote; and those who do not, seem marks to be pelted
at by fortune; or rather, as sign-posts, which point out the road to others, whilst
forced to stand still themselves amid the mud and dust.[1]
—Mary Wollstonecraft, *Letters Written During A Short Residence*

This chapter situates Wollstonecraft within philosophical debates circulating in
the late eighteenth century on the issue of the moral utility of public spectacle
(including state pageantry, public executions, and public rituals) and the effects
of sympathy. While philosophers like Smith and Mandeville ponder the potential
for theatrical simulation of sympathy, and Burke argues for his own brand of
the moral utility of theater, Rousseau, in his *Letter to D'Alembert on Theatre*,
resoundingly denies the capacity of spectacle to engage compassion, arguing
that theatrical spectacle weakens one's commitment to active social duty *outside*
the theater. This general question of the utilitarian ethic of theater or spectacle
informs Wollstonecraft's nonfiction works in a number of ways: the context of
philosophical and political foundations for both sides of this debate; the critique of
hollow forms or rituals performed in political and religious institutions; the role of
gender in considerations of the ethics of public spectacle; and finally, the potential
for a performative selfhood based on the spectatorial negotiations of theater.
I explore Wollstonecraft's divided, often ambiguous conclusions on this issue in
Thoughts on the Education of Daughters and especially *Letters Written During A
Short Residence*.

Samet's discussion of French Revolutionary theater and sympathy offers a
useful framework of eighteenth-century discourses on benevolence and the debate
about the moral utility of theater, especially as manipulated by Rousseau. In such
discourses, authentic charity or sympathy is counterfeited in pity which is then
counterfeited in theatrical imitation. Bernard Mandeville's 1723 "The Fable of
the Bees," for example, asks readers to imagine themselves in a locked room
unable to act but witnessing a small child be destroyed by a ravenous brute.
Mandeville's frozen spectator dramatizes the difference between theoretical
pity and sympathetic action. Rousseau invokes this conceit of the imprisoned
spectator in his *Discourse On The Origin of Inequality*, and it incidentally serves
the ends of his anti-theatrical prejudice in the *Letter to D'Alembert On Theatre*.

---

[1]   *Letters Written During a Short Residence in Sweden, Norway, and Denmark*, ed.
Carol Poston (Lincoln: University of Nebraska Press, 1976), 188.

Rousseau's point is that dramatic representation imprisons viewers in the chains of their depravity but with a cost. He argues that theater purges spectators' emotions such that by the time they get back outside the theater, they have no resources in reserve for real social action. As Samet summarizes it, theatrical contract negates the more important social contract, as it were, nullifying any potential moral utility in theatrical production.[2]

David Marshall's work on sympathy notes that the title normally written as *Letter to D'Alembert On Theatre* really should be translated as "on spectacles," emphasizing Rousseau's concern with "how we are affected by the theatrical relations enacted outside as well as inside the playhouse by people who face each other as actors and spectators."[3] Famously occasioned by d'Alembert's article in *L'Encyclopedie* describing the benefits of bringing theater to Geneva, Rousseau counterargues that such an action would harm the moral fabric of the community.[4] Using the specific issue of a theater in Geneva, Rousseau, not surprisingly, returns to a consistent premise: in the conflict between the simplicity of nature and the artifice of civilization, the theater and the actor are symbols of society and social man. This reading counters the more reductive readings of the *Letter* such as Barish's label of it as an "antitheatrical tract."[5] Many critics point out the hypocrisy of Rousseau's critique of theatrical arts given, first, his own creative and literary endeavors (he composed seven plays and three operettas between 1742 and 1752), and, second, the hypocrisy of critiquing theatricality in a work itself employing a variety of dramatic devices.[6] Rousseau's text invokes both literal and metaphorical concepts of theater: literally, he focuses on theater as a place for public entertainment, and the causes and effects of its existence; metaphorically he sees it as a sign of morality and collective social civilization. As far as the causes for a collective desire for public theater, Rousseau insists it is a sign of a weakening culture and an unhealthy populace who has given in to the "burden of idleness." Further arguing the point of human weakness, Rousseau characterizes theatergoers as those already ill at ease with themselves and experiencing an alienation within the community at large. He addresses the paradoxical nature of this assertion:

---

[2]   Elizabeth D. Samet, "Spectactular History and the Politics of Theater: Sympathetic Arts in the Shadow of the Bastille," *PMLA* 118.5 (2003): 1305–19. See 1306.

[3]   See David Marshall, *The Surprising Effects of Sympathy* (Chicago: University of Chicago Press, 1988), esp. 135–6.

[4]   For an excellent treatment of this issue, see Timothy M. Costelloe, "The Theater of Morals: Culture and Community in Rousseau's *Lettre a M. d'Alembert*," *Eighteenth-Century Life* 27.1 (2003): 52–71.

[5]   John Barish, *The Antitheatrical Prejudice* (Berkeley: University of California Press, 1981.), esp. Chapter. 9.

[6]   See Costelloe's summary of these arguments, esp. 53.

People think they come together in the theater, and it is there they are isolated. It is there that they go to *forget* their friends ... in order to concern themselves with fables, in order to cry for the misfortunes of the dead, or to laugh at the expense of the living.[7]

On the effects, Rousseau suggests that actors commit to a profession dishonorable in its essence, in addition to being associated with particular moral vices. The talent of the actor being "the art of counterfeiting himself," the person is degraded and seduced into vice from the very act of acting. A final concern he has is that theater is all-consuming and would take ordinary persons away from ordinary pleasures; theater would become "a metaphysic of all morality."[8]

In the more metaphorical sense, theater itself becomes a trope through which to argue for institutional foundations of a healthy state. Theater, thus, ceases to be simply an institution which occasions deleterious effects, but becomes an idea through which Rousseau expresses his view on the nature of human beings. As such it attains a symbolic status, representing the human condition and the corruption of nature wrought by the vagaries of human society. In this larger sense of metaphor, Burke, Paine, and Wollstonecraft are all cross-referencing Rousseau's arguments as they engage in polemical debate about the French Revolution. Given Burke's statements in the *Reflections* about the power of drapery and illusions of state pageantry being necessary ("To make us love our country our country ought to be lovely") and given his moral arithmetic that finds that vice itself can lose "half its evil" by "losing all its grossness," it would seem that Burke clearly favors theatrical displays by the state and its rulers.[9] Additionally, Burke consistently uses an ethics of theater in his political arguments. In the *Reflections* at the close of his description of the October Days episode, he asks how anyone could exult over tragedy in real life while only being distressed by it in theaters, basically asking what kind of fraud could weep at the theater and yet revel at the plight of Marie Antoinette. As Bromwich has pointed out, Burke joins the "standards of dramatic naturalness and moral naturalness" to suggest that "history is itself a theater of judgment, and human nature is embodied in the responses of the spectactors."[10] I take up Wollstonecraft's representation of French Revolutionary discourse as itself a kind of fall into theatricality in Chapter 5, but we need to note here that Paine's attack on Burke's "horrid paintings" and Wollstonecraft's attack in *VRM* on Burke's misguided sympathies build upon the philosophical debates spawned by Rousseau. Paine's castigation of Burke's theatrics culminates in his own dramatic unfolding of a "real" prisoner of misery, sliding into death in the silence

---

[7]   Quoted in Costelloe, 56.

[8]   Quoted in Costelloe, 58.

[9]   Edmund Burke, *Reflections on the Revolution in France*, ed. Conor Cruise O'Brien (New York: Penguin, 1968). The quote is from 170.

[10]   See David Bromwich, *Politics by Other Means* (New Haven: Yale University Press, 1992).

of the dungeon; thus, as Samet summarizes, "Paine does not ultimately condemn the play; he simply replaces the royal player with a populist understudy" (1315).

Another dimension to consider about Rousseau's *Letter* is the way in which his discussions of "good" spectacle—the rural festival—become a model and paradigmatic source for nationalist rhetoric. A balanced appropriation of sentiment and spectacle informs most discourses on nationalism in the period, and Rousseau's recipe for a rural festival is quite explicit:

> Plant a pole crowned with flowers in the middle of a square, assemble the people, and you will have a festival. Even better: put the spectators into the show; make them actors themselves; contrive it that everyone sees and adores themselves in others, and everyone will be bound together as never before.[11]

As Rousseau distinguishes it, theater is a corrupt form of entertainment because the distinction between the spectator and the actors perpetuates aristocratic notions of publicity, according a public role to a privileged few and consigning the rest to private obscurity; thus, the upper class rely on imposture in a ritual that reproduces the deceptions and divisions of feudal society. The festival, on the contrary, serves as a form of spectacle useful for a republic because it obliterates the distinction between actor and spectator.[12] Perhaps the most famous festival, the 1794 Festival of the Supreme Being, provides an interesting fulcrum of opposing reactions to the ritual. A massive pageant ordered by Robespierre and staged by Jacques-Louis David on 8 June 1794, in open air on the "Field of Reunion," formerly the royal army's parade ground, the festival boasted as centerpiece a huge mountain erected on the field. The June Festival, thus, incorporated a lot of military display, yet was inherently pastoral. An influential account of the festival from Helen Maria Williams likens it to terrorist principles and attacks the "coerciveness and hidden cruelty of Robespierre's utopian pageant" which was, in essence, a "lifeless simulation of republican feeling."[13] Similarly, in 1795, Charles Pigott's *A Political Dictionary* conveys this sense of a mystification attendant on such ritual, defining the word "Pageant" as "A spectacle, by the lure of which a minister may draw money for himself and his friends, by amusing the public mind; ... and whilst the People of England suffer their privileges to be restrained, their rights pillaged, and immunities plundered, the same pageants will be erected, and the same spectacles displayed."[14] Mona Ozouf's discussion of Revolutionary fêtes is helpful here in emphasizing how the very readability of such orchestrated events depended upon a denial of the ongoing complexity of the political process, an attempt to

---

[11] Quoted in Dart 110. See Gregory Dart, *Rousseau, Robespierre, and English Romanticism* (Cambridge: Cambridge University Press, 1999).

[12] See Dart's useful discussion on 110.

[13] See Dart's summary on 114.

[14] See David Karr's "'Thoughts that Flash Like Lightning': Thomas Holcroft, Radical Theater, and the Production of Meaning in 1790s London," *Journal of British Studies* 40 (2001): 324–56. The Pigott quote is from 334, n.48.

fix or to install a sense of revolutionary heroism or martyrdom, depending on the festival.[15] Wollstonecraft does not overtly comment on the festival at all, although she does write about attending a festival with Fanny and simply enjoying the entertainment.[16] The significant question is how Wollstonecraft would have interpreted this in terms of ethics of spectacle. Most critics agree that Robespierre was driven to seek civic unity through the manipulation of aesthetic effect: the form of the festival suited his purpose since virtue cannot be taught nor simply imposed by force. Dart's reference of Habermas on the role of legislator is pertinent here: "[he] could rely neither on force nor on public discussion ... he had to take refuge in the authority of an indirect influence which can compel without violence and persuade without convincing" (109). This idea of the "authority of an indirect influence" informs Wollstonecraft's analyses of the potentially positive ethics in all kinds of spectacles and the abuses that lead to destructive effects, as we will see in her *Thoughts on the Education of Daughters* and *Letters Written During a Short Residence*. Dart, in fact, argues that Wollstonecraft demonstrated a growing interest, highly characteristic of both French and English radicals during this period, in "the concept of aesthetic education, that notion that a people might have to be seduced to follow virtue rather than simply forced to obey it, and that therefore a project of cultural rather than political regeneration might offer the best means of recuperating the tarnished revolutionary ideal" (101).[17]

One final philosophical dimension to this issue of the ethics of theater has to do with to what extent Rousseau's consideration of public acts is gendered. Lynn Hunt, in her introduction to the excellent collection *Eroticism and the Body Politic*, points out both Rousseau's denunciation of the erotic potential of females on display in public salons and the irony of his statement. In arguing against women's propensity for self-display in public and its corrupting effect on masculine virtue, Rousseau misses the point that such denunciations, including his own, were often developed in an eroticized form; that is, Rousseau's writings about the public displays of women were themselves public displays of women's sensibilities and erotic potential. Hunt concludes that even the most vitriolic passages in the *Letter* are ambiguous because they virtually exalt women's powers. Also, when we talk about the question of "politics-as-seduction," we should remember that Wollstonecraft, Germaine de Stael, and Helen Maria Williams

---

[15] See Mona Ozouf, *La Fete Revolutionnaire 1789–1799* (Paris: Editions Gallimard), 1976.

[16] See the *Collected Letters of Mary Wollstonecraft*, ed. Janet Todd (London: Penguin, 2003) as she talks about Fanny's enjoying the music at the fete and her intentions to buy her a memorial sash: "... to honor J.J. Rousseau ... I intend to give her a sash, the first she has ever had about her—and why not?—for I have always been half in love with him." The letter discusses her attending the fete on 21 September 1794. See 263.

[17] Dart 101. I discuss Wollstonecraft's suggestion about how Louis XVI should have used the practical power of politics as seduction in Chapter 5, and Chapter 6 extends this concept to her views on acting and the stage as influenced by the performances and theory of Siddons.

all had a fervent interest in Rousseau's fictional and confessional writings while keeping a notably skeptical attitude to his political theory, which was misogynistic in consigning women to the private sphere. In her nonfictional writings *Thoughts on the Education of Daughters* and *Letters Written During a Short Residence*, Wollstonecraft presents herself as both spectator, actor, and theorist, with a conscious awareness of the influence of gender on one's participation in spectacle.

Written in 1786, in the familiar genre of a courtesy book, Wollstonecraft's liberal pedagogical treatise *Thoughts on the Education of Daughters* takes the form of 21 brief essays ranging from instructions on raising infant daughters to lessons for young women about dress, marriage, and reading. Conger, in her analysis of the text's complex depiction of sensibility, suggests the necessity of reading it carefully in light of Wollstonecraft's larger projects, demonstrating that far from simply relying on a critique of false sensibility and its baleful effects, Wollstonecraft dissects the issue very creatively and "casts sensibility in the role of an active tutor or internal monitor, a rhetorical move that transforms it from a passive propensity into a dynamic force within the mind."[18] My discussion of theatricality in the text offers a similar conclusion to Conger's on sensibility. While Wollstonecraft critiques hollow forms of "theater" throughout the text, her chapter "On Theater" offers an argument for the potential ethical function of theater and alerts us to read the text as a whole more carefully even as we note the familiar denunciations of fake performances, especially by women. On moral discipline, for example, Wollstonecraft repeats here her consistent assertion in *VRW* that "cunning," a kind of false dramatic posing, is "the natural opponent of strength."[19] Here she asserts, "Dissimulation and cunning will soon drive all other good qualities before them, and deprive the mind of that beautiful simplicity which can never be too much cherished."[20] Similar to the use of "cunning," she also cautions against imitation or "aping," especially with regard to physical beauty, as in the context of a grown woman attempting to pretend she is young: "It is very absurd to see a woman, whose brow time has marked with wrinkles, aping the manners of a girl in her teens" (13). On affectation in a chapter entitled "Artificial Manners," she conversely argues in favor of the artlessness of manners: "She who suffers herself to be seen as she really is, can never be thought affected. She is not solicitous to act a part; her endeavor is not to hide" (14).

In the chapter on theater, she begins with repeating the common maxim that theater can breed affectation, saying that one who is not formed in a healthy manner

---

[18]   See Conger's excellent discussion on 70–75: Syndy McMillen Conger, *Mary Wollstonecraft and the Language of Sensibility* (Rutherford, NJ: Fairleigh Dickinson University Press, 1994), 73.

[19]   *A Vindication of the Rights of Woman*, 2nd edition, ed. Carol Poston (New York: Norton, 1985), 11.

[20]   Wollstonecraft, Mary. *Thoughts on the Education of Daughters. The Works of Mary Wollstonecraft*, ed. Janet Todd and Marilyn Butler. 7 vols (New York: New York University Press, 1989), 4: 1–49. The quote is from 9.

of mind/heart may learn affectation at the theater. This denunciation, however, is part of the larger point that we should not compare intelligent minds with vacant ones. Also, she distinguishes authentic valuable plays that intelligently explore the passions versus those that are full of "declamation" only. Exalting the nuanced restrained emotion of the opening of *King Lear* as compared to Rowe's penitent heroine Calista, she claims,

> That start of Cordelia's when her father says, "I think that Lady is my daughter," has affected me beyond measure, when I could unmoved hear Calista describe the cave in which she would live "Until her tears had washed her guilt away." (46)

With the right play and a lively mind, then, theater does offer a moral function, and her instructions about this include a subtle political message as well:

> Young persons who are happily situated do well to enter into fictitious distress; and if they have any judicious person to direct their judgment, it may be improved while their hearts are melted. Yet I would not have them confine their compassion to the distresses occasioned by love; and perhaps their feelings might more profitably be roused, if they were to see sometimes the complicated misery of sickness and poverty, and weep for the beggar instead of the king. (47)

In a final reflection about theater's effect, she concedes discomfort with the representation of death on stage by actors. Unlike Burke's unease at this, however, hers is not about the dramatic effect that death has on the spectators but rather that it numbs the crowd to suffering. Allying it to the effects of public execution, she says that deaths on stage seem to "have much the same effect on a polite audience, as the execution of malefactors has on the mob that follow them to Tyburn" (47).

Her comparison draws attention to what is perhaps Wollstonecraft's most well-known discussion of "spectacle" in the *Letters Written During a Short Residence*, an account of the audiences at executions which I discuss at length below, but the text as a whole offers some of the most compelling discussions of theatricality in both private and public arenas. Begun as series of personal missives written to her estranged American lover Gilbert Imlay, and later collated and revised into a full-scale travel book offering an extensive narrative of social conditions prevailing in little-known Scandinavian countries, the text attempts to meld social discourse into new popular genre of travel literature. Both Conger and Dart offer useful discussions of the text's representation of sensibility. Dart points out the personal and confessional mode used throughout and contends "that this autobiographical element does not offer a repudiation or rejection of the project of social perfectability, but a tactical manipulation of it ... an intriguing return to and renegotiation of the sentimental writings of Rousseau" (131). Wollstonecraft, thus, comes to view sensibility more positively than in *VRW*. As Poovey has argued, the shift from ultra-rationalist feminism toward an acknowledgement of the power of feeling comes from biography—her growing acceptance of her own feminine susceptibility after Imlay, what Dart labels a brave new vulnerability.

Despite Wollstonecraft's philosophical and theoretical ruminations throughout the *Letters*, it is ultimately herself that is read as the subject of the work. This is a fair starting premise; her friend Amelia Anderson Opie posits Wollstonecraft as a melodramatic heroine, saying that this text replaces the "cold awe" of philosopher with the spectacle of Wollstonecraft as wronged woman. Wollstonecraft, aware of this inevitable reading perhaps, consciously presents herself as actor of sorts. She says in the Advertisement that she could not avoid being "the little hero of each tale," and in Letter One presents herself through the eyes of her Swedish host as subverting gender boundaries from the beginning as the host tells her she has incredible powers of observation in that she asked "*men's questions*."[21] As Conger beautifully puts it, "Whatever ostensible subject [*Letters*] pursues, it is always constituting or revealing the authorial subject, gesturing from the textual threshold toward some shadowy but intensely personal emotional life beyond the text."[22]

It does not take Wollstonecraft long to plunge into the issue of the theatricality of social performance as she takes up the Swedish reliance upon ceremony in Letter Two:

> The Swedes pique themselves on their politeness; but far from being the polish of a cultivated mind, it consists merely of tiresome forms and ceremonies. So far indeed from entering immediately into your character, and making you feel instantly at ease, like the well-bred French, their over-acted civility is a continual restraint on all your actions. (21)

Stressing the "over-acted," Wollstonecraft introduces into her text early on what will be a consistent, energetic critique of hollow rituals. The passage also gestures to the "well-bred French" as possessing an alternative, positive ability to enter "into your character," an observation that supports my contention in Chapter 5 that Wollstonecraft's perspective on the theatricality of the French is far more complex than most critics have observed.

The critique of ceremony pervades her observations of both public and private behavior, but especially that influenced by political and religious systems. In Letter Nine she denounces a religious orthodoxy that defines morality as obeying the right forms. She, for example, castigates towns where "the Sabbath is so decorously observed" in a "stupid stillness" that churchwardens are even sent out of the building during the device to try to "catch some poor person playing a game of bowls" (87, 88). She laments in Norway a turn to this kind of ceremoniousness which is a turn for the worse in morals because "observance of forms ... often supplies the place of that regular attention to duties which are ... natural" (88). And in an initial nod to the artifice of political class, she summarizes the powerful

---

[21] *Letters*, 5, 15.

[22] See Syndy McMillen Conger, "The Power of the Unnamed You in Mary Wollstonecraft's *Letters*," in *Mary Wollstonecraft and Mary Shelley: Writing Lives*, ed. Helen Buss, D.L. Macdonald, and Anne McWhir (Waterloo, Ontario: Wilfred Laurier University Press, 2001), 43–53.

Grand Bailiff in Norway as acting, like most "common minds" do: "aping a degree of courtly parade" (121). As Hadley's work on spectacle and state power demonstrates, it is in the arena of local governance where theatricalized power is most coercive and where theater itself is most distrusted. As one concerned citizen in London wrote after witnessing John Kemble portray a king's overthrow on stage, "Is it advisable to suffer the Theatre to become a school for opposition, to teach practically the effects of the voice of the people. ... May not the same voice which makes the Theatre resound ... aspire to shake the dome of more exalted structures?"[23]

In one of the most interesting letters, from Denmark, Wollstonecraft's discussion of the ill-fated life of Matilda, who died at the age of 24 after a disastrous nine-year marriage to King Christian VII, amplifies her sense of outrage at those who bow down to ceremony of morality as opposed to living by principles acquired by experience. Her defense of Matilda encompasses an intriguing consideration of how women's maternal/sexual identities are conflated and reductively judged in a somewhat similar way to her treatment of Marie Antoinette (see Chapter 5). Consistent with her method in the travel narrative, she records an incident that occurred in the street in which she hears some rude children and then some "invectives thrown out against the maternal character of the most unfortunate Matilda" (152). Having been married in proxy at age 15 to the notoriously depraved Christian VII, Matilda had a relationship with the gifted court physician Struensee, bore him a daughter, saw Struensee tortured and beheaded, was rescued by an English warship after orders to imprison her, and died at the age of 24. Wollstonecraft confesses that Matilda has "haunted [her] ever since [her] arrival" in Denmark, having heard her charged with licentiousness not only for her personal actions, but for her public causes, like founding an orphanage, and because of her sexual autonomy, which caused her to be publicly censured for being a bad mother. I disagree with Bahar's reading of this passage as one that evades the sensational details of Matilda's adulterous affair, instead focusing on her maternal virtue and social activism. Bahar says that Wollstonecraft "upholds her as a paragon by suppressing details of socially-sanctional sexual misconduct," but without belaboring any salacious details, Wollstonecraft does not evade her sexual actions at all; indeed, she confronts the hypocritical judgment of them and records a sympathetic identification with her.[24]

Empathizing with Matilda's victimization by empty forms of morality, Wollstonecraft asserts that she is "[d]isgusted with many customs which pass for virtues, though they are nothing more than observances of forms" (153). She goes even further in defense of Matilda's sexual choices, saying that attachment to Struensee "did not disgrace her heart or her understanding, the king being a

---

[23] See Hadley, 59.

[24] See Saba Bahar, *Mary Wollstonecraft's Social and Aesthetic Philosophy* (New York: Palgrave, 2002). The quote is from 126.

notorious debauchee, and an idiot into the bargain" (154). She concludes her letter
with complete disdain for the empty performative character of the Danish king:

> I cannot describe to you the effect it had on me to see this puppet of a monarch
> moved by the strings which count Bernstorff holds fast; sit, with vacant eye,
> erect, receiving the homage of courtiers, who mock him with a shew of respect.
> He is, in fact, merely a machine of state … [an] effigy of majesty. (154)

Wollstonecraft also includes the humorous anecdote of how the puppet king makes
a mockery of the serious business of governing: "A story is told here of the king's
formerly making a dog counselor of state, because when the dog, accustomed to
eating at the royal table, snatched a piece of meat off of an old officer's plate, he
reproved him jocosely, saying that he, *monsieur le chien*, had not the privilege
of dining with his majesty; a privilege annexed to this distinction" (168–9). She
returns in a serious way to this theatrical trope to describe the relationship between
the monarch and the count (who was the de facto administrator of the country) in
Letter Twenty, calling the count "the real sovereign, scarcely behind the curtain"
and exclaiming, "What a mummery it must be to treat as a king a being who has
lost the majesty of man!" Wollstonecraft's trope echoes Paine's attack in *Rights of
Man* on Burke's use of the drapery metaphor, describing monarchy as "something
kept behind a curtain, about which there is a great deal of bustle and fuss, and a
wonderful air of seeming solemnity; but when by any accident the curtain happens
to open, and the company see what it is, they burst into laughter."[25] She concludes
by acknowledging that Bernstorff's role as puppeteer is understandably seductive,
and she understands that at times, the count might in fact take on the part of the
King when it suited his needs: for instance in the giving of bad news, the count
"avails himself of it [the king's power] sometimes to soften a refusal of his own,
by saying it is the *will* of the king, my master, when everybody knows that [the
king] has neither will nor memory" (168).

From the spectacle of the suffering queen Matilda to the theater of public
executions, Wollstonecraft has reflected on spectatorial negotiations and ethical
consequences of it. But what about the incidental sketches of the suffering poor,
most frequently women? Bahar credits Wollstonecraft's ability to represent a
spectacle of suffering while avoiding a simple objectification of the woman
represented:

> Whereas her descriptions are certainly inscribed within a specular model
> of sympathetic understanding, she nevertheless attempts to recognize the
> subjectivity of the object of the gaze … to forestall the rapid degeneration from
> pity to contempt … and assur[e] the female her agency. (131)

In the most frequently cited example, Wollstonecraft's encounter with a wetnurse,
Bahar credits Wollstonecraft with making the woman a visible sign of social

---

[25] Thomas Paine. *Rights of Man*, ed. Henry Collins (New York: Penguin, 1984).

injustice but refusing a voyeuristic gaze of pity and suggests her method to achieve this is her "becoming absorbed *by* the spectacle of suffering and absorbed *into* it."[26]

Almost all of Wollstonecraft's concerns throughout the text coalesce in Letter Nineteen, which confronts the theatricality of executions, the moral efficacy of deaths acted on stage, false shows of justice, a revision of her earlier thoughts about the French, and the authority of speech acts. The incident of this letter is her meeting a crowd of people coming back from a spectacle of public execution:

> I could not help looking with horror around—the fields lost their verdure—and I turned with disgust from the well-dressed women, who were returning with their children from this sight. What a spectacle for humanity! The seeing such a flock of idle gazers plunged me into a train of reflections on the pernicious effects produced by false notions of justice. And I am persuaded that till capital punishments be entirely abolished, executions ought to have every appearance of horrour given to them; instead of being as they are now, a scene of amusement for the gaping crowd, where sympathy is quickly effaced by curiosity. (155)

The first thing to note about this passage is that its expression of contempt for well-dressed women who have taken their children to this gruesome public event significantly follows the previous narrative lament for Matilda, the victim of hypocritical censure against her sexual/maternal roles. Wollstonecraft thus implicitly compares those hypocrites who would judge Matilda to these complacent women who would most probably consider themselves good mothers for having exposed their children to the execution. Another significant feature of this passage is that her first response to the news, told to her by a servant's simple report, is a visceral reaction to the visual image in the report which included the fact that the man's body had been "afterwards burnt." Sounding like Wordsworth in his response to the gibbet where a man had been recently hung in *The Prelude*, she recalls it as a horror which drained the very fields around her of their "verdure."[27] Turning her narration from personal horror to judgment in disgust of the women to a more reflective analysis, she now labels the crowd "a flock of idle gazers," stressing their posing as passive witnesses to a spectacle rather than a feeling/ thinking audience. This reflection causes her to consider how such an event might be a useful ethical tool, arguing that it should be a genuine spectacle of "horrour" rather than merely a "scene of amusement." Wollstonecraft's careful deployment

---

[26] Bahar links this aesthetic turn to what Michael Fried has called the "absorptive plateau" in his study of eighteenth-century visual art; see Bahar 148.

[27] See William Wordsworth, *The Prelude: 1799, 1805, 1850*, ed. M.H. Abrams, Stephen Gill, and Jonathon Wordsworth (New York: Norton, 1979). The lines are from Book XI 287–301: "I led my horse, and stumbling on, at length / Came to a bottom where in former times / A man, the murderer of his wife was hung / In irons. Mouldered was the gibbet-mast / The bones were gone, the iron and the woods; / Only a long green ridge of turf remained / Whose shape was like a grave."

of theatrical tropes effectively conjures up the serious spectacle for the reader while censuring those who wrongly see it as amusement.

Having overtly conflated public execution with theater, Wollstonecraft next turns to the effects of more specifically staged deaths, that is, of actors pretending to die on stage. She begins by admitting her anxiety about an audience watching an actor pretend to die—she cautiously confesses she sees it as an "immoral tendency"—and then concludes that it is trifling when compared to "the ferocity achieved by viewing the reality as show." An important phrase because she inverts reality/show, the words imply that viewing a show as reality (like the verisimilitude moments of watching a play) is trifling compared to watching a death, for instance, and seeing it only as a show.

Returning to the issue of the theater of execution, she considers issues of class and motivation, saying that she observes that "in all countries the common people go to the execution to see how the poor wretch plays his part rather than to commiserate his fate." Very significantly, again, she emphasizes a passive act of watching a part being played and counters that with the potential effect of a real drama, which might cause one to "commiserate" the fate of the criminal (I take this up more substantively in Chapter 5 on subversive potential of acting). She further suggests that a potentially salutary effect of theater is the fact that spectacle causes not only a commiseration but also a chance to "think of the breach of morality which has brought him to such a deplorable end."[28] Given Wollstonecraft's complex ruminations on "morality" and "virtue," the phrase "breach of morality" offers two meanings: 1) that one would reflect on the crime committed by the accused and learn from it, or 2) that one would consider the "breach of morality" attendant in many supposed administrations of justice, echoing her concern in the first paragraph of this letter with the "pernicious effects produced by false notions of justice." Her insinuation that such spectacles should make viewers question the machinations of justice, as opposed to simply fearing retribution, becomes a more overt censure just a few paragraphs later when she suggests a cynical back story to the execution. Having suffered through a great fire in 1795, Copenhagen government officials might have thought an occasion of another fire (the criminal burned after his execution) would divert those who are "still distressed from the late conflagration"; in fact, Wollstonecraft concludes that she believes it is entirely probable that "the malefactor who died this morning would not, probably, have been punished with death at any other period" (156).

Having cast doubt upon the categorical validity of the players in the scene (justice versus crime), she delves further into the psychology of criminal acts, and her very goal in the *Letters* themselves. Accentuating the performative nature of self, she concludes that the "characters" of hero/villain are made out of the same substance: "I am more and more convinced that the same energy of character which renders a man a daring villain, would have rendered him useful to society,

---

[28] Compare Wollstonecraft's passage in *Thoughts on the Education of Daughters* on positive effects of bad stories.

had the society been well-organized" (156). Thus, her general aim in the work is to provide useful suggestions for improvement by offering various and varying scenes from her travels. As she emphatically states, her intention is *not* to "sketch a national character," but to "note the present state of morals and manners as I trace the world's improvement." That she sincerely believes that her presentation of dramatic scenes can foster ethical improvement testifies again to her belief that theatricality in a number of forms is morally useful.

Concluding this most important letter, Wollstonecraft clearly contrasts the hollow performative forms of virtue to an embodied enactment of virtue by the individual. Again dismissing religious ritual, she avers, "I do not perceive that a regular attendance on public worship, and ... other observances, make them [the Danes] a whit more true in their affections, or honest in their private transactions." Stressing the performative nature of language, especially official pronouncements—those forms of authoritative speech by those who, in Culler's words, declare "what is what" like the judge, priest, umpire—Wollstonecraft wryly debunks the discursive authority of religion and law, asserting, "It seems, indeed, quite as easy to prevaricate with religious injunction as human laws, when the exercise of their reason does not lead people to acquire principles for themselves to be the criterion of all those they receive from others" (162). Continuing with her broader, philosophical considerations of performance of virtue, she uses the occasion of seeing a beggar on the road to affirm her contempt for those who act with charity to bolster their own pride. Wollstonecraft shares Blake's suspicion of charity because as Blake's "A Divine Image" puts it, "Pity would be no more / If we did not make someone poor."[29] Casting such hypocritical postures of charity as performances, she says, "You know that I have always been an enemy to what is termed charity, because timid bigots endeavoring thus to cover their *sins*, do violence to justice, till, acting the demi-god, they forget that they are men" (182).

Finally, Wollstonecraft's travel narrative, which has both censured the coercive or simply vapid forms of theatricality and acknowledged the potentially positive ones, includes a final philosophical reflection about the incontrovertibly dramatic nature of human existence. Beginning with a well-known Shakespearean allusion, she writes, as quoted in the epigraph to this chapter,

> All the world is a stage, thought I; and few there are in it who do not play the part they have learnt by rote; and those who do not, seem marks set up to be pelted at by fortune; or rather, as sign-posts, which point out the road to others, whilst forced to stand still themselves amid the mud and dust. (181)

Catherine Burroughs in *Closet Stages* discusses this passage in a very general way, using it to demonstrate why Wollstonecraft should be considered in studies of Romantic theater theory because she "drew upon theater history ... for metaphors with which she could formulate her critical readings of women's

---

[29]   Wollstonecraft has quoted overtly from Blake's *Songs of Innocence* twice in the text, in Letter IV and Letter XXII, both times from "The Divine Image."

cultural position" (19). Wollstonecraft's emphasis in these lines, according to Burroughs, demonstrates her knowledge of a mode of performance we would call improvisatory, improv actors being those who can "point out the road to others." Accepting the improv role, Wollstonecraft rejects traditional social acting of roles "learnt by rote" and instead posits herself, and the *Letters* as a whole, to be a "sign-post" to instruct spectators in alternative ways of seeing.

Chapter 4
"The subterfuge of law":
Theatricality and Juridical Discourse

Convinced that the subterfuges of law were disgraceful, she wrote a paper, which she expressly desired might be read in court.
—Mary Wollstonecraft, *Maria, or The Wrongs of Woman*

A letter such as Maria writes might have remained unopened to this day, or been passed to the prosecution to make what they would of it. Maria's defence, in relation to the law and legal practice of her day, is a silent and fantastic (im)possibility.
—Elaine Jordan, "Criminal Conversation"

Elaine Jordan's observation that Maria's written defense is a "silent and fantastic (im)possibility" rightfully situates Wollstonecraft's fiction within the powerful legal discourses at play in the last decades of the nineteenth century.[1] In suggesting women's victimization by what she calls the "subterfuge of law," Wollstonecraft's character Maria foregrounds the author's interest in women's complex and vexing relationship to marital, economic, and national jurisdiction. Wollstonecraft's specific use of the term "subterfuge," with its connotations of dissimulation and deceptive cover, significantly implicates legal discourse within that of theatricality. In this chapter, I argue how competing notions of theatricality framed juridical discourse of the time and how these influence Wollstonecraft's representation of legal practices. My argument draws upon three historical juridical contexts: 1) the civil divorce trials of the 1790s, 2) the British treason trials of 1794, and 3) the 1793 trial of Marie Antoinette, all of which involve theoretical considerations of authoritative speech (judicial, legal, and theological) as binding performatives to be resisted and rewritten.

Culler's enormously cogent discussion of performative speech from J.L. Austin to Judith Butler, "The Fortunes of the Performative," emphasizes the shift from concern about what words do, as in Austin's *How To Do Things With Words*, to a question of how and in what way performative speech gains/maintains/challenges authority.[2] When Butler takes up the model of authoritative speech, she applies her theoretical arguments about the effect of the repetition of gender norms to the question of authority:

---

[1]   See Elaine Jordan, "Criminal Conversation: Mary Wollstonecraft's *The Wrongs of Woman*," *Women's Writing* 4.2 (1997): 221–34. The quote is from 224.

[2]   Jonathon Culler, "The Fortunes of the Performative In Literary and Cultural Theory," *Literature and Psychology* 45.1–2 (1999): 7–28.

Performative acts are forms of authoritative speech: most performatives, for instance, are statements which, in the uttering, also perform a certain action and exercise binding power. Implicated in a network of authorization and punishment, performatives tend to include legal sentences, baptisms, inaugurations, declarations of ownership, statements that not only perform an action but confer a binding power on the action performed.[3]

One of the main questions with the utterances of these agents of authority (judges, umpires, priests, president, lawyers, or any figures who, as Culler says, "declare what is what") is the common supposition that the utterance creates what it names because of the authority of the speaker. Butler insists that it is not through the externally granted authority of the figure but the "repeated citation of norms, the application of rules, that the authority of a mode of speaking is generated" (225). This qualification leads Butler to her interest in the force of the word "queer." In an original example that has added another dimension to the analysis of performative utterance, Butler asserts that the force of the insult comes not from any authority of the speaker who is, as Culler says, "likely some fool unknown to the victim" (22), but from the fact that the shout "Queer" repeats shouted insults from the past, or acts of address that produce the homosexual object through reiterated shaming:

'Queer' derives its force precisely through the repeated invocation by which a social bond among homophobic communities is formed through time. The interpellation echoes past interpellations, and binds the speakers, as if they spoke in unison across time. In this sense it is always an imaginary chorus that taunts 'queer.' (226)

Throughout my analysis of the three trial discourses that were circulating around Wollstonecraft in the late eighteenth century, I interrogate how authoritative speech enacts power or fails to do so, or in the case of Wollstonecraft's heroine Maria, how such speech acts are appropriated and manipulated for individual proclamations which, nonetheless, use collective force of repeated iterations over time.

We can be sure of Wollstonecraft's knowledge of the treason and divorce trials in England as well as the trial of Marie Antoinette in France. The seven volumes of *Trials for Adultery* was "known to Godwin," as Gary Kelly points out, and I agree with Caroline Franklin that Wollstonecraft would have doubtless made use of Godwin's personal copy of this text as she must have had first-hand knowledge of the intricacies of the adultery clauses in divorce cases from helping her sister Eliza escape her husband.[4] Her knowledge and engagement with the treason trials is just as certain. Godwin was, in effect, an informal consultant to figures in the criminal treason trials, like Holcroft and Gerrald, and Wollstonecraft was herself implicated in one of the trials. As Claire Tomalin points out, Wollstonecraft's name

---

[3]   Judith Butler, *Bodies That Matter* (London and New York: Routledge, 1993), 225.

[4]   See Caroline Franklin, *Mary Wollstonecraft: A Literary Life* (New York: Palgrave, 2006).

appeared before the public in the treason trial of William Stone. A letter from John Hurford Stone was read aloud in court, referencing Wollstonecraft's presence at Revolutionary Christmas festivities in Paris during the Terror. A huge public trial—Sheridan spoke in Stone's defense, Mr. Barbauld was a character witness, and Stone was ultimately acquitted—this event proves that Wollstonecraft would have had a personal investment in the discursive strategies of these trials.[5] Additionally, one of Wollstonecraft's correspondents was Amelia Alderson Opie, whom Pascoe characterizes as "a female court enthusiast."[6] Opie wrote to Wollstonecraft (or Mrs. Imlay, as she was calling herself then) and chronicled many of these trials. Even without Opie's (or other enthusiasts') accounting of the trials, public access would have been routine as the transcripts were published in popular periodicals, including the *Monthly Review*. Finally, while the trials of the French royals would have been as closely followed as today's media reports on the celebrity of the day, we can pinpoint Wollstonecraft's specific intersection with these French events: she was in France from 1792–1794 and records that she witnessed the king being taken to his trial, and she writes about the performative nature of Marie Antoinette in both her *Vindication of the Rights of Men* and *An Historical and Moral View of the French Revolution*, treated extensively in Chapter 5. Clearly, all these trials were part of the cultural fabric of the 1790s and rich sources for Wollstonecraft's representation of theatrical juridical discourse.

Both civil and criminal trials became wildly popular in the 1790s as both amusement for audiences and as dramatic roles for attorneys, defendants, and sometimes even spectators; as such, they serve as mirrors of the culture's ambivalence toward theatricality and as rich sources for fictionalizing. Scholarship of the last 15 years has brought to life both the politicization of theater and the theatricality of politics in the eighteenth century, especially Pascoe, whose *Romantic Theatricality* connects the performances of the treason trials, of Marie Antoinette, and of the actress Sarah Siddons (all of which this book treats with specific reference to Wollstonecraft). Criminal trials and execution made for "hideous but magnificent theater," to use Backscheider's phrase, Foucauldian spectacles that were elaborate visible manifestations of state power, governance as theatrical coercion.[7] On the other hand, performances in the courtroom from defendants, attorneys, and spectators alike, street performances in the forms of protests or assemblies, and "eye-witness" accounts written the morning after suggest a potentially powerful, enabling strategy: theater as subversion rather than coercion. Joseph Litvak, in his study *Caught in the Act: Theatricality in*

---

[5] See Claire Tomalin, *The Life and Death of Mary Wollstonecraft* (London: Weidenfeld and Nicolson, 1974) in which she quotes from a letter collected in *Thomas Poole and His Friends*. See esp. 191, n.12.

[6] Judith Pascoe, *Romantic Theatricality: Gender, Poetry, and Spectatorship* (Ithaca: Cornell University Press, 1977). The quote is from 44.

[7] For Wollstonecraft's responses to public execution and the effects on spectators' sympathies and ethics, see Chapter 3.

the Nineteenth-Century English Novel, reminds us of the "normalization of theatricality, its subtle diffusion throughout a culture that appeared to have repudiated it" and suggests that even though theatrical frameworks clearly enable various coercive mechanisms, those same frameworks could also threaten or subvert them: "acting ... frustrates the attempts to define—let alone to patrol—the border between the safely domestic and the menacingly foreign, between private and public, inside and outside."[8] The three historical contexts of juridical theater that are my subject here all offer significant and polyvalent representations of this question of coercive and subversive function of theatricality.

The London Corresponding Society (LCS) and the Society for Constitutional Information (SCI) came to be seen as seditious and potentially treasonous organizations during the context of repressive governmental measures to ward off revolutionary agitation in Britain following the French Revolution; in all, seven members of the LCS and six members of the SCI were charged in October 1794.[9] The treason trials overtly exposed a cultural anxiety about and yet reliance on theatricality, especially with regard to female spectatorship. Hadley's analysis of melodrama and audience solicitation reveals how audiences at theaters took on the dramatic roles available to them as a form of power. Interestingly, though, what appeared to be "power to the people" was itself theatrical posing—that is, some of the audience unrest was staged as theater owners bought off both sides, directing a kind of "acting up" that would caution against the unruly mob, a politics of fear. In any event, this inversion whereby the spectator becomes the player, or at least has a stake in the play, also informs the courtroom setting of the British treason trials. Pascoe's account of the 1794 British treason trials of Thomas Hardy and John Horne Tooke, which she calls the "most showy and famous of the proceedings" (33), astutely treats the theatricality of all sides within the courtroom, including the attorneys, defendants, spectators, and the larger public audience admitted "into" the courtroom scene through the lens of published transcripts. A brief overview of the key tenets of Pascoe's argument will provide a useful context to my argument that Wollstonecraft directly appropriates and manipulates juridical discourses, perhaps even specific trials.

Unlike earlier critics who have analyzed or, at least, commented on the theatrical nature of the trials, Pascoe's interest is in "the outer trappings, the costumes and poses adopted by proponents of both sides, the consciousness of an audience which colors every public move and ensures that every move will

---

[8]   See Joseph Litvak, *Caught in the Act: Theatricality in the Nineteenth-Century English Novel* (Berkeley: University of California Press, 1992), 8.

[9]   At this time Wollstonecraft was in France awaiting delivery of her illegitimate child; during this time in France she had become increasingly interested in the notion of French theatricality in both state spectacle and the criminalizing of Marie Antoinette. See Chapter 4.

be made public" (34).[10] Women, moreover, played important roles in the staging of the treason trials, both in the narrative content of the defense and prosecution and in the audience dynamic created by a "significant female presence in court" (34). The trials featured participants who took very seriously the rhetorical power of their addresses at court, not only to appeal to the judge but also because they knew their words would reach a larger audience through morning headlines in newspapers and ultimately through private eye-witness accounts and published trial transcripts. In fact, the defendant in one case whose address to the jury never happened (because the court acquitted him before he could deliver it) decided to print and distribute it anyway. Thomas Holcroft, whose trial was rendered unnecessary by the not guilty verdicts of Thomas Hardy and John Horne Tooke, published his *Narrative of Facts, Relating to a Prosecution for High Treason, Including the Address to the Jury, Which the Court Refused to Hear* (1795) after the judge's refusal to allow him to address the court. Including the phrase "which the court refused to hear" dramatically calls attention to the performance denied him. Although the judge had initially assented to the defendant's request to speak, he became, as Pascoe says, "much less tolerant, however, when Holcroft announced that he would speak for 'only' half an hour, a time span the judge finally ruled was 'not a thing to be endured'" (37).

Sometimes the defendants' narratives themselves were not only highly declamatory and dramatic performances, but more concretely constructed as theater. Thomas Hardy, for example, uses the third person to refer to himself, posing as a speaker who is allied to the reader in discovering the story of the "humble shoemaker" who joined the ranks of other "martyrs of freedom."[11] Godwin, in January of 1794, served as a consultant of a sort in the sense that he wrote letters to the imprisoned Joseph Gerrald. His admonitions are laced with performative instructions; he sounds more like a director addressing an actor than a consultant assisting a defendant in that he not only tells him what to say to the jury but also how to say it: "Let every syllable you utter be fraught with persuasion."[12] Aware of the need to perform sincerity, Godwin admonishes Gerrald, above all, to "be wholly yourself" (126), a paradox that Pascoe has termed a "theatrical double bind" (42):

---

[10] See John Barrell, "Imaginary Treason, Imaginary Law: The State Trials of 1794," *The Birth of Pandora and the Division of Knowledge* (Philadelphia: University of Pensylvania Press, 1992); Alan Wharam, *The Treason Trials, 1794* (Leicester: Leicester University Press, 1991); Phillip Anthony Brown, *The French Revolution in English History* (London: Crosby, Lockwood, and Son, 1918); Carl B. Cone, *The English Jacobins: Reformers in Late Eighteenth-Century England* (New York: Charles Scribner's Sons, 1968).

[11] *Memoirs of Thomas Hardy*, 23. See Pascoe 39 for details.

[12] Godwin, *William Godwin: His Friends and Contemporaries*, ed. C. Kegan Paul (London: Henry S. King & Co. 1876): 1: 126.

A discomfort with the disjunction between a theatrical imperative (the need to attract public attention and win public support) and an antitheatrical anxiety (the result of an equation between performance and falsity). (43)

Even more rehearsed than the defendants' statements were those of the attorneys. The similarity between lawyers and actors was a commonplace of public discourse in 1790s; Thomas Erskine, the main attorney for the radicals in the trials, was skewered in the press and in published caricatures for swooning and feigning. Amelia Opie, in fact, uses lines from a poem describing the great stage actor Garrick to describe Erskine's pose in the courtroom: "the adapted mien, / Faithful as nature to the varied scene."[13] Godwin, interestingly, had a quite different reaction to Erskine, especially after he failed to acquit Thomas Paine in 1792, namely, a frustration and suspicion that Erskine's "exhibition" might not be trustworthy:

> What sort of exhibition of himself does an orator make who employs himself for four hours as you did, in a pretended attempt to persuade an audience into the truth of a proposition, which in his personal opinion is confessedly false? What must mankind think of this purchased fatigue of the lungs ... .[14]

Calling Erskine's courtroom performances a "purchased fatigue of the lungs" overtly indicts them as being available to the highest bidder.

Finally, the audience was an integral part of the performance within and outside of the courtroom. Spectators who could not get in formed large audiences outside the Old Bailey, demonstrating their support for one side or the other. The pro-government newspapers accused the crowd outside Thomas Hardy's trial of having been paid off, calling them a "hireling mob," while the *Morning Chronicle* published examples of how easily a large sum of money "or a little beer" could sway the public's opinion.[15]

Women specifically played a major role in these proceedings as spectators, defense witnesses, and family members of the accused, and influenced the genre on which the trial participants drew most heavily, melodrama. Hadley situates melodrama within a variety of social settings, seeing it as a hybrid genre and stressing the fact that early melodramas were "audience solicitations" and that key features of melodrama were heightened emotiveness of acting, female victimization as subject matter, and, frequently, courtroom scenes. While female victimization at the hands of a violent husband or profligate rake functioned to sway audiences of melodrama, even more effective in the courtroom setting was

---

[13]   *Memorials of the Life of Amelia Opie*, ed. Cecilia Lucy Bridewell (London: Longman, Brown, and Co., 1854), 124.

[14]   Pascoe cites this from a unpublished letter of Godwin to Erskine. Housed in the Bodleian Library, Oxford, the letter is undated, but Pascoe suggests that it most probably was written very soon after the trial of Paine, to which it makes reference. See Pascoe 48, n.24.

[15]   The quotation from *The Morning Chronicle* is from March 8, 1793, while the statement from the *True Briton* is from Nov. 7, 1794. See Pascoe 46 for other examples.

the role of mother as victim, maternal pathos being the most effective means to gain audience support. And a person didn't even have to be alive to be a player in the proceedings; Hardy's dead wife, for example, haunted his trial. Having died in childbirth during his imprisonment, the wife was never far from the audience's mind as Hardy publicly testified that the "ruffian mob" who attacked his family home in protest of his revolutionary activities were responsible for the death of his wife and unborn child; Mrs.Hardy, thus, assumed in Pascoe's words "the stock pose of the female victim in melodrama, overcome with horror before a threatening masculine power" (61). The treason trials, thus, use stories of suffering women and introduce females, as Pascoe says, "into narratives in which there is no political or utilitarian space for them" (64). Whether the trials foregrounded it or not, most of them used stories of suffering women as appeals to audiences and used actual female spectatorship as a dramatic element in the proceedings, thus giving women a power that they did not have outside the courtroom (except, as we will see, in the theater), an irony which Pascoe emphasizes in her summary:

> That is, women were given featured roles in reconstructions of the trials—most notably as victims of crimes against their husbands—to engage other women who attended the trials, read the newspapers, and, ultimately, bought the memoirs and narratives penned by the defendants. Although at first glance women seem to have been entirely disenfranchised from the political and legal systems that produced the trials, they actually exerted a force over the proceedings by virtue of their collective presence as spectators. (64–5)

Pascoe asserts that this goes far to "counter the definition of female subjectivity predicated on the female as spectacle" (65). Yet, it is still their "collective presence" and primarily that of a domestic and maternal identity that "exerts" a force over the proceedings. While the treason trials' manipulation of females associated with the radical defendants spotlighted, whenever and wherever possible, a domestic/maternal pathos, the civil divorce trials used female erotic identity to various ends.

We know from her correspondence that Wollstonecraft received firsthand accounts of divorce and adultery trial transcripts which clearly reveal the legal processes by which separations could be obtained and, more frequently, damages could be awarded to betrayed husbands and which would have been part of the discursive juridical contexts from which Wollstonecraft could borrow. Civil divorce trials were reported in the metropolitan and provincial presses, and pamphlet accounts appeared subsequently.[16]

---

[16] The most thorough and comprehensive studies of divorce in the period remain Randolph Trumbach's *Sex and the Gender Revolution* (Chicago and London: Chicago University Press, 1998); David M. Turner's *Fashioning Adultery: Gender, Sex, and Civility in England, 1660–1740* (Cambridge: Cambridge University Press, 2002), and, of course, both of Lawrence Stone's masterful studies: *Road to Divorce: England 1530–1987* (Oxford: Oxford University Press, 1990), and *Broken Lives: Separation and Divorce in England, 1660–1857* (Oxford: Oxford University Press, 1993).

Trial transcripts, which were printed as pamphlets and then reprinted in collections, were popular and sensational amusement in what Janet Todd has called a pornographic-scandal culture. Interestingly, the fate of the collections of adultery trials is itself a dramatic story, as Bladon's collected transcripts of 1779 were supplemented in 1799 by Gill, whose printed collection of court reports included suggestive illustrations, the consequences of which led to censorship and destruction of these illustrations in 1802 by the Society for the Suppression of Vice.[17] It was the radical and spectacular growth in the 1790s of these trials—known as crim. con, the shortening of "criminal conversation," named for the offense itself—and, concomitantly, the growth of sensationalized accounts not only in the form of transcripts, but also in biographies of the infamous as well as satirical prints that made this kind of juridical discourse part of the discursive fabric of the culture.[18] In her "Amour in the Shrubbery: Reading the Detail of English Adultery Trial Publications of the 1780s," Lloyd explores the use of various discourses appropriated in the reporting of adultery as well as the trials themselves, focusing on landscape and linking such tropes to how the trials commented on fashion and female sexuality.[19] As Lloyd summarizes, evidence from 26 criminal conversation or divorce trials were published in pamphlet form between 1780 and 1789 and occasioned a variety of newspaper reports, verse satires, pseudo-biographical accounts, and caricatures, all part of a seeming obsession with female sexual infidelity (422). Lloyd points out the irony that there were fewer divorces in this decade and yet many more accounts; thus, the marketability (on which publishers like George Lister capitalized) of these materials demonstrates "adultery's apparent capacity to elucidate and capture broader cultural issues including class and gender politics and imperial security" (422). Lloyd's contribution to the existing historiography on these trials is that she is less concerned with reconstructing the characters' psychology or combing through all trial transcripts than with questioning "the processes by which late eighteenth-century knowledge about adultery was constituted" (422). In this way, it is important to gauge adultery's wider transgressive effects, linking it to ideas about "mobility, identity, commerce, print, and publicity, addressing issues that many historians place at the heart of modernity" (423).

Some of the public interest in adultery cases and trials stemmed from a curiosity about and a critique of aristocratic licentious behavior. Donna Andrew, particularly, has investigated this obsessive concern with aristocratic female libertinism, of which the Worsley case of 1782 was perhaps the most prominent. Lady Worsley used as her defense (in a move to protect her partner in adultery, the defendant) her apparently legendary sexual repertoire.[20] The fact that the

---

[17]   See Jordan, 230.

[18]   See *Fashioning Adultery*, 172, for a nice summary of sources for these accounts.

[19]   Sarah Lloyd, "Amour in the Shrubbery: Reading the Detail of English Adultery Trial Publications of the 1780s," *Eighteenth-Century Studies* 39.4 (2006): 421–42.

[20]   See Donna Andrew, "'Adultery a-la-Mode': Privilege, the Law, and Attitudes to Adultery, 1770–1809," *History* 82 (1997): 5–23.

Worsleys were connected to both Parliament and the military entwined anxiety about adultery to larger national anxiety about the potential corruption of gender and class hierarchies, a conflation we see in Wollstonecraft's queries about the idle, effeminate military in *A Vindication of the Rights of Woman* and in Maria's defense of herself in her court appearance at the end of *Maria, or The Wrongs of Woman*. What these trials and their subsequent manipulation by all kinds of discursive channels make apparent is that the issues of freedom and liberty at the heart of much of 1790s discourse in British literature were already central to the debates about female liberty that these civil cases foregrounded. The publicity around adultery trials highlighted that a vulgar and threatening female liberty was one form freedom could take; thus, liberty might usher in an illicit and corrupting discourse. Finally the significance of these divorce trials to an understanding of the period cannot be overestimated: it represented and amplified cultural anxieties about women, aristocratic society, the moral and legal ramifications of marriage, national and imperial British identity, print culture, and interclass relations.

I contend that Wollstonecraft appropriated historical cases from the adultery trials much in the same sense that Aphra Behn did. Backscheider's work on Aphra Behn, in *Spectacular Politics: Theatrical Power and Mass Culture in Early Modern England* demonstrates how Behn appropriated historical trial facts and juridical discourse. Bachscheider used the 1682 case of Henrietta Berkeley, who denied being abducted, claimed a shame marriage, and illicitly cohabitated with Lord Grey in a case that was labeled "the most notorious case of seduction in a profligate age" and which spawned 60 years of published accounts under the media heading "Whoredom Fornication and Adultery, detected and laid open." Correspondingly, Wollstonecraft may have appropriated cases from the also notorious transcripts of *Trials for Adultery* (1779), most of which record pursuit of damages by a husband who sued a seducer for "criminal conversation" with his wife. Only two studies have treated crim.con in Wollstonecraft, and while neither uses the lens of theatricality, both Jordan and Komisaruk provide useful historical and legal interpretations.

Using Bladon's collection not merely as mimetic narrative sources, Jordan suggests that Wollstonecraft offers a radical opposition both to the ways in which women are constructed in these reports and to the editor's stated motivation for publishing them, which was to deter "wavering wantons" from consummating their wishes and thus reduce seduction (230). In civil actions, neither plaintiff nor defendant could actually give evidence in their own cause: the opposing claims were pleaded by lawyers and supported by witnesses. Prosecution witnesses were often servants economically dependant and therefore loyal to the husband. But the husband and the one charged with seduction would not appear before the judge and certainly not the wife. Thus, in *Maria, or The Wrongs of Woman*, as Maria is said to have taken "the task of conducting Darnford's defence upon herself," she inserts herself into a legal arena which would have left her literally unrepresented, focusing on the legal action between the husband and the seducer. On Maria's defiance of this lack of representation, Jordan concludes, "A letter such as Maria writes might have remained unopened to this day, or been passed to the prosecution to make what they would of it. ... Maria's defence, in relation to the law and legal practice of her day, is a silent and fantastic (im)possibility" (224). My interest in this fantastic (im)possibility (the phrase from my second epigraph) lies in the intersection between Maria's conclusion, being "convinced that the subterfuges of law were disgraceful," and her decision to "write a paper" to be read in a courtroom, one of three physical sites in the novel that can be read as theatrical stages (both of Maria's residences—her house and the asylum/prison—become transformed into staging grounds, but the courtroom is obviously the most spectacular of the three).

Long before the courtroom scene, Maria directly comments on the nature of these trials, although she does not use the term "crim.con." As Maria argues that she could have easily found a lover once she finds herself "Bastilled for life" with a husband who neglects her, she wryly castigates both lover and husband, saying that the lover will dote on the "forlorn state of the neglected woman" even while "foreseeing that he may afterwards be obliged to pay severe damages" to the man who "never appeared to value his wife's society, till he found there was a chance of his being indemnified by the loss of it" (87–8). Exposing the cynical monetary motivations of husbands who want renumeration, Maria suggests here a kind of prophetic awareness of what will become of her while, at the same time, suggesting a dissimulation, a theatrical pose, on the part of the husband. In fact, Maria moves from an explicit acknowledgment of binding theatricalized social norms to a sense of the potential inherent in a conscious self-staging. As Chapter 2 discusses, Maria simply performs her freedom, with Mr. S as her first audience in the scene which serves as a turning point from spectator to actress of her part:

> Then turning to Mr. S, I added, "I call on you Sir to witness" [and I lifted up my hands and eyes to heaven] "that as solemnly as I took his name, I now abjure it" [and I pulled off my ring and put it on the table] "and that I mean immediately to quit his house never to enter it more ... . I leave him as free as I am determined to be myself." (95)

I turn now to the transcripts themselves and one in particular that resonates as a source text. The title page of transcripts, reprinted in seven volumes in 1985, promises a record of "Select Trials" for "Adultery, Fornication, Cruelty, and Impotence, &c. From the Year 1760 to the present Time."[21] Sounding like a playbill designed for a salacious audience, the rest of the title promises "INTRIGUES, and AMOURS of many Characters in the most elevated Sphere" and swears that "every Scene and Transaction, however ridiculous, whimsical, or extraordinary" will be "fairly represented." Many of these adultery cases include effusive letters which have been, again according to the title page, dramatically "intercepted between the amorous parties." The cases include effusive letters by wives who refer to themselves as fictional characters, for example, the "penitent," alluding

---

[21]   *Trials for Adultery; Or, The History of Divorces* (Clark, New Jersey: Lawbook Exchange, 2006).

to Rowe's wildly popular play *The Fair Penitent*. One of the real-life penitents writes, "happiness and peace of mind is gone ... I may say with Calista, I have bound up for myself a world of woes" (7). This adoption of a dramatic, fictional character in the service of legal proceedings underscores not only the powerful cultural legacy of Rowe's plays (see Chapter 2), but also the clear interdependence between theatrical and social stages. All of the transcripts can be read as theater and vividly demonstrate how theatrical metaphors were manipulated by both sides in complex agendas—with voices ranging from wronged and injured spouse, to an enraged, justice-seeking spouse, to a sorrowful and penitent accused spouse— and in that sense would have been part of the discursive juridical contexts from which Wollstonecraft could borrow. The statements of both plaintiff and defendant strike layers of theatrical poses, exemplifying how the "subterfuge of law," as Wollstonecraft calls it, is answered by an oppositional theatricality which adds another layer to the "theatrical double bind" of Romantic radicals.

The case I argue here as source text, Cibber vs. Sloper, overtly dealt with theatrical mores since the plaintiff was himself a player; the wife, an actress; and the Drury Lane theater part of the context for the proceedings. While the facts of this case parallel scenarios in Wollstonecraft's novel in many ways, more significant is the fact that the courtroom arguments offer potentially important premises about theatrical character and self-invention, including the potentially enabling and therefore subversive instrumentality of "acting." In the case of Mr. Cibber against Mr. Sloper for criminal conversation with Mrs. Cibber, the Solicitor General (who in this case was the writer who records the plaintiff's statement) observed "that it is true, the plaintiff was a player, but he was also a gentleman."[22] The solicitor's opposition between actor/gentleman becomes an explicit, unifying part of the proceedings, as he goes on to acknowledge the public assumption about the bad reputation of actors:

> He said, he knew it was attempted, by some, to have the players considered in a matter of this nature, as not upon the same footing with the rest of the subjects; as if it were more lawful to invade their properties than those of other people; but he knew no law that deprived them of those comforts and rights which other subjects ought to enjoy. (7)

After this suggestion about the hypocrisy of anti-theatrical prejudice, he then appeals to theatergoers in the audience (and the jury) to remember that

> the stage has been cherished and encouraged by the politest and wisest states, as a school of virtue and good morals, and that many receive good lessons and impressions from what they hear at the theatre, who perhaps don't incline to go to seek for instruction elsewhere. (8)

---

[22] *Trials for Adultery*. The quote is from 7.

The plaintiff's father Mr. Cibber, also an actor, testified to the wife's talent as an actress, and "Mr. Fleetwood, Master of Drury Lane Playhouse" seconded her being "much in the favour of the town" (8).

While the principals in this trial were themselves actors which brought to the forefront of the trial prejudices against and arguments for the moral utility of theater, this case also suggests the extent to which illicit and adulterous relationships conducted in rented rooms and "secret" closets were entertaining theater to the voyeuristic peeping toms who made it their business to spy on them and to then offer official court statements about it. In this case, the adulterous couple apparently met some 20 times in the rented room of a friend, and the owner of the boarding house reveals that he had "bored holes through the wainscot" of the wall between his closet and that rented room and, thus, could "see them plain." Offered merely as a insignificant detail in order to verify that he had firsthand knowledge of the criminal conversation, Mr. Hayes reveals himself as a secret audience of illicit love scenes played out in his own lodgings. This overt act of voyeuristic spectatorship is an example of the behavior Wollstonecraft condemns in the novel in two distinct ways. First, she offers a very different kind of spectatorial scene as Jemima watches Maria and Darnford engage in an affair in stolen moments in the asylum and rather than voyeuristic pleasure in illicit activity, Jemima is educated in the potential of honest expression of emotion and in fact is prompted to "begin an account of herself" as a consequence of viewing these scenes. Secondly, Wollstonecraft specifically comdemns the perverted and hypocritical morality of self-satisfying spectators, the "women at the opera" who judge and reject Maria for having admitted to a sexual affair while maintaining the morality of the cloak over their own indiscretions. In this case M. Hayes offers such explicit descriptions of the mutuality of the sexual encounter that the public voice of the proceedings, the judge, must intervene to stop him: "... his Lordship interposed to this effect: there is no occasion to be more particular; we are not trying a rape" (10). While the witness casts himself as a passive spectator and casts the lovers as theatrical adulterers, he obviously in his recounting of the sexual scene becomes quite theatrical himself, again underscoring the courtroom and witness stand as a powerful stage.

A third way in which this case intersects with Wollstonecraft's concerns in her novel is the explicit parallels to Maria's being bartered as a sexual object by her husband. Here the plaintiff husband, Cibber, is accused of being, at the very least, complicit in the affair, recalling George Venable's attempt to sell Maria into prostitution, to a sexual relationship with a friend, for everyone's mutual benefit. The defense attorney, Mr. Serjeant Eyre, very astutely uses the theatrical context to argue both that 1) the actors in theater have a different sense of "appropriate" behavior, and 2) that Cibber (the husband plaintiff) is himself guilty. Mr. Eyre begins his defense with a sarcastic statement that "he never heard that [the theater] was a place celebrated for virtue," and undermines the husband plaintiff's moral position by confirming him as a consummate actor of love scenes himself since "all theatrical performances abound with [love]" (12). Having cast the husband then as a player, in all senses of that word, the attorney accuses the husband of having known and approved of any sexual flirtation that might have been going on. Citing the *Tragedy of Cato*, in which Cato "lent his wife out to a friend to breed out of her, and when they had done, he took her back again well contented," Mr. Eyre inserts this allusion without attempting to prove its truth in the present case as a mark of what "theater" people do. He concludes that he hopes nothing "criminal" passed between the two but assures the jury that "if there had, the plaintiff had certainly encouraged it, and had no pretense to come to a jury for damages." The case goes a bit farther, finally, than exposing this potential pimping activity as the Solicitor General himself concurs with the defense on this fact, observing the "ill consequence of letting it pass for a law that men might sell their wives" (12), the fact that Wollstonecraft so ironically presents in her statement that some husbands only value their wives when they realize they can be "indemnified" by it.

Finally, this trial is particularly resonant as a source for Wollstonecraft in its debates about the effects (good and ill) of acting. The defense attorney's final statement would have suggested to Wollstonecraft, in ways that Mr. Eyre never intended, the kind of potential power inherent in acting, in the sense that Siddons means it, in the sense that Litvak means it about acting as outside police boundaries, that is, as a tool for morality, an impetus to imaginative identification which is the heart of moral behavior. Eyre's contentions, again used for his own agenda to show the amorality of the theater circle and thus the unconvincing moral grab of Cibber, are worth quoting in full. The record says that Eyre contended that

> the players are a people who act, and enter into all manner of characters; that their men and women are made to fall in love with each other every day; this day with one, tomorrow with another; that this practice in variety must give them an uncommon propensity to love, without any confinement of the passion to a particular subject; that it is very likely this enters into their common course of life. (7)

Wollstonecraft would have seen in this "uncommon propensity to love" a potentially positive construction of selfhood, a theatrical construction played out by Maria in the final scene in the book. Maria's navigating of the judicial system—her move from prisoner in the asylum to defendant, judge, and jury in her own case—offers a compelling representation of competing notions of the theatrical (as I have discussed in Chapter 2); here I focus just on the courtroom scene and its very specific appropriation of trial discourse.

Seeking a potential at least for a sincere performance, and convinced "that the subterfuges of law were disgraceful, she wrote a paper, which she expressly desired might be read in court" (130).[23] Exposing the fake theatrics of the

---

[23] Jordan cites one historical possibility for this narrative fact of writing a letter to the court in that Amelia Opie, as a spectator at Norwich ecclesiastical court proceedings for divorce, records that after the trial, court officers found an unopened letter in the file from the wife of one of the participants. Jordan credits the work of Marjorie Nevill on records from Norwich courts. See Jordan 233, n.6.

court—the "subterfuges of law"—a social stage where defendants, attorneys, and spectators try to perform innocence, her choice to write a paper to be read aloud in effect takes her out of that loop. Her act then is a defiant resistance and rewriting of the "guilty" role: 1) a refusal to "speak" the language of penitence; in fact, the published transcript of this trial will disappoint the audience hungry for titillation; 2) a refusal to be a visual spectacle, both in the Foucauldian sense of being the object of spectacle of state power and in terms of being the object of the gaze in the courtroom; for example, she refuses the position of being the defense attorney, she refuses to play the penitent or even the wronged, if seductive woman; and 3) a refusal to be a female body, a sexual object, visible in front of a judge while she proclaims sexual autonomy. This creative narrative decision on Wollstonecraft's part should not be underestimated since the spectacle of the wronged woman in the courtroom made for sensational theater. Rowe's play, *Lady Jane Grey*, for example, casts Jane in a trial scene that made tears flow from audience members; as Marsden's analysis of this suggests, Jane became a spectacle of male gaze in the courtroom as men looked at her with "lovers' eyes."[24]

Other than visually and verbally absenting herself from the scene, her silence can also be read as performance. I take issue with Rajan's reading of this scene as a defeat for Maria. Using Peter Brooks's discussion of the figure of the mute in nineteenth-century melodrama, Rajan says:

> Silenced by society, forced into a nightmarish reality, the mute is a radicalizing figure with a specific rhetorical function. In the courtroom Maria has been muted and feels compelled to present her case in a paper that is read out.[25]

Contesting this portrait of Maria as mute, my reading suggests her conscious manipulation of performance. Choosing to be silent is not the same as being mute.

Finally, in perhaps the most significant detail in terms of the theatricality of the scene, she has her words read aloud by a presumably male officer of the court. What are her reasons to use another body and voice to speak her words? She positions herself as spectator on equal footing with the judge; they get to watch a male declare, as he reads her statement, the intellectual and sexual autonomy of a female. She therefore scripts nothing short of a brilliant ventriloquizing moment. Like her performance of the dissolution of her marriage vows as she discards her wedding ring in front of Mr. S, her words perform their content. First, she ceremoniously forgives George: "I pardon my oppressor." After enacting this public act of pardon, appropriating and performing a theological language of authority, Maria can reject the charge of adultery because she rejects "any tie … between me and my what is termed lawful husband" (132). Consistently demarcating purely legal motives from inherently moral ones, Maria dismisses

---

²⁴   See Jean Marsden, "Sex, Politics, and the She-Tragedy: Reconfiguring *Lady Jane Grey*," *Studies in English Literature* 42.3 (2002): 501–22.

²⁵   Tillotama Rajan, "Wollstonecraft and Godwin: Reading the Secrets of the Political Novel," *Studies in Romanticism* 27 (1988): 221–51. The quote is from 233.

"those laws to which the policy of artificial society has annexed punishments" (132). An extraordinary redefinition of morality versus the "policy of artificial society" allows Maria to perform her defense with declarative statements as she declares, protests, and claims her own innocence:

> "I appeal to my own sense of justice and declare that I will not live with the individual who has violated every moral obligation which binds man to man."
> "I protest ... any charge being brought to criminate the man whom I consider my husband ... *freeing him*, as I solemnly do from the charge of seduction."
> "I claim then a divorce." (133)

The judge's inflammatory response suggests the power of this performance as he equates her "newfangled ideas" with "French principles," thus demonstrating the cultural anxiety about role-playing as that which, as Litvak says, frustrates the attempts to define—let alone to patrol—the border between the domestic and the foreign, the private and public.

The anxious borders between domestic and foreign are highlighted when we turn to the third juridical context at play, the most notorious trial of Marie Antoinette. While the treason trials spotlighted maternal and melodramatic suffering and the civil divorce trials targeted erotic female seduction or complicity in sexual liaisons, the trial of Marie Antoinette manipulated both of these female performances. In Chapter 5, I argue how Marie Antoinette's life as a queen was a series of costumed events culminating in a persistent pornographic pamphlet campaign against her, and that Wollstonecraft's opinions of her are much more complex than earlier critics have documented. Here I focus exclusively on her final public act, one set in a courtroom, which included a performance of maternity that, to some extent, won over a female crowd and perhaps inaugurated the image of the domesticated queen that dominated Victorian iconography of her. Colwill's "Just Another *Citoyenne*? Marie-Antoinette on Trial, 1790–1793" uses material from Jacques-Rene Hebert's celebrated newspaper *Le Pere Duchesne*—3,000 pages written by Hebert from 1790–1794—to argue that the

> dominant representation of the queen as quintessential unruly woman had multiple political ramifications. On the one hand, it undermined the legitimacy of the monarchy and provided a rallying cry for the new republic; on the other it provided a negative model against which non-elite women were to define their own identity ... a watershed in the ideology of womanhood. (64)[26]

Hebert's newspaper used a fictional protagonist, Pere Duchesne, traditionally a stove merchant and a popular burlesque figure long before the Revolution. By September 1790 he emerged as patriot, family man, pipe in mouth and stove-pipe in hand, on the cover of each issue of the newspaper, and provided a common sense

---

[26]   Elizabeth Colwill, "Just Another *Citoyenne*? Marie-Antoinette on Trial, 1790–1793," *History Workshop Journal* 28 (1989): 63–87.

voice inimical to highminded seriousness, a common voice which nonetheless struck deep registers of fear within the populace with regard to the dichotomous maternal/sexual body of the queen, and, by extension, of all women.

Just as Maria's judge worries over her defense in terms of its use of "newfangled ideas" from the French, the queen's trial highlights and amplifies the troubling intersections between public and private, collective and individual, especially in terms of the female body. No other trial in France ever attracted the same attention. Unusual in the first place to even have a trial of a queen in a country that specifically excluded women from ruling, the long separation between the trial of the king and that of the queen (from December to October of the next year) seemed to weaken the linkage. Additionally, unlike Louis, Marie Antoinette was not tried by the Convention itself, but was brought before the Revolutionary Criminal Tribunal like all other suspects in France, and her fate decided by male jury and nine male judges. After the king's execution, Marie Antoinette was transferred from the Temple to the Conciergerie on August 2, 1793, in the face of powerful counter-revolutionary forces, who hoped in one blow to eliminate the symbol of Austrian tyranny—thus the escalation of the queen's trial caused by the battered republic's attempt to stave off counter-revolutionary forces. As Colwill asserts, the Revolutionary Tribunal thus decided Marie Antoinette's fate in the context of a state of siege (75). This explosive, taut moment between the warring forces once again figures woman as a performative site of chaos that is at once sexual, social, and symbolic. Unlike the king's trial which, as Lynn Hunt argues, remained entirely restricted to a consideration of his political crime, the trial of the queen, especially in its strange refractions of pornographic literature, offers a unique perspective on the revolutionary political imagination.

The proceedings began by comparing the queen to legendary infamous women. As Pierre Saint-Amand asserts, with each new name Marie Antoinette "acquired a new narrative for which she would have to stand trial before a tribunal of men. ... A phantasmic delirium is staged around these signifiers."[27] At the beginning of her trial in October 1793, the notorious public prosecutor Fourquier-Tinville began with an extraordinary accusation against her, even in those inflamed times: "In the manner of the Messalinas-Brunhildas ... Marie Antoinette has been since her time in France the scourge and bloodsucker of the French" (Hunt 109). Invoking one of the most cruelly ambitious women of ancient Rome, and one whose name evokes sexual aggression and greed, the prosecution originates its case through an act of performance in a sense, casting the queen in a damning role. Strikingly, the focus on her sexualized body in the pornographic pamphlets against her was carried over to the trial, which included frequent references to the orgies at Versailles. In his closing statement, the prosecutor, in Hunt's summary, "collapsed sexual and political references" denouncing the "perverse conduct," "criminal liaisons,"

---

[27]   Pierre Saint-Amand, "Terrorizing Marie Antoinette," trans. Jennifer Curtiss Gage, *Critical Inquiry* 2.3 (1994): 379–400.

and "intimacies with a villainous faction"; in short, Marie Antoinette had used her sexual body to corrupt the body politic (Hunt 111).

Spotlighting her misuse of public money and secret contributions to her Austrian brother Emperor, the bill of indictment also singled out her more amorphous crime, that of theatricality: that she "taught the king how to dissimulate—that is how to promise one thing in public and plan another in the shadow of the court" (Hunt 109). Because dissimulation had been denounced as the chief characteristic of court culture, this charge may not seem at first to be gender specific, but the focus on the queen's body as mask certainly was. The body became a site for others to attempt to read; Herman (the President of the Tribunal), in his summary of the accusations, included the process whereby people had tried to read her motives not by looking at facts, but by the "ability of the people or their representatives to 'read' her body"; thus, Herman writes that he hopes her imprisonment would begin to tear off the veil from the "threatening ability to hide her true feelings from the public" (Hunt 111). This threatening ability to act as a means of self-preservation is analogous to Wollstonecraft's use of a kind of transgressive mimicry, a subversive form of self-fashioning claimed by the fictional Maria. The entire juridical proceeding against Marie Antoinette—a damnation of a sexual female who claims the rights of self-definition—is clearly an influence on Wollstonecraft's depiction of the courtroom performance that a judge labels full of "French principles."

The most important similarity between the two trials exists in the intersection of the erotic/maternal body and a profanation of the sacred, albeit in different directions. Laying the groundwork for the infamous charges of incest against Marie Antoinette were perverse attacks on her as a maternal figure, especially a nursing mother. This strategy is nowhere more apparent than in the imagery Hebert uses, days before the execution, to strengthen public outcry against her. Using a parable about a simpleton who discovers a nest of serpents in his fields, Hebert asks what would one say if the man destroys only the father snake, feeling sympathy for "a poor mother in the midst of her children" and then brings the mother and baby serpents in the house as amusement. His foolishness would obviously be a crime since the serpents would repay his kindness by destroying his family. Just as the mother serpent deserved no sympathy, Hebert says "No Mercy" should be extended to Marie Antoinette (76). Hebert's profaning of a sacred image of nursing mother testifies to the ideological climate of the queen's trial; that is, the representation of Marie Antoinette as venomous serpent nursing at her breast a brood of vipers was a counterattack against royalists' attempts to repaint the portrait of the former queen as model wife and mother since they could no longer rely on the language of monarchical authority to sway the populace.[28]

Significantly, this debate rallied women across party lines who saw in these slanderous representations a collective threat to women in all classes. Colwill's analysis summarizes the trajectory by which royalists had to switch from defending the queen by reference to the language of authority to defending her

---

[28] See Colwill, 76.

motherly nature. The queen, for instance, appears in De Stael's account as a heroic mother whom republicans would do well to emulate. During the invasion of the Tuileries in June 1792, De Stael claimed the queen's courage faded only when she lost sight of her son in the crowd. When he was returned unharmed, she "fell on her knees, prostrate" before the National Guardsman who returned him. De Stael's attempt did influence subsequent generations as the trial foreshadowed the victory of domesticity, for royalists and revolutionaries alike sought converts by cloaking political arguments in the vocabulary of sentimental womanhood (77).

If the competing discourses in the October Days episode were class/gender, the most publicized trial of the revolution highlighted the many competing bodies of the queen in a performative event that inversely echoes the adversarial discourses in Wollstonecraft's heroine Maria (and more broadly Wollstonecraft's concern with the erotic/domestic binary forced on women). Just as Maria appears in a courtroom with a triangulation of performed selves to defend, the revolutionary trial pitted the queen's political, sexual, and maternal bodies against one another. We do well here to recall Culler's words on the force of the performative. Commenting on Butler's analysis of authoritative utterance, Culler posits that many diverse utterances "derive their force precisely through the repeated invocation by which a social bond among [...] communities is formed through time." Since no social bond is stronger than those among mothers, and we see the power of, and the challenges to, authoritative maternal discourse in the queen's trial. Hebert's parabolic image linking the maternal/sexual by use of the poisonous breast-feeding serpent stands as representative of the nature of adversarial staging of Marie Antoinette at her trial. Replicating Hebert's charges in the newspaper in more elegant language but with the same vehement scorn, the prosecutor opposed the queen's attorneys' arguments of her as a good wife and mother. In a political vocabulary rife with sexual innuendo, he pronounced Marie Antoinette guilty of "intimate liasons with infamous ministers, perfidious generals, and unfaithful representatives of the people."[29]

The climactic moment in the trial, however, came with the charge of incest, a culmination of years of public outrage against her failure to produce heirs soon enough and her miscarriage. Hebert, of course, was the agent who testified in the newspaper and to the Revolutionary Tribunal that Marie Antoinette had committed incest. Hebert records that he was informed by the boy's guard Simon that he was found masturbating, committing "indecencies" on himself. Colwill says that Hebert's eagerness to get high ranking commissioners involved "is testimony to Hebert's eagerness to exploit the event for political gain and throws suspicion on the confession extracted from Charles" (86, n.74). Whether Marie Antoinette had been forewarned of the charges and, therefore, prepared for her answer is unknown, but the strategy with which she answers the charges was carefully fashioned for the audience in the galleries: "If I have not responded it is because nature refuses to respond to such a charge made to a mother. I call upon every mother here." The queen's famous appeal to "all mothers here" did much

---

[29]   See Colwill, 78.

to replace her sexual identity which had been so foregrounded and perverted in the course of the trial with her maternal persona and reportedly brought part of a hostile crowd over to her side. We could say that this performative utterance is the queen's only authoritative speech in the trial. Reaction in the galleries was mixed between sympathy and vocal distaste, according to Colwill, who uses the queen's lawyer's account of reactions.[30] While we cannot know the extent of the crowd's sympathy or outrage, just as we cannot judge the verity of the claims, the aftereffects of Marie Antoinette's jarring swerve, repudiating lurid accusations of her by adopting the maternal persona, were enormous.

Both this nexus of maternal/sexual identity and the queen's performative utterance are strikingly similar to what we have seen in Wollstonecraft's most performative character, Maria. As she moves from spectator to actress, from victim to judge and jury in her own trial, Maria demands equal maternal/sexual autonomy. Where Marie Antoinette engaged a maternal persona while being persecuted for a sexual one, Maria insists upon her right to sexual autonomy even after having her infant taken from her. Seeing no incompatibility between claiming sexual autonomy and dramatically narrating having her nursing baby taken from her breast, Maria challenges the discursive and legal boundaries of woman''s bifurcated roles. While Maria does not win over the judge or gain a divorce, she does simply perform her defense with declarative, authoritative statements similar to the queen's. And very significantly, the judge, in equating Maria's "newfangled ideas" with "French principles," invokes the mélange of conflicting representations of the queen by accusing Maria of "opening [the] flood-gate for immorality," specifically the premises of the French Revolution on English soil. He concludes, "We [do] not want French principles in public or private life" (133).

Finally, the "poetics of impossibility" that is the cultural legacy of Marie Antoinette is made of the same semantic fabric as Maria's fictional vindication of her rights to a judge. If Marie Antoinette's life as a queen was a series of costumed events culminating in a persistent pornographic pamphlet campaign against her, her final public act included a performance of maternity that perhaps inaugurated the image of the domesticated queen that dominated Victorian iconography of her. Similarly, if Wollstonecraft's career was dedicated to a "revolution in female manners" that required intellectual and moral education, the final public act associated with her, Godwin's *Memoirs*, eclipsed that work and replaced it with tawdry, titillating details of a woman driven by sexual and emotional urges. Engaging the "discourse of infamy" associated with these performing women reminds us that attention must be paid to the theatrical constructions of the body politic which may, indeed, do serious damage to the bodies that get staged within it.

---

[30] See M. Chaveau-Lagarde, *Note historique sur les process de Marie-Antoinette d'Autriche, Reine de France, et de Madame Elisabeth de France, au Tribunal Revolutionnaire*, Paris 1816. p. 25.

Chapter 5
"The gallery is in place of the house": The French Revolution and State Theater

Nothing can equal the fondness which the French suck in with their milk for public places, particularly the theatre; and this taste ... has produced so many stage tricks on the grand theatre of the nation, where old principles vamped up with new scenes and decorations are continually represented. ... And after this kind of education, is it surprising, that almost every thing is said and done for stage effect?
—Mary Wollstonecraft, *An Historical and Moral View of the French Revolution*

Plots, massacres, assassinations, seem to some people a trivial price for obtaining a revolution. Cheap, bloodless reformation, a guiltless liberty appear flat and vapid to their taste. There must be a great change of scene; there must be a magnificent stage-effect; there must be a grand spectacle to rouse the imagination, grown torpid with the lazy enjoyment of sixty years' security and the still unanimating repose of public prosperity.
—Edmund Burke, *Reflections on the Revolution in France*[1]

Stage tricks and grand spectacle. Plots, massacres, assassinations. That Burke and Wollstonecraft, two iconic, ideologically opposite writers, employ a theatrical trope by their common use of the phrase "stage effect" suggests the high stakes in the widespread conflation of political discourse and theatrical metaphors in the 1790s. The dialogue between Burke and Wollstonecraft on the ethics and tactics of the primary players in the French Revolution documents how revolutionary and counter-revolutionary writers consistently invoke attention to what Wollstonecraft calls the "grand theatre of the nation." Disturbingly, however, critical attention to such passages has effected a reductive reading of Wollstonecraft's complex appropriation of the theatrical trope in her representations of history, particularly of the French Revolution and Marie Antoinette. Despite the obvious fact that Burke's "stage-effect" refers to the actions of the Revolutionary activists whereas Wollstonecraft's "stage effect" points to the machinations of the monarchy and, by extension, the counter-revolutionaries, these epigraph passages sound deceptively similar, leading one to assume that both Burke and Wollstonecraft vehemently critique the theatricality, the "stage effect," of French culture. A closer read, however, opens up a number of differences in the assumptions behind their common use of the phrase (complexities similar to those my discussion in

---

[1]   Mary Wollstonecraft, *An Historical and Moral View of the French Revolution* (New York: New York University Press, 1989), 25. Edmund Burke, *Reflections on the Revolution in France* (New York: Penguin, 1968), 130.

Chapter 2 develops regarding Wollstonecraft's use of the same phrase "stage effect" in terms of aesthetics in her preface to *Maria, or The Wrongs of Woman*). Far from being a blanket denunciation of theatricality or of the stage in general, Wollstonecraft's phrase targets very specifically the "tricks" by which the nation keeps worn, "old principles" acceptable to the multitude through "new scenes and decorations." Whereas here Wollstonecraft implies that a theatrical bent in the French culture or taste "produced" the stage tricks going on in the public political sphere, elsewhere she argues the opposite, that a state-sanctioned "courtly insincerity" (*VRM* 5) are to blame for the French people's taste and, in a larger sense, the failures of the French Revolution's earliest promise. Indeed, in *Letters Written During a Short Residence*, Wollstonecraft lauds the ability of the French people as a whole to adopt an empathetic pose, in essence to "act" in relation to others, as opposed to the Swedes who "pique themselves on their politeness; but far from being the polish of a cultivated mind, it consists merely of tiresome forms and ceremonies. So far indeed from entering immediately into your character, and making you feel instantly at ease, like the well-bred French, their over-acted civility is a continual restraint on all your actions."[2] As this praise of the French indicates, critics have simply reductively missed the complexity of Wollstonecraft's thinking about the epistemic nature of theater in French Revolutionary political discourse, such that even the most thorough critical discussions rely on an assumption of her anti-theatricality bias.[3]

In this chapter I argue that notions of theatricality, spectatorial relationships, and performative speech pervade Wollstonecraft's historical writings, both her political utopianism and her analyses of the French Revolution's (ultimate) failure. To do so, I explore Wollstonecraft's immersion in French Revolutionary political discourse from her earliest defense of Richard Price and her rebuttal to Burke in *A Vindication of the Rights of Men* (1790) to her writings on the French Revolution, all in terms of Wollstonecraft's multivocal renderings of theatricality and performative politics. Most significantly, I offer new critical attention to a difficult text, *An Historical and Moral View of the French Revolution* (1794), arguing that what unifies this most baggy monster of a book is Wollstonecraft's persistent attention to the theatricality motif in all these discursive premises: 1) very specific references to both British and French theater; 2) an analysis of public riots and protests as street theater; 3) state theater in three of King Louis XVI's encounters with French parlement and the National Assembly (the *lit de justice, cour pleniere*, and the *séance royale*); 4) the members of the National

---

[2]   See my discussion in Chapter 3 of *Letters Written During a Short Residence*. The quote is from Letter II, 21.

[3]   Furniss offers a comprehensive look at the Burke/Wollstonecraft dialogue, particularly in reference to the characterization of the French mob, and righly interprets a Wollstonecraftian anti-theatricality as a condemnation of the ancien regime. See Tom Furniss, "Mary Wollstonecraf's French Revolution," *Cambridge Companion to Mary Wollstonecraft*, ed. Claudia L. Johnson (Cambridge: Cambridge University Press, 2002), 59–81.

Assembly contrasted to the key figures in the court; 5) the drama of the October Days episode, already narrated to great "stage effect" by Burke's *Reflections on the Revolution in France* and in her own *A Vindication of the Rights of Men*; and 6) her take on the most performative figure of the 1790s, Marie Antoinette.[4] Finally, while all these specific analyses of historical spectacles as theater constitute a central, unifying thread, I here continue my broader exploration of the potential agency in certain kinds of "acting"; thus, the *HMV*, which at times seems to trudge through day to day events in early Revolutionary France repetitively or formulaically, also participates in Wollstonecraft's interrogation of the power of the performative in the making of individual identity.

My study of Wollstonecraft's manipulation of theatricality in her representations of history builds upon the cultural analyses of Gillian Russell, Marc Baer, and Betsy Bolton. Gillian Russell's *The Theatres of War: Performance, Politics, and Society 1793–1815* analyzes how the "theatre of war" affected self-perception in England at a time when the "theatre functioned in a world where performance, display, and spectactorship were essential components of the social mechanism" (17). Baer, in *Theater and Disorder in Late Georgian London*, a book about the meanings of the last great theater riot in English history (67 nights of rioting at Covent Garden and its aftereffects), takes up the relationship between theatricality and stability, which is at the heart of Wollstonecraft's discussion of French theater audiences. Baer hypothesizes, "Unlike the French Revolution, where theatricality contributed to social and political transformation, it is possible in Britain that theatricality helped maintain the status quo" (13). Betsy Bolton's study *Women, Nationalism, and the Romantic Stage: Theatre and Politics in Britain, 1780–1800* similarly highlights this question of British theater as a stabilizing force for the status quo or as subversive model. Bolton points out that the Glorious Revolution offered an analogy between spectator and citizen, and, correspondingly at this time, theater was seen as offering a model of a political state in which a socially mixed public maintained power. Bolton, however, attributes the challenge to this perspective to the upheavals of the last two decades of the eighteenth century, anxieties surfacing as British citizens looking across the Channel saw a culture where "theatre seemed inextricable from Revolution" (12). Bolton specifically addresses Wollstonecraft, Burke, and Paine in her discussion of the ambivalence of attitudes toward theater in nationalistic terms, arguing that the theatrical analogies were comprised of both national fears and national fantasy—fears of unruliness and fantasies of differing classes brought together as one (16). Wollstonecraft, according to Bolton, clearly rejects the French model: "England benefited from its

---

4   Since Wollstonecraft had already, in her *A Vindication of the Rights of Men*, remarked on Burke's characterization of the spectacle of the October Days, her return to the subject here after a close analysis of all theatricality of French government is particularly enlightening. Also, while this chapter discusses the French monarchy extensively, Wollstonecraft's discussion of the public trials of Marie Antoinette and Louis XVI is treated more fully in Chapter 4 on trial discourse.

spectatorial negotiations and compromises, avoiding thereby the French evils of an absolutism both moral and political" (16). The argument in these critical texts— either that England's theatrical state apparatus preserved a status quo or that it offered a more fruitful model of what Bolton calls "spectatorial negotiations"—is central to my exploration of Wollstonecraft's historical discourses; what we find is much less clear and much more provocative than either side of the argument.

The last 20 years of historical and literary criticism about the French Revolution debate in England—including my edited collection *The French Revolution Debate in English Literature and Culture*—constitute a scholarly industry so productive that some Romanticists believe that we know all we need to know about political writing in this period, yet as Daniel O'Neill's 2007 book *The Burke–Wollstonecraft Debate: Savagery, Civilization, and Democracy* asserts, the Revolution Debate is now seen as foundational not just for an understanding of Romantic writers but for "the emergence of political modernity itself" (O'Neill 3). O'Neill's study, the only book-length account of the clash between Burke and Wollstonecraft, focuses on both writers' reinterpretation of Scottish Enlightenment philosophy and generates an interesting new context for their dialogue, yet fails to offer a close, analytical reading of Wollstonecraft's Revolutionary texts. Significantly, though, O'Neill emphasizes that Wollstonecraft's *HMV* is important because in it she "interpreted … [Revolutionary] milestones from the perspective of the Terror, and 'philosophically,'—that is, from within the framework of her broad historical thesis concerning manners and their relationship to moral development" (247); more specifically, his assertion that both Burke and Wollstonecraft were driven by the potential advent of "deep democracy," as Furniss succinctly summarizes it in his review of the book, is crucial for my reading of Wollstonecraft's deployment of theatrical tropes:

> … the fear or hope that the French Revolution was not just a change of regime but was driven by an ideological commitment to a total revolution that would democratize all institutions, from the family up to the church and the aristocratic state. (162)

For Burke, the fear seemed warranted in the radical displacement of hierarchical order apparent in the National Assembly. Burke complains that the lower orders of the gallery are running a "burlesque" show, applying the metaphor of the playhouse to Revolutionary activists:

> They act like the comedians of a fair before a riotous audience; they act amidst the tumultuous cries of a mixed mob of ferocious men, and of women lost to shame, who, according to their insolent fancies, direct, control, applaud, explode them … as they have inverted order in all things, the gallery is in place of the house. (161)

Burke's condemnation of a "mixed" assemblage is a political fear of democracy itself, where the gallery audience "is in place of the house." By contrast, Wollstonecraft heralds the change and sees a gradual, systemic emergence into a truly "democratic" reorganization of all human institutions as a hopeful possibility. Her appropriation of the theatricality trope, then, functions not only as critique of coercive political mechanisms but also as a sign of subversive potential for revolutionizing democratic paradigms.[5]

To begin with Wollstonecraft's immersion in the French Revolution debate is to follow a standard trajectory of reading Wollstonecraft as activist. Her participation, beginning in 1787, in the Joseph Johnson circle of radical artists and thinkers, initiated or substantiated through her work as a critical reviewer for Johnson's *Analytical Review*, and her support of Dissenting minister Reverend Richard Price, deeply embed her in radical political scenes. As we situate her historical text, *A Vindication of the Rights of Men*, the first of over 50 published rebuttals to Burke's *Reflections on the Revolution in France*, within the context of this radical group during the early 1790s, it is imperative to see Wollstonecraft not just as political thinker/theorist or as a protofeminist poised to translate this text's anti-hierarchy arguments against class into arguments against gender bias four years later in her second *Vindication* but rather, as part of a group who were, as Todd says, "not the sages of more peaceful periods, but engaged polemicists who believed that their ideas might soon be put into practice ... [and] that their publishing might have political and social consequences for their personal lives" (Todd, *VRM* vii).[6] Wollstonecraft's experiences in France from December 1792 until 1795 included, as Godwin in his *Memoirs* relates, her horror at seeing the streets of Paris literally running with blood from the guillotine. Ralph Wardle even suggests that Wollstonecraft's name may have been mistakenly listed in Parisian papers as one imprisoned briefly during the Terror.[7] While Burke visited France only once, in 1773, Wollstonecraft interpreted the unfolding of the French Revolution from a much closer and more perilous position. Not just a spectator of events but an actor in them, in a sense, Wollstonecraft consistently appropriates theatrical metaphors in her historical texts all the while calling Burke out for his own gaudy show.

Burke's description of Wollstonecraft as one of "that class of desperate, wicked, and mischievously ingenious women who ... bring ruin and shame upon all that listen to them" (*Correspondence* 8: 304) acknowledges her "mischievous" influence, although he claimed not to have ever read her response *A Vindication of the Rights of Men*. In this first published response to Burke's *Reflections*, Wollstonecraft aligns Burke's aristocratic privilege, the "intoxicating bowl"

---

[5]   On the other hand, Wollstonecraft cautions against the kind of blind mimicry that characterizes class positioning: "It would be an arduous task to trace all the vice and misery that arise in society from the middle class of people apeing the manners of the great" (22).

[6]   All quotations from *A Vindication of the Rights of Men* taken from this edition: *A Vindication of the Rights of Men, A Vindication of the Rights of Woman, An Historical and Moral View of the French Revolution* (Oxford: Oxford University Press, 1993). Todd's introduction is vii–xxx.

[7]   See Ralph Wardle, *Mary Wollstonecraft: A Critical Biography* (Lawrence: University of Kansas Press, 1951), 194–5.

of his rhetoric, and the superficial theatricality of the *ancien regime*. From the first sentence, she attempts to perform authenticity as she contrasts her own stance—she refuses "courtly insincerity" (5)—to the "specious garb" (3) of his rhetoric, using Burke's favorite trope of drapery against him. Foundational to his representation of civilization is a reliance upon what he calls "the decent drapery of life," which can be read as a system of manners influenced by chivalry that beautified the state and gave the illusion that power and obedience were natural. Such delusory drapery has, then, the effect of mystification, obscuring power struggles and forced subjugation, a point Wollstonecraft identifies as she announces one of the aims of her book: to "shew you to yourself, stripped of the gorgeous drapery in which you have enwrapped your tyrannic principles" (37). That this drapery metaphor is itself infused with notions of theatricality, the costume versus the body per se, Wollstonecraft insists in the fifth paragraph of the text. Furthering her critique of his style, she characterizes it as popular to those who love theater and avers that his "ornamental feelings" are applauded by the "fashionable world":

> Even the Ladies, Sir, may repeat your sprightly sallies, and retail in theatrical attitudes many of your sentimental exclamations. Sensibility is the *manie* of the day, and compassion the virtue which is to cover a multitude of vices, whilst justice is left to mourn in sullen silence, and balance truth in vain. (6)

Here she not only condemns Burke's audience as full of "theatrical attitudes," but also begins her consistent condemnation of his troubling claim that a covering of vice produces a kind of virtue. In his *Reflections*, Burke claims that evil loses "half its evil" by "losing all its grossness" (170). We should attentively follow Wollstonecraft's progressive denunciation of Burke's strange, mathematical (loses "half" evil by losing "all" grossness) ethical formula (this recalls Hazlitt's label of Malthus as "moral arithmetic"). Wollstonecraft persistently returns to this passage because it demonstrates that Burke's argument is not simply a politics with which she disagrees but a pernicious and immoral "moral" philosophy.[8] This dimension to her thinking sets her response to Burke apart from the more famous rebuttal, Paine's *Rights of Man*, which similarly attacks Burke's use of the drapery metaphor, but for overtly political ends, describing monarchy as

---

[8]   Her second reference to Burke's vice passage occurs in her famous attack on Burke's sentimentalizing over the downfall of Marie Antoinette: "your tears are reserved ... for the declamation of the theatre, or for the downfall of queens whose rank alters the nature of folly, and throws a graceful veil over vices that degrade humanity ..." (14). A third occurs as she links this immoral fondness for appearance to the acquisition of wealth; "numberless vices, forced in the hot-bed of wealth, assume a sightly form to dazzle the senses and cloud the understanding ... and vice 'loses half its evil by losing all its grossness'—What a sentiment to come from a moral pen!" (23–4). Her attention to this mathematical application recalls Hazlitt's label of Malthusian utilitarianism as a "moral arithmetic."

> Something kept behind a curtain, about which there is a great deal of bustle and fuss, and a wonderful air of seeming solemnity; but when by any accident the curtain happens to open, and the company see what it is, they burst into laughter. (22)

Wollstonecraft finds this no laughing matter.

Her first attempt, in *VRM*, to characterize Burke's argument foregrounds his claim that concealment, the curtain behind which "grossness" may be hid, is a virtue:

> ... if there is anything like an argument ... in your wild declamation behold the result: that we are to reverence the rust of antiquity ... nay, that if we do discover some errors, our *feelings* should lead us to excuse, with blind love ... the venerable vestiges of ancient days. These are gothic notions of beauty—the ivy is beautiful, but when it insidiously destroys the trunk from which it receives support, who would not grub it up? (8)

Using the organic metaphor of ivy adorning/destroying the tree, Wollstonecraft both incorporates a Burkean metaphor of the English state as sturdy oak tree and suggests that the drapery/costume metaphor he uses is dangerous because it not only is predicated on a superficial appreciation of artifice, but also extols a destructive agent.[9] In terms of performance studies, we can (re)view such passages in terms of spectatorial negotiation. Paine's descriptions of monarchy versus democracy utilize such premises: monarchy is "something hid behind a curtain," whereas representative government is played out in the "open theater of the world" (22). As Russell has argued, Paine's description blurs the boundary of audience and performers, democratic structure becoming a theater in which the audience is not subordinate to the performers but would in fact become the performance (24).[10]

Wollstonecraft's condemnation, in *VRM*, of Burke's hollow ethical formula, his "smearing a sentimental varnish over vice" (24), which echoes her label of his style as essentially "subterfug[e]" (28), culminates in her response to Burke's treatment of one key scene in Revolutionary history, the spectacle that pointedly spotlights two different groups of women and Burke's melodramatic reactions to the radical crossing of boundaries: the October Days episode, which functions as the rhetorical and argumentative center of the text (126). Wollstonecraft will return to this textual site again in her *HMV*, but at this point, she mercilessly exposes Burke's particular horror at the scene, a fear of female monstrosity. In "'The Furies of Hell': Women in Burke's 'French Revolution,'" Chapter 3 of *Signifying Woman: Culture and Chaos in Rousseau, Burke, and Mill*, Linda Zerilli definitively decodes Burke's juxtaposition of women labeled as the "furies of hell"

---

[9]   Burke cautions against listening to half a dozen grasshoppers under a fern instead of recognizing the thousands of great silent cattle "beneath the shadow of the English oak" who though silent are more significant than the "little shriveled, meager, hopping, though loud and troublesome insects of the hour" (181).

[10]   This model parallels Rousseau's description of a rural festival as offering the perfect blend of spectator/performer relations, as I discuss more fully in Chapter 3.

with the ultimate lady in distress, the Queen. To understand Burke's narrative of the "atrocious spectacle" of October 6, we should note the event and the social actors that led up to it, the famous October 5 Women's March on Versailles. As Zerilli summarizes, it was

> a march of almost six thousand women—market woman, wage earners, wives of artisans, craftswomen, small business women, and some women from the middle class—exercising their time-honored right as mothers to demand bread for their families; a march that provoked the municipal government to send the National Guard to hold off counterrevolution by bringing the king to Paris; a march that, in the early hours of the sixth, would lead "a crowd of women and a *few* men," as Ruth Graham writes, to enter the "palace door leading to the queen's chambers."[11]

Knowing this context alerts us as readers to pay attention to the symbolic economy of Burke's narration in which the protesters are a savage mob bent on destroying the social and cultural values of civilized France. He first compared the procession to Native American savage rituals similar to his descriptions in his *Account of the European Settlements in America*, saying the mob resembled "American savages, entering into Onandaga, after some of their murders called victories, and leading into hovels hung round with scalps, their captives, overpowered with the scoffs and buffets of women as ferocious as themselves ... ."[12] Thus, in that earlier narrative, the *Account*, the particular signification of savagery was, as O'Neill says, "seen most clearly in its peculiar effect on the nature of women" (126), and accordingly Burke shifts attention here to how the horrors wrought by the Revolutionary actions threaten the civilized figure of woman:

> Whilst the royal captives, who followed in the train, were slowly moved along, amidst the horrid yells, and shrilling screams, and frantic dances, and infamous contumelies, and all the unutterable abominations of the furies of hell, in the abused shape of the vilest of women. (165)

Burke's opposition to the Revolution's "unnatural" order is grounded in the spectacle of women acting out in the public sphere, women "lost to shame, who according to their insolent fancies, direct, control, applaud, explode ... and sometimes mix and take their seats amongst [the men]," making a "profane burlesque" of civilized government. Burke is horrified by the figure of woman, or rather the "unutterable" that is nonetheless named in his evocation of the "furies

---

[11]   Zerilli uses language from Ruth Graham's "Loaves and Liberty: Women in the French Revolution," *Becoming Visible: Women in European History*, ed. Renate Bridenthal and Claudia Koonz (New York: Houghton Mifflin, 1977), 241.

[12]   See O'Neill 126; for extensive discussion on relationship between *VRM* and Burke's *Account*, see Luke Gibbons, *Edmund Burke and Ireland: Aesthetics, Politics, and the Colonial Sublime* (Cambridge: Cambridge University Press, 2003).

of hell." Thus, his conflation of events of October 5 onto the event of the October 6 morning assault on the palace betrays his obsessively gendered lens.

Wollstonecraft's first response in *VRM* to this spectacularizing passage is to expose Burke's classist, misogynist assumptions: "Probably you mean women who gained a livelihood by selling vegetables or fish, who never had had any advantages of education; or their vices might have lost part of their abominable deformity, by losing part of their grossness" (29). As Furniss shrewdly asserts, "Wollstonecraft deflates Burke's display of outraged sensibility with a precise socioeconomic description of the kind of women who participated in the Versailles march" (61). The effect of this rhetorical move is demystification and denaturalization of Burke's depiction of the furies embodied in the "shape" of vile women, further revising Burke's metaphor of concealment and exposing the real working class women whom Burke had, in effect, staged/dressed as furies.

The other female subject in Burke's passage on the October Days, Marie Antoinette, even more powerfully displays Burke's problematic representation of female bodies. If he were unable to describe the women in the mob as anything other than a hideous "shape," his alternating views of Marie Antoinette—from disembodied, etherealized vision to an "almost naked" victim of sexualized violence—portray both his inability to confront her as a real woman behind the staged beauty and his obsession with doing just that. Numerous critics have noted Burke's chivalric evocation of Marie Antoinette as lady in distress: O'Neill argues that, for Burke, the queen is "the sentient embodiment of European civilization"; Isaac Kramnick argues that Burke coped with feelings of sexual and political ambivalence by exposing "the horror inflicted by unleashed masculinity"; J.G.A. Pocock attempts, as Zerilli says, to salvage Burke's political theory by rescuing the author from his chivalric, figurative excess.[13] In *VRM*, her earliest rebuttal to Burke, Wollstonecraft simply labels his narration of the attack on Versailles pure theater: "… your tears are reserved … for the declamation of the theatre, or the downfall of queens, whose rank alters the nature of folly, and throws a graceful veil over vices that degrade humanity" (14). As Bahar points out, Wollstonecraft shrewdly uses the plural ("the downfall of queens") to demystify the exceptional status of the rank of queen and therefore "moves the term from the register of social hierarchy to that of the theatre, where the downfall of queens is frequently recited" (142). I read Wollstonecraft's reaction to this passage more fully later in this chapter because it is in *An Historical and Moral View of the French Revolution* that she confronts and exposes the complex performative politics of Marie Antoinette.

While *A Vindication of the Rights of Men* does present a thorough rebuttal to Burke and in so doing a defense of the French Revolution and a critique of the French monarchy, it is the little-known *An Historical and Moral View of the Origin and Progress of the French Revolution* that offers readers a rewarding,

---

[13] O'Neill 146; see Isaac Kramnick, *The Rage of Edmund Burke* (New York: Basic Books, 1977), 152, and Pocock's *Virtue, Commerce, and History: Essays in Political Thought and History* (Cambridge: Cambridge University Press, 1985), 198.

complex view of Wollstonecraft's revisionary thoughts about the Revolution from the vantage point of time. Written in 1794 about the events in France during 1788 and the early months of 1789, the book is informed by Wollstonecraft's knowledge of the later violent events of the Jacobin period under Robespierre. By the time she wrote this book, she had accepted that the Revolution, in spite of the barbaric nature that she deplored and her disillusion chronicled in her brief 1793 *Letter on the Present Character of the French Nation* (a text which O'Neill labels a "contrapuntal prologue" to her *HMV*), was, indeed, a sign of intellectual and social improvement. As Dart suggests, Wollstonecraft takes a broad view of revolutionary history, like Condorcet, subsuming the birth pangs of the new nation into a broader narrative of historical progress (121).[14]

Unsurprisingly, this six-volume tome has received little sustained critical attention aside from its famous return to the October Days episode so well analyzed by numerous critics, notably Jones and Furniss.[15] Two recent studies, however, have included some limited discussion of the book in interesting contexts. First, Angela Keane's "Imperious Sympathies," which situates Wollstonecraft's discourses within the contexts of a "matriphobic" culture shaped by population discourse of the 1790s, acknowledges the general premises of *HMV*: that Wollstonecraft contextualizes the French Revolution in a broad historical trajectory, struggles to absolve revolutionary agents from blame for violence, and projects an optimistic long-term end (Keane 33). Keane argues that a significant part of Wollstonecraft's diagnosis of revolutionary failures is an indictment of commercial culture, which she often describes using analogies of sexual degradation and in terms of its impact on the status of women. Referring frequently to the debased tastes of the French court, Wollstonecraft, according to Keane, also implicates the bourgeoisie, for whom trade in female bodies—prostitution or marriage—is just another kind of business. Emphasizing her overall contention that Wollstonecraft's ambivalence toward the maternal body was grounded in population discourse of the 1790s, Keane points out that Wollstonecraft punctuates her narrative repeatedly with the maxim that reason progresses more slowly than passion and, thus, that "the strongest conviction of reason cannot quickly change a habit of body (*HMV* 6.53). Despite her interest, in theory, that this text evinces Wollstonecraft's integration of "body matters" and revolutionary history, Keane, nonetheless, devotes no more than a page and few specifics to the text she understatedly calls a "somewhat digressive narrative" (32).

---

[14]   Dart argues that Wollstonecraft, in the next two years, shifted from political commentary to autobiography in the Letters of 1796 as a deliberate attempt to wrest meaning and value from the unaccountable chaos of the revolutionary history (103). For an excellent, concise discussion of Wollstonecraft's brief "Letter on the Present Character of the French Nation," see O'Neill, 229–32.

[15]   Vivien Jones, "Women Writing Revolution: Narratives of History and Sexuality in Wollstonecraft and Williams," in *Beyond Romanticism: New Approaches to Texts and Contexts, 1780–1832*, ed. Stephen Copley and John Whale (London and New York: Routledge, 1992), 178–99; Furniss, "Mary Wollstonecraft's French Revolution," 59–81.

Alex Schulman speaks more directly to this critical inattention, calling *HMV* a "text to which Wollstonecraft scholars have tended to devote comparatively small space, understandable in light of the book's length, wealth of minutiae, and historical inconsequence next to the two *Vindications*" (44). Schulman's "Gothic Piles and Endless Forests: Wollstonecraft Between Burke and Rousseau" analyzes Wollstonecraft's seemingly contradictory stance toward reason/emotion, intellect/ sentiment in terms of what he calls a "strategy adopted, whether consciously or not, in her support of the French Revolution" (42). Specifically, Schulman suggests that Wollstonecraft realized the multifunctionality of the "politics of sense and sensibility," that far from being relevant only to gender issues in England (and thus her persistent attention to the reason/emotion dichotomy in *VRW*), a deployment of sensibility would work "as much in the service of the French Revolution as in the counter-revolutionary project" (43–4). Offering a useful summary of critical attention to this quandary, Schulman repeats Todd's succinct argument that Wollstonecraft "tried to rescue good from bad sensibility" and, more specifically to the French Revolution, Syndy Conger's hypothesis that Wollstonecraft returned to defenses of sentiment after witnessing the Jacobin terror: "her firsthand observation of the revolution in the name of reason causes her to temper her faith in reason, and to restore a measure of her faith, if now subdued, in sensibility."[16] Schulman's study acknowledges that Wollstonecraft and Burke use the politics of sensibility against one another, one context of such politics being the function of theatrical tropes: "In fact, [Burke] uses the concept of the theater as a cudgel against the revolutionaries just as Wollstonecraft would use it against him and his imagined audience of weeping ladies" (44). My reading of *HMV* develops what is in Schulman just a suggestion and goes beyond a development of this argument between Burke and Wollstonecraft to a thorough examination of Wollstonecraft's complex analysis of performative politics in the Revolutionary era.

To begin the discussion with the most overt deployment of performance issues in *HMV*, its representation of actual, material French and English theater, we might expect a critique of French performance. A critique of the theatricality of the French is not the same as a critique of French theater; the conundrum is worth sorting out. To return to my first epigraph for this chapter, Wollstonecraft sarcastically describes the French fondness for public theater as inbred ("they suck [it] in with their milk") and, yet, her slam is not against theater itself as she goes on to indict a nation who maintains "old principles" through "new scenes and decorations." In a similar move, she conflates the French taste in theater with the

---

[16] See Janet Todd, *Mary Wollstonecraft: A Revolutionary Life* (London: Weidenfeld and Nicolson, 2000), especially 163, and Syndy McMillen Conger, *Mary Wollstonecraft and the Language of Sensibility* (Rutherford, NJ: Fairleigh Dickinson University Press, 1994), esp. 133–4. Conger's discussion of Wollstonecraft's *HMV* as negotiating a fine distinction between "'true sensibility' and its counterfeits" makes claims about the need for close analysis of true/false sensibility similar to mine about positive/negative power of theatricality; see especially 136.

pageantry inherent in Catholic ritual, developing a point she had pushed earlier in 1790 in *VRM*. Directed against Burke's lachrymose declamations, she famously indicts in that text "the idle tapestry that decorated a gothic pile," "the dronish bell that summoned the fat priest to prayer," and "the empty pageant of a name" (62). As O'Neill stresses, Wollstonecraft's *VRM* consistently rejects the civilizing function of the "bulwarks of the *ancien regime*, the church and the nobility" and indicts "the medieval church as a sublime instrument of terror that tricked the people by threatening them with divine punishment" (234). In the first pages of *HMV*, she similarly describes Catholic ritual as a low, vulgar kind of theatrical entertainment:

> Voltaire leading the way, and ridiculing with that happy mixture of satire and gaiety, calculated to delight the French, the inconsistent puerilities of a puppet-show religion, had the art to attach the bells to the fool's cap, which tinkled on every side, rousing the attention and piquing the vanity of his readers. (18)

Wollstonecraft dramatically exposes the meretricious and "inconsistent" nature of the national "puppet-show religion," which she later in the chapter admonishes for replaying the same scenes over and over—"the eating of the apple, the theft of Prometheus, the opening of Pandora's box and the other fables, too tedious to enumerate, on which priests have erected their tremendous structures of imposition" (21)—to persuade their members of their inherent inclination toward evil and the necessity of institutional orthodoxy. This critique of the melodramatic nature of public religious practice no more indicts theatricality per se than it does religion; context is all-important here. In fact, her denunciation of the manipulations of the "puppet-show religion" is accompanied and attenuated by praise of Voltaire's strategy or "art" of attaching "the bell to the fool's cap," or playing the role of jester/writer in order to rouse and pique his audience. Admiration for the role-playing strategy of Voltaire leads into her discussion of how the French, as opposed to the English, respond at the theater:

> At our theatres, the boxes, pits, and galleries, relish different scenes; and some are condescendingly born by the more polished part of the audience to allow the rest to have their portion of amusement. In France, on the contrary, a highly wrought sentiment of morality, probably rather romantic than sublime, produces a burst of applause, when one heart seems to agitate every hand. (19)

This analysis of the difference between theater audiences in Britain and France serves as an opening volley in this work's sustained debate about and Wollstonecraft's complicated position toward the coercive/subversive potentials in theater and, more generally, in performativity. The lines suggest to some critics a Wollstonecraftian emphasis on the heterogeneity of English versus absolutism of French taste (although she does not discuss *HMV*, Russell celebrates Paine's "theater," in which "the audience is not subordinate to the performers but would in fact become the performance" [24]). To what extent this is a critique of the French is, however, a matter of debate. In fact, Wollstonecraft's later direct comments about her own analysis of the French as a people rebuke the very kind of critical myopia that has dominated the criticism; in *Letters Written During a Short Residence*, she confesses, "I believe I should have been less severe in the remarks I have made on the vanity and depravity of the French, had I traveled toward the North before I visited France" (161) and even adds a footnote that says "See *Historical and Moral View of the French Revolution.*" Her admonition demands that we read this text more critically. A careful reading of *HMV*, for example, provides this interesting context for the line quoted above—her description of French theater as one where "one heart seems to agitate every hand." She appears to express the same kind of admiration for such audiences as for Voltaire's wearing of the fool's cap. Wollstonecraft, indeed, sounds impressed as she asserts that new opinions in France "fly from mouth to mouth with an electrical velocity unknown in England" (19). If we as readers still interpret this line as critique of a French custom, we can no longer do so as she finishes the sentence: she goes on to theorize that this electrical discourse reduces class distinction "so that there is not such a difference between the sentiments of the various ranks in [France] as is observable in [England]" (19).[17]

Building on this collapse of distinction between classes in terms of taste, and implying a potentially positive energy in the French passionate attraction to expression of ideas, Wollstonecraft goes on to use vulgar, common street theater as a trope for a diseased monarchical performance. Similar to her critique of Catholic ritual as a "puppet show" religion, she critiques lower class amusements by comparing them to diseased, meretricious displays of the powerful. Her only consistent point is contempt for those who fall prey to "show":

> If we turn then with disgust from ensanguined regal pomp, and the childish raree-shows that amuse the enslaved multitude, we shall still feel more contempt for the order of men, who cultivated their faculties, only to enable them to consolidate their power, by leading the ignorant astray. (23)

Her comparison of "regal pomp" to "raree-shows" shrewdly suggests the spectatorial negotiations inherent in street theater and public processionals. Johnson's *Dictionary* of 1755 defines the "raree-show" as "a show carried in a box" so called "in imitation of the foreign way of pronouncing rare show." Peep shows or raree shows can be traced back at least to the fifteenth century and were usually a wooden box with a hole or several holes containing a set of pictures which the show-man set into a viewing position by pulling corresponding strings. Common subjects included exotic views and animals, scenes of classical drama or ceremonies, and, of course, lewd pictures. Wollstonecraft's equation of royal ceremony with these vulgar

---

[17]   This statement appears to contradict her critique, in *A Vindication of the Rights of Men*, of the "subtle magnetism" of Burkean rhetoric. While she cautions against a kind of knee-jerk reaction to seductive rhetoric, she also seems to in this context acknowledge the democratic power of such "velocity."

displays will coalesce/culminate in her representation of court figures, especially French ministers as key performers who require passive spectators.

The most frequently cited evidence of Wollstonecraft's anti-theatricality is her complete disdain for the artifice of the French court, not just in the era of the *ancien regime*; she traces "courtly insincerity" back to the seventeenth century and the reign of Louis XIII, especially the power of Richelieu and Mazarin, chief ministers of Louis XIII's reign, whose rise to power institutionalized "favoritism" and "the Italian mode of governing by intrigue" and who were, according to Wollstonecraft, "dissimulation personified" (24). Further weakening any strength of mind in the act of governance, Louis XIV, the "haughty and inflated," quickly accelerated "the perfection of that species of civilization," and Wollstonecraft invokes again Burke's immoral mask trope in her metaphorical description of insincerity:

> Endeavoring to make bigotry tolerate voluptuousness, and honor and licentiousness shake hands, sight was lost of the line of distinction, or vice was hid under the mask of it's [sic] correlative virtue. (24)

Again, Wollstonecraft dialogues with Burke's contention that vice itself loses half its evil when it loses all its grossness. Appropriating the trope of the mask functions like the drapery/curtain/cloak metaphors to indict the concealment of vice (here, bigotry and licentiousness), leading Wollstonecraft progressively into a discussion of French theater, which she maligns only in terms of how closely it simulates/ copies the artifice of the court; she critiques theater which presents "the manners of the court ... imitating the drapery of manners which points out the *costume* of the age" (24). Only Moliere, she asserts, was able to write on the "grand scale of human passions" (24). Wollstonecraft's argument that the seventeenth-century political history of favoritism and corruption at court shaped an idle and meretricious form of theater centers on Racine, indicting his emphasis on "the courtly propriety of behavior" and labeling him "the father of the French stage" (25). It is within this context that she unleashes her scathing critique of French theatricality used as my first epigraph to this chapter, and she goes on to align this kind of "phosphorical, sentimental gilding" that is "constantly observable at the theatres" (26) with destructive political policies attacking liberty: "ranting sentiments, which, with mock dignity, like the party-coloured rags on the shriveled branches of the tree of liberty, stuck up in very village, are displayed as something very grand and significant" (26). This image of the rags tied on the shriveled branches of the tree of liberty leads her to equate meretricious theater with monarchical displays of power and might: "The wars of Louis [XIV] were, likewise, theatrical exhibitions; and the business of his life was adjusting ceremonials" (26).

Having distinguished Moliere's admirable theater of real "human passions" from the false theater that takes its cue from the artifice of courtly manners, Wollstonecraft's next move is to align the ceremonial performance with licentiousness. Significantly, Wollstonecraft had earlier made this association with regard to British aristocracy in both her *Vindications*. Equating luxury and effeminacy, idleness and debauchery, she attacks the "contagion of restless idleness, and its concomitant, vice," and argues that the system of aristocracy is itself to blame for the wanton behaviors of "the fine lady," who would otherwise "superintend her family and suckle her children in order to fulfill her part of the social compact" (*VRW* 24). Schulman's remarks on this passage link it to Burke's representation of immoral women of the French mob:

> She reverses Burke's gendering of the French Revolution as the spectacle of "unsex'd" monsters wreaking havoc on the streets of Paris. It is in fact the decadent aristocracy that has introduced the truly pernicious gender confusion by plucking men from their Spartan countryside duties, and women from the natural (and rational) suckling of their children, to idle at court. (47)

Within her brief discussion of the regency and reign of Louis XV, Wollstonecraft similarly exposes the overtly profligate manners of the regency, linking the "bare-faced" sexual debauchery of the king to the system of "false refinement" that had been in place before him:

> During the regency, vice was not only bare-faced but audacious. ... In the character of the regent we may trace all the vices and graces of false refinement ... [and] atrocious debaucheries. ... Impotence of body, and indolence of mind, rendered Louis XV the slave of his mistresses, who fought to forget his nauseous embraces ... . (27–8)

Once masked for so long, the court figures' vices now are "bare-faced," audacious, strengthened by the falsity so long at play, and in her description of the "nauseous embraces" of a king, Wollstonecraft sets up what will be her complex and, at first glance, contradictory discussion of the French state theater of which she and her generation were keen spectators, the French Revolutionary stage of Louix XVI and Marie Antoinette.

Because her complex representation of Marie Antoinette and her relationship to Louis XVI hinges on identifying the theatrical ploys required of the queen in the most performative political reign in history, I begin with Wollstonecraft's attention to Louis' performances with parlement, in particular two fights in 1787 and 1788. In the last use of the judicial proceeding known as the Bed of Justice (*lit de justice*), Louis XVI flaunted what Wollstonecraft scornfully calls the "gaudy and meretricious pageant of the court" (37) in an attempt to intimidate the representative body. The term "bed of justice" refers to the seat or platform occupied by the kings of France whenever they were present at sessions of the French royal court or in Parlement. In French judicial history, the term was also used to denote a session of Parlement held in the presence of the king and called specifically to overrule previous decisions or to force the acceptance of royal edicts or ordinances that the Parlement had rejected. This usage was based on the theory that the authority of the Parlement was derived from the Crown, and that in the physical presence of the king (the source of authority), this delegated authority ceased to exist. Under this legal fiction, the Parlement was legally incapable of resisting any demand that the king might make, as long as it was made from this platform, the bed of justice. Louis XV used the device repeatedly to try to control the rebellious Parlements of the eighteenth century, but these attempts at coercion usually only intensified resistance to royal authority. In exposing the "gaudy pageantry" of such a theatrical proceeding, Wollstonecraft calls attention to the performative nature of such rites and rejects the authority of the process, pointing out the hypocrisy of "what was termed a bed of justice, though in reality of all justice a solemn mockery" (37). Thomas Carlyle's representation of the dramatic nature of the proceeding is unparalleled:

> When a Parlement refuses registering, the remedy, by long practice, has become familiar to the simplest: a Bed of Justice. One complete month this Parlement has spent in mere idle jargoning, and sound and fury . ... On the 6th of August let the whole refractory Body roll out, in wheeled vehicles, as far as the King's Chateau of Versailles; there shall the King, holding his Bed of Justice, order them, by his own royal lips, to register. They may remonstrate, in an under tone; but they must obey, lest a worse unknown thing befall them.

> It is done: the Parlement has rolled out, on royal summons; has heard the express royal order to register. Whereupon it has rolled back again, amid the hushed expectancy of men. And now, behold, on the morrow, this Parlement, seated once more in its own Palais, with 'crowds inundating the outer courts,' not only does not register, but (O portent!) declares all that was done on the prior day to be null, and the Bed of Justice as good as a futility! (118)[18]

Parlement's power of resistance here, what Carlyle can in retrospect call a portent, gains strength in a second attempt by the court to circumvent and subdue the power of the elected assembly, the calling of a *cour pleniere*, which elicits Wollstonecraft's closer analysis of the power of the court's theatrical maneuvers. Summoned by the finance minister Brienne, the *cour pleniere* was an aristocratic assembly designed to bypass an obstructive parlement. Wollstonecraft writes that the assembly tried to pass itself off as "an heterogeneous assembly of princes, nobles, magistrates, and soldiers," which Brienne conceived as a "happy substitute" for parlement which "by restoring the ancient forms of the kings of France, would awe and amuse the people" (38). It is this attempt to use "forms" of ritual to "awe" the people that ultimately succeeded in "awaken[ing] the sensibility of the most torpid" and which instigated the French audience of these antics to actively observe the corruption of the court which Wollstonecraft vehemently casts as "the labyrinths of sophistry and tergiversation" and "the very dens of ... nefarious machinations" (39).

---

[18] See Carlyle, *The French Revolution: A History in Three Volumes*, published by James Fraser, 7. Carlyle's depiction of the resistance to and recoiling of the king's command recalls Blake's similar representations in *The French Revolution and America*.

Awakening a French populace into acknowledging these "machinations," the *cour pleniere* sparked a number of public rallies and protests, which Wollstonecraft considers in terms of performance. She alludes particularly to Paris protests of 1788 after the imprisonment of Duval and Montsabert, who had attempted to circumvent the calling of the *cour pleniere*. While the people burned in effigy several of the ministers, without violence, the government hired a number of people to start a riot which could then be crushed by the cavalry, the event Wollstonecraft describes as one in which the "hired slaves of despotism" initiated a "riot purposely excited" (40). Again linking theatrical display to political corruption, Wollstonecraft exposes that the court, having "purposely excited" a riot, then progressed to "artfully excit[e]" a fear of famine "in order to have a pretext to form magazines of provision for an army" (43). Within the context of this fear of famine, the court also, just on the evening of the meeting of the Estates-General in May 1789, initiated a hysterical fear of bread shortage against a respectable and liberal-minded manufacturer. Of this propensity to use fear of survival, Wollstonecraft says of the court agents,

> The scarcity, real or factitious, of this article [bread] has always been taken advantage of by those who wished to excite tumults in Paris; and at this juncture the duped Parisians rose, at the instigation of court agents, to destroy themselves. The riot was allowed to get ahead before any ferocious attempts to quell it ... and established an opinion, that the turbulent mob [was] required to be awed by the presence of troops. (56)

Gillian Russsell's discussion of street protests in England in the French Revolutionary mania is helpful here in seeing Wollstonecraft's view of these tactics. Russell analyzes how mock executions, especially of Paine, went on routinely on the streets in 1792–1793 in an attempt to harness a form of political protest, suggesting that these events were not only allowed to go on by the British government, but encouraged to make visible a kind of anti-revolution sentiment to counter all the radical subversive protests. Like any public spectacle, however, those in authority had to be careful that the energies let loose in these events were still contained, framed, by the ritual boundaries of the proceedings and thus would not go too far. On the issue of Paine's mock executions, Cowper, for example, advised that the rulers should be careful about "playing with the passions of the multitude" since such passion might then be used just as easily against the government (Russell 23). This strategy of permitting license in these political protests in hopes to contain ultimately the "wrong" kind of protests again returns us to the questions of the social utility of masquerade as release valve—containment as traditional or subversive—and ultimately back to my central question of theater (broadly defined) as coercive or liberating. And at this point in *HMV*, Wollstonecraft overtly moves from exposure of the negative, repressive mechanism of state theater to the potentially enabling appropriations of it as she turns attention to performers in the other camp, figures of the National Assembly. O'Neill, in fact, summarizes the plot trajectory of *HMV* in terms of these major historical events of 1789:

"the convocation of the Estates General; its transfiguration into the National Assembly; the taking of the Bastille; the abolition of feudalism on the night of 4 August; the *Declaration of the Rights of Man and the Citizen*; and the October Days" (247).

In the calling of the Estates General, the courtiers adapted the "ceremonials of reception" (55), even adjusting the requirements of dress for the session; as Wollstonecraft wryly notes, "true to the inveterate prejudice in favour of precedents, the nobility were gaudily caparisoned for the show, whilst the commons were stupidly commanded to wear the black mantle" (55). Wollstonecraft treats the opening of the Estates General session with special detail to the (in)effectiveness of the performative speech of both parties. Louis XVI's opening speech she labels a performance, exposing it as pure "cant" with the posture of servility: "... in the true cant of courts, dictating while complimenting, he assured them, that he depended on their wisdom and moderation; concluding with the words of course *the humble servant of king*" (57). This hollow utterance contrasts with the authentically performative nature of the declaration that is at the heart of the French Revolution: the day, 17 June 1789, on which the Estates General "declared themselves a NATIONAL ASSEMBLY" (61). Celebrating the exemplary performative utterance, she praises "the novelty of the measure" and suggests that it was an utterance heard across Europe: "Europe also heard with astonishment what resounding through France excited the most lively emotions" (61). The "novelty" of the declaration is one that Wollstonecraft spends a good deal of time on, emphasizing first that the lawmakers' "calm prudence" of actions effected important, consequential business through the power of their speech acts: using their self-appointed power to "pronounc[e] that all taxes not enacted by the consent of the representatives of the people were illegal" and to "declar[e] their intents to liquidate the national debt," the assembly performs its power through words, and Wollstonecraft stresses the power of "[t]hese decrees" (63).

Against these authentic performatives, the court, on June 20, called an infamous *séance royale*. Like the *lit de justice* session, where the king presided over a plenary session of the Paris Parlement, this royal session of the Estates General normally assured the power of the king's pronouncements over the will of the people. For the king to attempt to corral the newly established National Assembly in a *séance royale* was, for Wollstonecraft, another example of the court's "subterfuge," as they "affected in some degree to yield to the prayer of the nation" in a "trick as palpable as the design was flagrant" (64). Accordingly, on the 20th June, the herald proclaimed a *séance royale*; and a detachment of guards surrounded the hall of the National Assembly so that it could be prepared for the reception of the king, or so was the "shallow pretext" (64). A selection of members who were wise to the "ministerial wiles" calmly advised others to adjourn to the neighboring tennis court. The moment of what has come to be known as the Tennis Court Oath Wollstonecraft treats as a performance, complete with audience:

> Assembled at the tennis-court, they encouraged each other; and one mind actuating the whole body, in the presence of an applauding crowd, they joined hands solemnly, and took God to witness, that they would not separate, till a constitution should be completed. (65)

While the court could not fathom the potential of power residing in an assembly that did not also have the "ceremonials," the pageantry that attended royal ensembles, they, nevertheless, went on with their planned *séance royale* the next day, an event which Wollstonecraft considers in terms of spectacle and concludes that a change in the power of the spectators, the French people, signaled a new kind of liberty:

> The following day, the *séance royale* really took place, with all the exterior splendour usually exhibited at these shows; which hitherto could scarcely be termed empty, because they produced the desired effect. But the public ... now viewed with contempt, what formerly inspired almost idolatrous respect. (66)

The intention being to annul the proceedings of the National Assembly, the King's speech offered certain benefits as "lures to submission" (66), pretending to be a reform when in actuality the language of each offer maintained the king's privilege to interpret as he saw fit, with the "*ifs* and *buts*, that were to render [reform] void" (67). Ironically, it is instead the King's language that was rendered null and void. His final conclusion—a barrage of attempts at performative utterance—Wollstonecraft treats with sarcastic demystification, saying that he was obviously "forgetful that this was not the period to imagine himself reigning at Constantinople" (67): "I *command* you to separate immediately, and to attend, each of you, tomorrow, at the chamber appropriated for your order" (67). Wollstonecraft scornfully points out that a majority of the nobles and some of the clergy obeyed this empty command, following the king "like the trained horses of his court" (67). The brave representatives of the assembly, however, make an important stand against this order, and Wollstonecraft carefully emphasizes their response as an exposure of the hollowness of the king's performative utterance at this stage in their revolutionary actions:

> [They] remained sitting, preserving a silence, more menacing and terrible, than the *I will*, or *I command*, of the cabinet; when the grand master of the ceremonies entered ... and reminded [them], in the king's name, of the order given to separate immediately. The president answered "that the assembly was not constituted to receive orders from any person." (67)

Wollstonecraft's emphasis on the menacing power of *silence* contrasts sharply with the hollow pronouncements and reminders of the king's authority, which the president of the assembly negates by referring to him as "any person." Even more striking is the discursive power of Mirabeau. whose words Wollstonecraft heralds as a potentially empowering manipulation of public discourse on two separate stages, both in the newly formed National Assembly. Clearly impressed with the power of Mirabeau's attention to the power of discourse, Wollstonecraft records his response to the orders of the grand master of ceremonies, a repetition of the king's orders, directly quoting him: "Yes, we have heard the intentions which the king has been induced to utter ... . You, who have neither seat, nor right to speak, ought not to remind us of his discourse ... if you are charged to make us go from hence, you should demand orders to employ force; for only the bayonet can oblige us to quit our places" (67). Against the power of the king's discourse, Mirabeau asserts that the words alone will no longer signify. Like Blake, Wollstonecraft characterizes the power of the revolutionary's words, as opposed to the supposedly performative power of the courtly decrees, as able to effect change in the world, saying that Mirabeau's "eloquence" was a "fire [that] flew from breast to breast, whilst a whisper ran round, that what Mirabeau had just uttered, gave a finishing stroke to the revolution" (67). The entire course of the ensuing revolution Wollstonecraft dates from this battle of words: "From this moment we may consider the nation and court at open war" (67). Wollstonecraft's representation of the power of language is very similar to Blake's unpublished, unfinished prophetic book *The French Revolution.*[19]

One further distinction she makes between performative utterance and staged political performance is when she contrasts the performative power and presence of royal minister Calonne to Mirabeau's. Of Calonne, she writes that he

> possessed the showy talents necessary to procure instantaneous applause in a popular assembly—a deceiving, rather than a commanding eloquence ... .Mirabeau, on the contrary, seems to have had from nature a strong perception of a dignified propriety of conduct; and truth appearing to give earnestness to his arguments, his hearers were compelled to agree with him out of respect to themselves. (124)

Thus Mirabeau taught the National Assembly dignity and Calonne deceit: 'Mirabeau appears to have been continually hurt by the want of dignity in the assembly—By the inconsistency, which made them ... heroes one moment, with a true theatrical stride, and the next cringe with the flexible backs of habitual slaves" (124).

In the narration of events from June to August 1789, Wollstonecraft's account becomes much more retrospective, using her own reflections on the meanings of the primary events, calling the reader to pay specific attention to "the arts of the acting parties" (105). The dismissal of Necker who had been retained in place by the king "only to hoodwink the people," according to Wollstonecraft, becomes an occasion for her to express a philosophical anxiety about the origin of growing violence of both sides. Upon the news of Necker's departure, an aroused crowd rushed into theaters at opening hour and demanded they be shut down, suggesting the spectacle on the street was theater enough; crowds, for example, seized

---

[19]   Cf. Blake's representation of the power of the voice in *The French Revolution.* See my article "'Ancient Voices': The New Language of Blake's *The French Revolution*," in *The French Revolution Debate in English Literature and Culture,* ed. Lisa Plummer Crafton (Westport, CT: Greenwood Press, 1997).

sculptors' busts of Necker and Orleans and paraded them through the streets (82). Wollstonecraft's divided opinion becomes very apparent here as her tone changes to sarcasm; of the orders for the public to remain calm and avoid riots, she writes, "But this was not the moment to talk of peace, when all were making ready for battle ... To arms! To arms! re-echoed from all quarters" (83). At this point, before narrating the events of 13 July and 14 July, Wollstonecraft's narrative abruptly shifts in one of the most memorable scenes in the text as she admits that she cannot fully rejoice with the happy throng as a spectator in her imagination, knowing what she and we readers all know about the sinister events to come, and conjuring up a starkly opposing scene in her narrative apostrophe to Versailles. In a fascinating reversal of scene and manipulation of spectatorial dynamics, Wollstonecraft shifts from a record of events on the street to a scene where she herself is visitor to the palace at Versailles and places readers as spectators of her, following in the empty corridor in a rich gothic scenario:

> The solitary foot, that mounts the sumptuous stair-case, rests on each landing place, whilst the eye traverses the void, almost expecting to see the strong images of fancy burst into life.—The train of the Louises, like the posterity of the Banquoes, pass in solemn sadness, pointing at the nothingness of grandeur ... whilst the gloominess of the atmosphere gives a deeper shade to the gigantic figures, that seem to be sinking into the embraces of death. (84)

Her invocation of *Macbeth* initiates the double consciousness that attends the rest of her narration, which is about, as much as anything, her own divided heart and intellect. Rather than a cold, philosophical discussion about the complexities of violence and the cycles of despotism, Wollstonecraft stages herself in the site of contests, an embodied performance that enables her to connect with all sides of the controversy. Her attention to spectatorial dynamics is manifest in her shift from self as subject of the gaze ("the eye traverses the void") to object as she imagines her "fleeting shadow ... reflected in long glasses, that vainly gleam in every direction ... [and which] slacken the nerves" (85). This image of multiple selves refracting in different directions, as Blakemore suggests, casts her as "both the blood-guilty Macbeth and his haunted queen, fearful even to extinguish her brief candle."[20] A final imagined encounter with another concludes the scene: "I tremble, lest I should meet some unfortunate being, fleeing from the despotism of licentious freedom, hearing the snap of the *guillotine* at his heels; merely because he was once noble, or has afforded an asylum to those whose only crime is their name" (85).[21] As she meditates on loss—"How silent is now Versailles. ... Lo!

---

[20] These words are Kelsom's in a review of Blakemore's book *Crisis in Representation: Thomas Paine, Mary Wollstonecraft, Helen Maria Williams, and the Rewriting of the French Revolution*. See Malcolm Kelsom, *Modern Language Review* 94.3 (1999): 794–5.

[21] This encounter with a specter-like figure occurs in similar fashion in *Maria, or The Wrongs of Woman* near the end of the narrative where Maria runs into a figure whose "form was scarcely human" as she leaves the madhouse; accosting her with Jesus' words

Was this the palace of the great king! ... the abode of magnificence"—she represents herself breaking down: "Weeping, scarcely conscious that I weep, O France! Over the vestiges of thy former oppression" (85). It is only after these projections of spectacle that she returns to philosophical discussion, concluding in a panegyric over the substitution of one kind of despotism for another: "Down fell the temple of despotism: but—despotism has not been buried in it's [sic] ruins!—Unhappy country!—when will thy children cease to tear thy bosom?" (85). This intermission of sorts prepares the reader for her narration of events which turn from celebratory to salacious, from honorable to horrific. Although she never abandons her critique of monarchical artifice, she conjures up a country whose center cannot hold, whose trajectory toward regicide becomes inevitable.

Her representation of the months after the fall of the Bastille and before the October Days presents a nuanced, and yet unmistakable interest in more subtle appropriations of "acting." Taking a cooler, detached stance towards Louis, she theorizes that in a more reasonable and equitable cultural climate, even kings might gain some sympathetic understanding of their subjects by simply *pretending* to do so. That is, if an "affectation of humanity" is the "affectation of the day," then it has potential to affect the player. With some optimism, she wonders whether pretenses of humanity by kings might put a "gloss of morality on their actions though it may not be their spring" (112).[22] This kind of reflection seems to be in her mind as she narrates an event which had the imaginative potential, at least, to reverse the spectatorial dynamic. On the morning after the Bastille was taken, the king appeared before the assembly standing without ceremony but addressed the people with "artful affection" (103) and "contemptible duplicity" (103). On 17 July the king decided against the counsel of his family and ministers to leave Versailles and go to Paris in hopes of assuaging the people. Wollstonecraft imagines his decision-making: "considering the little effect the pageantry of the court had produced at the *séance royale*, [the king decided] to meet the people without the parade of robe or guards" (120). Thus she posits Louis as a spectator of the crowd who is seen shouting not *vive la roi* "but the menacing memento—vive la nation!" (120) and who was reported to have said, "My people! My people may always rely on my love" (121). This temporary instability of boundaries and roles exacerbated an aura of suspicion, as rumors concatenated simple public disagreements into minor riots. Wollstonecraft tells substantially of one event that animated the National Assembly and that typifies the misreadings of even generous events. A civic feast was given at a nobleman's castle for the inhabitants

---

"Woman ... what have I to do with thee?" and yet described as a "hellish" "devil" the figure enacts a similar kind of ambiguous identity, a manifestation of her own divided loyalties. See 125.

[22]   Similarly, of the assembly fight against the idea of giving the king veto power, Wollstonecraft suggests it would have been better to give him that power so as to let him gently down, so that a "semblance" of his former authority would gratify him and induce him to submit to other restraints (337), again the power of mimicry.

of the village. He himself was not present. All the festivities ended by abrupt explosion from a nearby mine. The people, seeing treachery, got rustic weapons and went to neighboring castles and burned them or demolished them. The recital of this atrocity produced a great effect in the National Assembly, and Mirabeau acknowledged the difficulty of substantiating anything "as fact" especially since even "great assemblies are often too susceptible of theatrical emotions " (129). In this destabilized arena, Wollstonecraft notes, an inconstant people were found "always running after theatrical scenes" (133) such that while alarm bells were rung to denounce finance minister Necker, at the same time in another quarter of the city was he celebrated as a patriot (133).

One final narration before she turns to the spectacle of the October Days episode exemplifies Wollstonecraft's careful reading of historical events as spectacular performances. An October "magnificent entertainment" given in the name of the king's bodyguards was punctuated by a seemingly impromptu performance: "When their heads were heated by a sumptuous banquet, by the tumult of an immense crowd, and the great profusion of delicious wines and liqueurs, the conversation ... became unrestrained, and a chivalrous scene completed the folly. ... This acting, for it is clear the whole was a preconcerted business, was still more intoxicating than the wine" (194). The music chosen was a well known air "O Richard! O my king! The universe abandons thee!" Then a scene was played out for effect. With murmurs of scorn against the assembly, one "grenadier" darted from his group and asserted that he had not been as faithful to his king as he should have been and proceeded to endeavor several times to plunge his sword in his bosom. Wollstonecraft wryly and ironically narrates this "performance": "His held arm was not indeed allowed to search for the disloyal heart; but some blood was permitted to flow—and this theatrical display of sensibility, carried to the highest pitch, produced emotions almost convulsive in the whole circle, of which an English reader can scarcely form an idea" (195). Having produced such effect, the court sent invitations for a "similar treat" next week (341).

This theatrical social event is well known, not for the facetious performance that Wollstonecraft amusedly narrates (pointing out that the sword was "not indeed allowed to search for the disloyal heart") but for the queen's presence at the party, a performance that would be cited again and again as evidence against her immorality and licentiousness, as the course of the Revolution required:

> The queen, to testify her satisfaction for the homage paid to her ... exhibited herself to this half-drunken multitude; carrying the dauphin in her arms, whom she regarded with a mixture of sorrow and tenderness, and seeming to implore in his favor the affection and zeal of the soldiers. ... This acting, for it is clear the whole was a preconcerted business, was still more intoxicating than the wine. (341)

A gesture that would be invoked and reinterpreted by the pornographic campaign against Marie Antoinette, this exhibition by the queen at such a scripted event prompts Wollstonecraft's shift to consideration of gender in such performances inside and outside the palace. The French women who enjoyed, according to Wollstonecraft, "more freedom than the women of other parts of the world," were vulnerable to the ploys of men who decide to "wor[k] them up to some desperate act, and then ter[m] it a folly, because merely the rage of women, who were supposed to be actuated only by the emotions of the moment" (196). And here her narration of the October days begins:

> Early then on the fifth of October a multitude of women by some impulse were then collected together, and hastening to the *hotel-de-ville* obliged every female they met to accompany them.

> The concourse, at first, consisted mostly of market women, and the lowest refuse of the streets, women who had thrown off the virtues of one sex without having power to assume more than the vices of the other. A number of men also followed them, armed with pikes, bludgeons, and hatchets; but they were strictly speaking a mob, affixing all the odium to the appellation it can possibly import; and not to be confounded with the honest multitude who took the Bastille—. In fact, such a rabble has seldom been gathered together … . (196–7)

Wollstonecraft clearly regrets the loss of dignity in the mob's later actions but still explains it as effect of oppression: "The behavior of the hardened children of oppression in all countries is the same; whether in the amphitheatre at Rome, or around the lantern post in Paris" (125). Where she had earlier in *VRM*, as Furniss points out, strongly rebuffed Burke's characterization of "the vilest of women," here Wollstonecraft accepts to some extent his description: "they were, strictly speaking, a mob," yet also tries to maintain a distance between this "set of monsters, separate from the people" and the "honest multitude who took the Bastille." And, a final point about this passage, Wollstonecraft's conscious gendering of this context—arguing that women were deployed, worked up to "deplorable acts" and then made to carry the blame because of their sex—should inform our reading of Wollstonecraft's portrait of Marie Antoinette, the most performative woman of the historical scene. Vivien Jones has argued that this second rendition of the October Days episode relies on the "mechanisms and images of the bourgeois novel of seduction: Marie Antoinette is cast as the Clarissa-like heroine whose sense of virtue has yet to triumph over the advances of the archetypal sexual libertine."[23] Heeding Jones's suggestion, we do need to pay attention to the discursive echoes of melodrama, especially how Wollstonecraft subtly differentiates between Burke's unconscious lapses into sentimentality and eroticized fantasy and her own sharp critiques of the roles that each party played in the event. Overall, however, I concur with Bahar's comment that Jones ignores the fact that Marie Antoinette is not the heroine of this story; Mary Wollstonecraft is, her narrative voice always returning to her own sense of what the body of the queen means for her own female

---

[23]   Jones's influential article "Women Writing Revolution" argues overall how the linear rationalist narrative is disrupted by novelistic paradigms of Gothic fiction, with the queen as stock victim and Orleans as aristocratic villain manipulating the mob. See esp. 197.

body and for the body of women who will endure the legacy of the persecution of the queen. At any rate, Wollstonecraft's relationship to Marie Antoinette in this text (and metatextually) is of powerful significance in my consideration of French Revolutionary rhetoric and spectacle.

Wollstonecraft's exposure of Marie Antoinette as "complete actress" comes in the context of an empathetic connection to her, as one who was required to act by a culture's expectations, and as one who resorted to performance for very good reasons. Theoretical work on the body of Marie Antoinette underscores the profound impact that collective representations can make, mythic dimensions that are difficult to logically unravel. Saint-Amand began his 1994 essay with a famous analogy between Hillary Clinton and Marie Antoinette, made infamous perhaps by his use of *Spy* magazine's photomontage of Hillary as dominatrix. Arguing that both powerful, iconic women were implicated in positions of power and spectacle not entirely of their own making, Amand inscribed them together in what he called a "discourse of infamy." His two-part semiotic study, "Adorning Marie Antoinette" and "Terrorizing Marie Antoinette," charts the trajectory through which the queen's life can be read as a series of costumed events. Marie Antoinette's body—both as female sexual body and figure of the state—became an overdetermined sign.

The semiotic body of Marie Antoinette is a compelling part of my broader study of Mary Wollstonecraft and theatricality. Despite Wollstonecraft's politics, the collective cultural conflation of state corruption with criminal female sexuality which occurred in France would certainly trouble the woman whose intellectual legacy was marred by scandal, a series of posthumous attacks spawned by Godwin's *Memoirs*, resulting in such labels as Polwhele's "unsex'd female" or the tertiary "harpy, shrew, and whore" catalogued in Adrienne Rich's "Snapshots of a Daughter-in-Law." My juxtaposition of these notoriously scandalized women explores three key issues: the obviously competing arguments of class and gender; the question of how bodies refract on female public figure's legacies (especially given the public campaigns against sexual license for both women); and Wollstonecraft's ambivalent responses to two seminal events in Marie Antoinette's life—the October Days episode of 1792 (which featured a working class female mob attacking the body of the queen), and her trial of August 1793 (which pitted her social, sexual, and maternal bodies against each other and which I analyze at length in Chapter 4). Overall, my interest is in the performative nature of these public events and of authoritative speech. Reading Marie Antoinette, the most performative woman of the period, through Mary Wollstonecraft and the "theatrical double bind" of Romantic culture provides a unique lens with which to explore the essential question of this study: does theatricality act as a coercive or subversive mechanism of power? How we answer that question shapes our understanding of how much female self-fashioning was possible and of Wollstonecraft's ultimate contributions to that. Her representations of Marie Antoinette, then, are much more complex and multilayered than critics have acknowledged, thus the legacy of Marie Antoinette as what Saint-Amand calls an "impossible image" and "the scandal of representation itself."

Because the character of the queen has been exhaustively caricatured, Dorinda Outram calls for a "retraumatization" of the French Revolution, focusing on violence perpetrated on bodies (the queen's body, the working class women seen as "furies of hell"), a revisioning that would help underscore that the public obsession in England against Wollstonecraft's scandalous and ultimately scandalized body participates in this cultural moment.[24] Outram's *The Body and the French Revolution* is an essential contribution to this subject, as are two other collections of essays: Dena Goodman's *Marie Antoinette: Writings on the Body of a Queen* and Lynn Hunt's *Eroticism and the Body Politic*. Goodman investigates the queen as a "set of sites of contestations" (3), crediting the critical method of Joan Scott, a historian who presents ninettenth-century feminists as "sites—historical locations or markers—where crucial political and cultural contests are enacted and can be examined in some detail."[25] Arguing that this does not rob these female figures of individuality, Scott instead stresses the need to "recognize the many factors that constitute her agency, the complex and multiple ways in which she is constructed as a historical actor."[26] Significantly to my study, Backscheider uses virtually the same phrase about Sarah Siddons, calling her a "Foucauldian site for the representation of warring sexualities and powers," and Siddons, Wollstonestonecraft, and the queen form, in my study, a network of performative women whose political differences become elided by their collective fate as female bodies. Sheriff, in Goodman's collection, points out that feminist historians today increasingly draw attention to relation between Marie Antoinette's fate and that of all French women (as opposed to simplistically drawing the line between upper/lower class). Olympe de Gouges dedicated the "Declaration of the Rights of Woman" to the queen to emphasize that French women of all political alliances had a stake in the queen's status. Germaine de Stael, in 1793, similarly warns that sexual slander is a "genre of calumny" (11) that could be used to ruin any woman. Regarding the process by which the queen became the target of the Revolution's attempt to rectify the errant sexuality of women, Wollstonecraft could similarly commiserate about a culture's linkage of fearful political change with an autonomous female sexuality, demonstrating independent women's tenuous relationship to country—as Wollstonecraft's heroine Maria ponders, if women can be said to have a country.[27] The divergent positions of the king and queen are central to Lynn Hunt and Louis Marin's work on the "mystic fiction of the King's Two Bodies," whereby the monarch had both a visible,

---

[24]   See esp. 159.

[25]   See *Only Paradoxes to Offer: French Feminists and the Rights of Man* (Cambridge: Harvard University Press 1996), esp. 16.

[26]   Goodman, 2.

[27]   See Chapter 2 of this study on Wollstonecraft's appropriation of the political/sexual subtext within Nicolas Rowe's *The Fair Penitent* in her novel fragment, *Maria, or The Wrongs of Woman*.

corporeal, mortal body and an invisible, ideal, "body politic" which never died. Adding to this a third, Marin suggests the queen holds a "semiotic sacramental body": "This is the body as it is represented in the form of portraits and narratives. It is primarily a body of signs, fabricated for representation, offered to the imagination of the subjects" (14), and thus acknowledges the erotic, not just the corporeal, body. Given the fascination in the queen's body, especially in the circulation of pornographic pamphlets, Hunt rightly concludes that "the queen had, in a manner of speaking, many bodies" (110).

The complex route by which Marie Antoinette came to personify excess and perversity must be understood through her performative identity. She became, in effect, the court's supermodel. Conceived as a brilliant calculated strategy, her early ornamentation was a way of stabilizing the Bourbon monarchy by putting an end to its reputation for adultery. Thus she was trapped in a "compulsive self-beautification project" (almost as if she was being made to atone for past sexual indulgences of male kings and mistresses by becoming overly ornamentalized, an obvious object of desire).[28] This kind of compulsory overdetermination and suppression of her individual female desires in service of being the court's supermodel is in accord with the kinds of normalizing regulatory codes for English women that Wollstonecraft denounced. The fact that her body was to be spectacularized to erase prior sensationalizing about adulterous affairs of the monarchy and yet she then became a stand-in for female sexual excess of the nation would serve as a fascinating and frightening example to Wollstonecraft, whose own scandalous life continues to overdetermine critical reactions to her as a public figure. Saint-Amand goes on to label this swirl of events around the queen a "theatrical system of commerce":

> Marie Antoinette was progressively perceived as usurping the spectacular role of the king ... what [she] did was to efface the king, to render him invisible, by orienting all circuits of desire toward her body. While the king appeared divested of an image, of political *figurability*, the queen became the nexus of a theatrical system of commerce. (390)

The queen then became a voyeuristic enterprise for a whole nation, an erotic fantasy that culminated in revolutionary mass frenzy against her.

As studies of spectacle and monarchy point out, the "very essence of a court, of a king, is *parade*, an ornamentalism that enhances what is mundanely universal"; Marie Antoinette turned the king's parade into *masquerade*.[29] Using theories of masquerade and its relation to both performative and authoritative speech, we can debate the subversive versus coercive functions of this kind of theatricality and further theorize performance through Irigaray's claim that if mimicry is the only

---

[28] Saint-Amand, 389.

[29] Mitchell Greenberg, *Subjectivity and Subjugation in Seventeenth-Century Drama and Prose: The Family Romance in French Classicism* (Cambridge: Cambridge University Press, 2006).

option in some female contexts, it can be subversively affirmative: "One must assume the feminine role deliberately. Which means already to convert a form of subordination into an affirmation, and thus to begin to thwart it" (76).

Emphasizing Wollstonecraft's obvious opposition to the artificiality of the queen, a symbolic, iconic figure of aristocratic excess, critics have not considered how Wollstonecraft represents the spectacle of the "many bodies" of the most performative woman of the 1790s. O'Neill typifies the common response:

> Indeed, one can read Wollstonecraft's indictment of Marie Antoinette as a measured response to Burke's celebration of her as the personification of the *ancien regime*. For both writers, Marie was a living archetype, a cultural touchstone. For Burke, she was the glittering apotheosis of the old system of natural manners; for Wollstonecraft, she epitomized a morally bankrupt world ... moral poison. (244, 245)

Pascoe's chapter on Marie Antoinette in *Romantic Theatricality* comes close to acknowledging Wollstonecraft's attention to performance, but suggests only that Wollstonecraft "perhaps unintentionally" underscores the power of performance in paralleling the queen with Burke's dramatic rhetoric. I argue, instead, for Wollstonecraft's deliberate and sustained treatment of the queen as a fabricated sign, one that highlights conflicts between maternal/sexual identities and as such informs Wollstonecraft's stagings for her fictional heroines.

We have seen how in *HMV*, Wollstonecraft asserts that "a court is the best school in the world for actors" (74) and accuses the king of a "criminal insincerity." These seemingly absolute assertions, however, change when she turns from the king's theatricality to the queen's. Calling her the unfortunate queen of France, Wollstonecraft introduces her as one who

> ... possessed a very fine person ... her manners were bewitching. ... But her opening faculties were poisoned in the bud; for before she came to Paris she had already been prepared ... for the part she was to play. ... The person of the king, in itself very disgusting, was rendered even more so by gluttony and a total disregard for delicacy ... he treated her with great brutality till she acquired sufficient finesse to subjugate him. (73)

That she here sides with the queen in appropriating whatever "finesse" is required to deal with "the disgust she had for [the king's] person" is made overt in this completely overlooked line, a mini-history of the queen's turn toward the performative in the next sentence:

> Is it then surprising, that a very desirable woman, with a sanguine constitution, should shrink abhorrent from his embraces; or that an empty mind should be employed only to vary the pleasures, which emasculated her circean court? (73)

Lost then in the most luxurious pleasure of "managing court intrigues," "the queen," Wollstonecraft simply announces, "became a profound dissembler" (73).

Thus, it is in this context that she utters the famous line used by some critics to prove her antimony to the queen and an anti-theatrical bias: "the court is the best school in the world for actors; it was very natural then for her to become a complete actress, and an adept in all the arts of coquetry that debauch the mind, whilst they render the person alluring" (74). Significantly, then, her diatribe against the artificial theatricality of monarchy itself occurs *after* a sympathetic rendering of the queen's choices, or lack of choices. It is in this context, almost lauding the queen's "finesse," that she labels Marie Antoinette one who "became a profound dissembler."[30]

Wollstonecraft's focus on the loathsome nature of the king's embraces suggests her awareness of the country's fascination with the sexual activity of the queen and king. Very early, only four years after Marie Antoinette's arrival in France, the pornographic public campaigns began against her, fueled by rumors of Louis XVI's impotence; thus her sexual body became immediately fair game for caricature. Lynn Hunt, in her edited collection *Eroticism and the Body Politic*, stresses how the multivalence of the female body was especially striking in the eighteenth and nineteenth centuries. At the time of a reorientation in European politics, there was an accompanying set of issues about women's place in the public sphere, which led to an obsessive association of erotics and the body politic. Hunt argues that although it might seem that the erotic is a transhistorical category, it was exactly in the late eighteenth and nineteenth centuries that the separation between erotic and pornographic began and suggests that the development of a modern notion of pornographic as obscene (versus an earlier Greek sense of the word as meaning "writing about prostitution") is linked to new worries about woman's participation in public life and thus concerns with the place of women's bodies.[31] Even before Marie Antoinette became the center of a pamphlet pornographic campaign, this conflation of body/body politic had a hold over the French populace. Pamphlets throughout 1770s and 1780s denounced the eroticization and feminization of power under Louis XV, who had notorious mistresses. But when Louis XVI came to power, "Marie Antoinette became the target of choice for those who associated the overlapping of the female sexual and political activity with the political decay of the nation" (Hunt 7). Sara Maza, in her thorough analysis of the Diamond Necklace Affair (which in itself offers fascinating issues with regard to theatricality since it was a prostitute who was hired to "play" or impersonate the queen) argues that this incident provided a thematic source and repository for

---

[30] Her empathizing with Marie Antoinette's being forced to find a way to endure a "disgusting" partner is paralleled in her discussion of Matilda, queen of Denmark, whose affair with the court physician was understandable to Wollstonecraft; as she says in *Letters Written During a Short Residence*, "it did not disgrace her heart or understanding; the king being a notorious debauchee, and an idiot into the bargain." See my discussion of this letter in Chapter 3.

[31] See Hunt's introduction, 3.

venomous literature against the queen that began to appear in 1789 and occurred ad nauseum in the 1790s.[32]

Two French texts in particular demonstrate how the denunciations of the queen's body manipulated theatrical tropes. The queen took center stage in the grand synthesis on the subject, the 500-page *Les Crimes des reines de France* (whose author was a woman, Louise de Karalio). The introduction asserts that power corrupts and that female power corrupts with a vengeance, and the text chronicles the history of the queens of France, emphasizing their performative powers of dissimulation.[33] More significantly, the 1789 *Essai historique sur la vie de Marie-Antoinette* demonstrated the rising tone of personal hostility that would characterize revolutionary pamphlets. One of the most detailed vignettes purported to give the queen's own voice, staging Marie Antoinette as speaking to the audience in the first person. She calls herself a barbarous queen, an adulterous spouse, a woman polluted with crimes and debaucheries and traces her lesbian amours back to Austria; she even confesses at one point to poisoning her own son. Hunt points out the curious alternation between frankly pornographic staging— descriptions in the first person of her liaisons and political moralizing. Where earlier pamphlets were in effect telling dirty stories, this text moves beyond the distribution of rumors to engage a wider audience by casting Marie Antoinette herself as the confessional actress telling all. Obscene engravings with first person captions worked to the same effect, achieving a spectatorial dynamic such that the reader is made into both voyeur and judge. Wollstonecraft's perceptive discussion of the queen as a "profound dissembler" then evinces an awareness of the questionable moral stance of those who denounce the queen as a body; thus a line like "[the king] treated her with great brutality till she acquired sufficient finesse to subjugate him" (323) unsettles any complacent self-righteous attempt to judge the queen for her performative acts and exemplifies the complexity of Wollstonecraft's representation of her.

This multivalent account of the queen's role-playing informs Wollstonecraft's narration of some of Marie Antoinette's most notorious moments: the October Days and the trial. As we have seen, her first comments on the march to Versailles in her 1790 *VRM* provided a response to Burke's classist and sexist representation where he contrasts the beauty of the *ancien regime* to the uncivilized barbarity of the mob, and yet in her second treatment of the same event in the 1794 *HMV*, she accepts that "they were strictly speaking a mob" who "acted like a gang of thieves." While this may appear a capitulation to Burke, the full context includes a subtler, yet pointed, contrast to Burke as made apparent by their representation of gender, the queen in particular. Burke's version of the October Days, as we have seen, culminates in his narration of an attack upon a victimized, "almost naked" queen by a "hundred strokes of bayonets and poniards," which supposedly "pierced" the bed. Despite his

---

[32]   Maza interprets this incident beautifully as an example of the culture's assumption of interchangeable female identities.

[33]   See Hunt's discussion of this, esp. 116.

authoritative rhetoric that "History will record [the attack on the queen]," Burke's symbolic rape scene is not recorded by any historical records. As Zerilli points out, the *Moniteur* account of the event did not record anything like the queen's nakedness, but "no eye-witness account is going to stop the fecundity of [Burke's] imagination" (88). Burke's eroticized phantasia of the queen running almost naked from her pike-carrying persecutors concludes by warning against a culture where "the king is but a man, the queen is but a woman." Wollstonecraft's representation of the mob, in contrast, comes in the context of her re-reading the royal Versailles apartment as simply the bedroom of a woman, for, as she says, "I consider the queen only as one [woman]." Quite simply, the shifting allegiances and competing agendas of the Parisian market women and the French queen intersect with the vulnerability of *all* women, herself among them, as she concludes this passage by staging a dramatic scene of herself alone in Paris. Writing by herself in a Paris hotel room, after having seen Louis XVI being taken to his death, she recounts that she imagined "eyes glar[ing] through a glass door opposite my chair and bloody hands shak[ing] at me" (324). This striking narration of herself as threatened by "bloody hands" juxtaposes her alongside the royals; when compared to her earlier narrative apostrophe to Versailles, where as we have seen, she stages herself walking alone through empty corridors, haunted by her reflection in mirrors, this gothic fantasy aligns her with the queen, who is no more and no less than she, a woman caught up in the chaotic clash of political agendas, entrapped in the melee of competing dramatizations, a chaos which culminates in the role of lifetime, the trial which pitted erotic/maternal performances against each other.

Because of the intensely theatrical nature of the trial itself, I analyze it specifically in Chapter 4; here I want to end this chapter of French Revolutionary history with the legacy and aftereffects of the trial/execution of this most embodied woman. While reports of the king's execution were formal and restrained, the published accounts of Marie Antoinette's execution again stressed her body, using bestial metaphors, such as the "dangerous beast, the cunning spider, the virtual vampire … ."[34] Wollstonecraft had witnessed the king being taken to his execution and had responded to it as a spectacle of human misery, one that as we have seen, caused her to imagine herself in his [and the queen's] place. Gutwirth's analysis of the final poses of the queen beautifully points out that the king went to death in royal carriage garbed in court dress.[35] The queen rode in an open cart, as spectacle, in a humiliation reserved for the woman queen. The spectacle was to be a lesson for all women and inaugurated a vehement crackdown on female public assemblies and burgeoning female solidarity. Marie Antoinette had been a supporter of the arts for women, reinvigorating the *Journal des Dames*, which was then suspended, and strongly supporting female painters, like Lebrun. Revolutionary antagonism toward political prerogatives of queenship quickly

---

[34] Hunt, 123.

[35] Madelyn Gutwirth, *The Twilight of the Goddesses: Women and Representation in the French Revolutionary Era* (New Brunswick, NJ: Rutgers University Press, 1992).

evolved into a general proscription of female political action. Only two weeks after the execution, the Convention banned women's clubs. Within a month the Girondin leader Madame de Roland and feminist actress and playwright Olympe de Gouges were guillotined, and at the Festival of Reason at Notre Dame, a living woman appeared as Liberty, Marianne. "In killing the wicked witch, the Republic had given birth to the good daughter" (81).

If we return to the scholarly debate—Baer's hypothesis that in England the theatricality of social mechanism helped maintain the status quo whereas theater was inextricable from and contributed to transformative revolution in France versus Bolton's assertion that England embraced its own version of spectatorial negotiation—my reading suggests that Wollstonecraft's complex historical texts deny either. Instead, they comprehensively and consistently chart both the subversive and coercive functions of theatricality, within theater itself, within the pageantry of government, and within individual bodies, especially female bodies, staged within those histories.

Chapter 6
Retaliatory Self-Invention:
Siddons, Wollstonecraft, and Theatricality

"So many people know me. I wish I did. I wish someone would tell me about me."
"You're Margo. Just Margo."
"What is that? Besides something spelled out in light bulbs, I mean?"
—*All About Eve*[1]

"I supped in company with Mrs. Siddons last night. When shall I tell you what I think of her?"
—Mary Wollstonecraft, Letter to Godwin, 1796[2]

Joseph Mankiewicz's 1950 film *All About Eve* begins with the New York theatrical community's annual awards dinner, bestowing the Sarah Siddons award upon a new actress. In the film, which manipulates the border between fact and fiction and the performance of one's identity (on and off stage), director Joseph Manckiwiez offers up a satiric portrayal of theater. The totem which the film's characters covet, a fictional equivalent of the Oscar, is called the Siddons Award. Mankiewicz explains how, while rummaging around for set design ideas, he came across Reynolds' painting *Mrs. Siddons as the Tragic Muse*, and he knew that he had found his inspiration. Deciding to create a fictional Sarah Siddons Society to give the award in the film, he then had artists design an actual physical statuette based on the painting. What better way to launch his satiric portrayal of theater, especially aging actresses on screen, than through this manipulation of fact and fiction? As fact is always stranger than fiction, however, what happened in the culture unintentionally underscored his satirical point. Contemporaneous with the film, a Chicago hotel initiated a Siddons Society meeting to give a "real" award to a "real" actress, as part of a publicity gimmick for their restaurant. Manckiewicz's sharp comments on this are revealing:

> Could anyone conceivably have been taken in by such an award? With *All About Eve* and its satiric connotations about awards still playing in the theaters ...?
> With ... Sunday supplements, and lobby displays still filled with ... layouts from the film always featuring the Sarah Siddons award which I had dreamed up as an

---

[1] *All About Eve*, dir. Joseph L. Mankiewicz, perf. Bette Davis, Anne Baxter. 1950. The film itself posits interesting thematic questions about female agency and sexuality; for a provocative reading, see Roger Corber, "All About the Subversive Femme: Cold War Homophobia in *All About Eve*," in *American Cold War Culture* (Edinburgh: Edinburgh University Press, 2005).

[2] Ralph M. Wardle, ed., *Collected Letters of Mary Wollstonecraft* (Ithaca: Cornell University Press, 1979), 346.

object of satire? An award of which the Chicago gimmick version was in fact an exact replica? You can bet your ass it was taken seriously.[3]

An intended satiric fantasy became an unintended satiric reality. When we rewind about one hundred fifty years to a production in Covent Garden, we might see this: the real Sarah Siddons performing the role of Calista (a famous penitent heroine) in 1796, and in the audience Mary Wollstonecraft, at that time still going by the name of Mary Imlay, all the while confessing publicly that she was not nor ever had been officially Mrs. Gilbert Imlay, engaging in an intimate relationship with William Godwin, and drafting a novel about a repressed woman who goes to the theater to see Sarah Siddons play Calista![4] Embodying a multiplication of identities, Wollstonecraft would certainly have paid attention as Siddons's character on stage critiqued the hypocrisy of those who perform off stage as well as on.

In a tangible demonstration of the cultural currency of Sarah Siddons, two hundred years after her heyday on the London stage as the tragic muse, the Hollywood community rallied around concurrent Sarah Siddons events in 1999: exhibits at the Huntington and the Getty, an original play by Frank Dwyer, and an academic conference. A *Hollywood Reporter* called her the "patron saint" of Hollywood publicists, and the *Los Angeles Times* referred to her as a calculating celebrity. If we think of acting as a more ephemeral artistic activity than writing, an action that disappears after the curtain closes, this enduring celebrity of Sarah Siddons challenges that assumption; more importantly, it offers a substantive field of inquiry about the nature of female performance and acting on theatrical as well as social stages. The images on display at the Huntington and the Getty, as McPherson notes, call for more comprehensive consideration of how the visual representations of Siddons coincide with acting styles, female performance, and the overlap of studio and stage in the period. In any consideration of Mary Wollstonecraft and theatricality, Siddons is an essential subject, both as a person—a friend, a colleague, an ex-friend—and as a cultural phenomenon and aesthetic artifact. This chapter explores the historical, cultural, and theoretical connections between Siddons and Wollstonecraft in a number of arenas: 1) in her material presence as a friend to Wollstonecraft who then overtly rejected her when scandals broke about her morality; 2) in the cultural currency she earned through her portrayals of tragic female victims, who are analogues to Wollstonecraft's representations of wronged women; 3) and, most intriguingly, as a theorist of acting whose performances persistently destabilized gender roles (whether as a spectacle of female passion, as a maternal body who performed pregnant many times, or cross-dressed as a host of male characters, notably Hamlet) and whose written commentaries (notes

---

[3]   See Joseph Mankiewicz, "All About the Women in *All About Eve*," *New Yorker* 16 Oct. 1972. The quote is from 42.

[4]   Wollstonecraft had registered as Gilbert Imlay's wife while in France for safety and to be allowed to stay there and retained the name in England, but as Godwin points out, never tried to keep secret the fact that she was not ever his wife.

on acting and her *Reminiscences*) persistently invoke theatrical and performative language in social critique and in reflections about the nature of being the object of the gaze. For Wollstonecraft, whose celebrity was also fashioned posthumously by Godwin's *Memoirs*, in which Siddons figures, Siddons is a pivotal figure in questions central to this study, including the conflation of private and public role-playing, the reciprocity between theatrical and social performances, and, most importantly, both the coercive and subversive potential in acting. Siddons functions to alert us to the many roles played by Wollstonecraft in her lifetime, her conscious representation of theater and performance throughout all her texts, and despite her apparent anti-theatricality regarding mandated gender performance, her belief in the transgressive potential of consciously performative self-fashioning.

The public exhibitions in California centered around visual representations of Siddons, and as her epithet of "Tragic Muse" derives from the most celebrated of these, Sir Joshua Reynolds' magisterial and definitive *Mrs. Siddons as the Tragic Muse* (1784), I preface my discussion about Siddons and Wollstonecraft with the fascinating scholarly and theoretical attention to this painting in the late twentieth century. While the most intense flurry of critical and theoretical attention followed the exhibits in Los Angeles in 1999, the reconsideration of the painting itself was perhaps stimulated by technological advances earlier in that decade. As Heather McPherson, in her 2000 essay "Picturing Tragedy: *Mrs. Siddons as the Tragic Muse* Revisited," describes it, technical advances, including the use of composite x-rays, demonstrated that Reynolds reworked the picture substantially during the painting process, including some color variations and, most significantly, a revision in the figure of the attendant in the upper right of the picture, originally painted as a figure of melancholy but modified to be a figure of terror, emphasizing the iconography of tragedy.[5] Traditional allegorical depictions of Melpomene, the Muse of Tragedy, included her principal attributes, the dagger and the cup, and often presented her in timeless apparel; Romney's *Mrs. Yates as the Tragic Muse* had depicted Tragedy in classical garb, for instance. Reynolds's decision to represent Siddons in eighteenth-century dress, regal and majestic, and as a strong figure of resolution and intellect, challenges the allegorical aesthetic.[6] At this point it becomes clear that "readers" or spectators of the painting invariably gravitate toward one of two readings of the figure: is it a painting of the Tragic

---

[5]   McPherson offers a substantive analysis of the effects of these compositional changes in a provocative study of the reciprocity between portraiture and the stage in Georgian England. See Heather McPherson, "Picturing Tragedy: *Mrs. Siddons as the Tragic Muse* Revisited," *Eighteenth-Century Studies* 33.3 (2000): 401–30. See also Shelley Bennett, "New Light on British Paintings at the Huntingdon," *Burlington Magazine* 137 (1995): 512–13.

[6]   Reynolds was known for creating several unconventional portraits of allegorical figures, notably Fortitude and Justice at New College, Oxford, and Theory for the ceiling of Somerset House, all of which, as McPherson summarizes, "transform formulaic allegories into powerful embodiments of feminine majesty, resolution, and intellect and anticipate his depiction of *Mrs. Siddons as the Tragic Muse*." See 412.

Music, represented by the famous actress Sarah Siddons, or a portrait of Mrs. Siddons in her most famous role? If the latter, how does its stark difference from Gainsborough's famous painting of Siddons as simply herself, a work that renders Siddons more natural, less allusive, and simply more "readable" to use Ronald Paulson's term, offer us a different subject, a different Siddons?[7] Joel Weinsheimer's "Mrs. Siddons, The Tragic Muse, and the Problem of 'As'" shrewdly assesses the philosophical issues surrounding the "as"; I am interested in the performative dimension of the question itself, and the differing narratives of the genesis of Siddons's pose offer a number of provocative premises.

The same technological advances that uncovered Reynolds's revisions confirmed, on the other hand, that Siddons's pose and attitude were *not* modified in the painting— her original sitting captured and unchanged as it were. The genesis for the pose, offering a kind of ontological indeterminacy for the painting, is the subject of many a scrutiny; McPherson clarifies these studies by summarizing that Reynolds scholars frequently rehearse at least three different accounts.[8] I leave the definitive, particular scrutiny of these varying accounts to art historiographers; my interest is in how the decision to pose "as" an allegorical figure was made since it strikes at the heart of my concern about female embodiment and performance. In one narrative of the event, Samuel Rogers, a friend of Siddons present at the sitting, states that the pose was quite by accident. Siddons apparently arrived breathless and late and threw herself into an armchair, whereby Reynolds counseled her to stay "just as you are." A second account given by Siddons to painter Thomas Phillips explains the genesis of the pose as Siddons's spontaneous turning around to gaze at a picture on the wall, prompting Reynolds at that point to ask her not to move. Finally, in her *Reminiscences* composed at the end of her life, Siddons provides a more artful scenario:

> When I attended him for the first sitting, after many more gratifying encomiums than I dear repeat, he took me by the hand, saying, "Ascend your undisputed throne and graciously bestow upon me some grand idea of the Tragick Muse." I walked up the steps and seated myself instantly in the attitude in which She now appears.[9]

While Weinsheimer mentions only the first two accounts, both of which, in suggesting instanteous perception by Reynolds, thus support his contention that Reynolds immediately perceived the nature of "*as*" in the title of the painting, McPherson suggests that all three accounts "propound the dubious myth of 'miraculous conception,' insisting that the pose was arrived at spontaneously, and

---

[7]   Ronald Paulson, *Emblem and Expression: Meaning in English Art of the Eighteenth Century* (London: Thames and Hudson, 1975), 80–94.

[8]   I am indebted to both McPherson and Joel Weinsheimer for astute discussions of these accounts; see McPherson 410 and Weinsheimer, "Mrs. Siddons, The Tragic Muse, and the Problem of 'As,'" *The Journal of Aesthetics and Art Criticism* 36.3 (Spring 1978), 317–28. See 321.

[9]   *The Reminiscences of Sarah Kemble Siddons, 1773–1785*, ed. William Van Lennep (Cambridge: Cambridge University Press, 1942), 17.

thus privileging nature over art" (410). Siddons's discussion in the *Reminiscences* is interesting in the ways that she distinguishes herself, a body who walked up some steps and sat down, from the "She" in the painting. Out of context her narration of the event could be read as her crediting herself with the "attitude" of the pose; McPherson, for example, says that Siddons's account "underscore[s] her innate ... genius in immediately assuming the pose, while minimalizing the conceptual and aesthetic contributions of Reynolds" (410). Yet, her account indisputably gives Reynolds the genius, saying that *his* decision was "instantaenous" and occurred "in the twinkling of an eye" (17). Siddons thus represents herself both as herself, a body, and as an allegorical "grand idea," to use Reynolds's term, from the painter's eyes. The spatial dynamics of Reynolds's studio also offer a provocative, material paradigm for this merging of the I/She that Siddons references. As Wendorf describes, Reynolds's studio was a collaborative space, where sitters posed on a raised dais but not in isolation or as objects: they were encouraged to converse with the painters and others in the room and Reynolds himself walked around as he painted, sometimes using a mirror as part of the creative representational process.[10] Similarly, Siddons, in her *Reminiscences*, offers a continuous discussion of both the coercive/repressive consequences of being object of the gaze and the potential for self-fashioning that comes from a willingness to see oneself as subject and object, to be both the "I" walking up the steps and the "She" for posterity.

Contemporary critical reviews of the painting attest that some viewers obviously missed the balance that Siddons herself apparently felt. Gilbert Stuart's 1784 review of the Royal Academy exhibit, for example, faults Reynolds's revision for presenting an idealized representation of despair rather than Siddons's reenactment of the emotion:

> ... by endeavouring to correct [the original] we think he has lost considerably some of [its] spirit and energy. It is not a strong likeness of the original, it is rather an ideal representation of despair than a copy of Mrs. Siddons' countenance when affected by that passion.[11]

Modern writers primarily regard the painting as a preeminent example of the blend of the particular and the ideal, and Reynolds's own thinking on this dynamic is central to consider. While fascinated by the stage as an alternate form of representative art, he mistrusted the artifice, especially costumes and poses: "If a Painter should endeavour to copy the theatrical pomp and parade of dress and attitude, instead of that simplicity, which is not a greater beauty in life, than it is in Painting, we should condemn such Pictures as painted in the meanest style."[12] Mistrusting the artifice, the theatricality in the pejorative sense of the term, Reynolds successfully interrogates the potential power of a consciously

---

[10] See Richard Wendorf, *Sir Joshua Reynolds: The Painter in Society* (Cambridge: Harvard University Press, 1996), esp. 112–24.

[11] See McPherson, n.6.

[12] Quoted in McPherson, 409.

embodied pose, a kind of "acting" that Siddons initiated and modeled, and what I believe Wollstonecraft's works evince, in the rhetoric of the title for this book, a *transgressive theatricality*.

Siddons's professional influence in histories of acting and theoretical performance studies is indisputably legendary, her life as "Sarah" or "Mrs. Siddons" equally celebrated, marketed as it were. Like Wollstonecraft, Siddons became notorious for all kinds of rumored misbehaviors, and yet Siddons's popularity and fame allowed her to withstand biting caricatures and even being hissed off stage. The fact of Siddons's public rejection of Wollstonecraft after the truth broke about her own role-playing (going by the name of Mary Imlay while never actually having been married to Gilbert Imlay while also involved with Godwin) demands that we start at the level of historical, material ties between these two women who now share a position as cultural icons.

Both the relationship between Siddons and Wollstonecraft and its ultimate rupture offer a complex example of the pervasiveness of the theatricality of social mechanisms. During the 1790s, Wollstonecraft, like almost everyone else breathing in London, was a Siddons fan, describing one of her illnesses in 1796 by saying "even Mrs. Siddons would not have tempted me out today" and confessing to Mary Hays in 1797 that she has "had [her] eye on the papers" so as not to miss any of Mrs. Siddons's "best parts."[13] The admiration was mutual. Godwin's *Memoirs* references a letter in which Siddons acknowledges Wollstonecraft's power as a writer, even labeling herself the best possible audience: she says that no other reader could have more "reciprocity of feeling" or be more "deeply impressed with admiration" for Wollstonecraft.[14] Despite such a claim of reciprocity, though, Siddons joined her polite circle in dropping connections to Wollstonecraft in 1797 as soon as irrefutable evidence surfaced that she had never been married to Imlay but had used his name, the truth of which became undeniable when Wollstonecraft and Godwin announced their marriage and her pregnancy. The most significant fact in this event of scandal is that everyone knew and yet *refused to know* all along that Wollstonecraft and Imlay were never married. Narrating the event with a sense of outrage over the hypocrisy and dissembling nature of the crowd, Godwin rhetorically resembles Wollstonecraft in her lacerating condemnations of false ceremonies of morality (see Chapter 2 on ethics and theatricality, especially in her *Letters Written During a Short Residence*).

Initiating his version of events with a brief lecture of sorts against the ceremony of marriage ("nothing can be so ridiculous ... or so contrary to the genuine march of sentiment, as to require the overflowing of the soul to wait upon a ceremony"), Godwin prefaces his narrative with the conclusion that it will "expose certain regulations of polished society, of which the absurdity vies with the odiousness" (278, 282). While Wollstonecraft, in Godwin's words, "made no

---

[13]   The first quote is from her letter to Godwin of 12 Dec. 1796 and the second one to Mary Hays is dated 15 Feb. 1797. See Wardle, *Collected Letters*, 383, 397.

[14]   *Memoirs of the Author of A Vindication of the Rights of Woman*, ed. Cynthia Richards (Glen Allen, VA: College Publishing, 2004), 284–5.

secret of the nature of her connection with Mr. Imlay," and, in fact, in one instance "put herself to the trouble of explaining it to a person totally indifferent to her, because he never failed to publish everything he knew, and, she was sure, would repeat her explanation to his numerous acquaintances," the social crowd refused to acknowledge the unconventional life history (283). Godwin's description of the reasons for the public rejection repeat almost exactly Wolllstonecraft's heroine Maria as she denounces the theater crowd for rejecting her once she leaves her husband and gets involved with a new lover whom she does not try to hide. In *Maria, or The Wrongs of Woman*, Wollstonecraft writes,

> She ... was refused admittance ... at the opera or Ranelagh. ... Had [she] remained with her husband practicing insincerity, she would have been respected. If instead of openly living with her lover, she could have called into play a thousand arts to allow those not deceived to pretend to be so, she could have been caressed and treated like an honorable woman. And Brutus is an honorable man.[15]

Godwin similarly rails about the real-life rejection by the social posse:

> These persons, however, in spite of all that could be said, persisted in shutting their eyes and pretending they took her for a married woman. Observe the consequences of this! While she was, and constantly professed to be, an unmarried mother, she was fit society for the squeamish and the formal. The moment she acknowledged herself a wife ... the case was altered. Mary and myself, ignorant as we were of these elevated refinements, supposed that our marriage would place her upon a surer footing in the calendar of polished society, than ever. But it forced these people to see the truth, and to confess their belief of what they had carefully been told; and this they could not forgive. (283)

Only two women are mentioned by name as friends Wollstonecraft regretted to lose, actress, playwright, and novelist Elizabeth Inchbauld and Siddons. Siddons, however, gets a little reprieve from the sharp condemnation, Godwin explaining if not excusing her rejection: "Mrs. Siddons, I am sure, regretted the necessity, which she conceived to be imposed on her by the peculiarity of her situation, to conform to the rules I have described" (284). While Godwin is "sure" she regretted the rupture, we have little to go on in making that determination ourselves, there being no discussion of Siddons in Wollstonecraft's nuanced references to this event in two letters of April 1797. She does, however, mention Inchbauld and leaves no doubt as to her contempt for her. In a letter to Amelia Alderson dated 11 April 1797, following her marriage to Godwin on 29 March, Wollstonecraft relates the "very rude" conduct of Mrs. Inchbauld. Inchbauld had written to Godwin about securing a box at the theater for her, but once hearing of Godwin's marriage, she wrote again, "I most sincerely wish you and Mrs. Godwin joy—But, assured that your

---

[15] The quote is from 127. See my full discussion of this passage, including the allusion to *Julius Caesar*, in Chapter 2.

joyfulness would obliterate from your memory every trifling engagement, I have entreated another person to supply your place and perform your office in securing a Box. ... If I have done wrong—when you next marry I will act differently."[16] This response Wollstonecraft labels "Nonsense!" and Wardle's note informs us that it is clear from Godwin's letters that Wollstonecraft and Inchbauld did both attend the theater that night, were hostile, and avoided any further contact. Apparently the incident caused a major quarrel between Wollstonecraft and Godwin that night, evidence of the increasing anxiety caused by the fallout. In the same letter to Amelia Alderson, Wollstonecraft goes on to confess that she has also lost the friendship of Mr. and Mrs. Twiss, whom she had been in the habit of dining with every month, and her account of it emphasizes her strength of character and unwillingness to compromise principles:

> I shall be sorry to resign [their] acquaintance ... but my conduct in life must be directed by my own judgment and moral principles: it is my wish that Mr. Godwin should visit and dine out as formerly, and I shall do the same; in short, I still mean to be independent ... I am proud perhaps, conscious of my own purity and integrity; and many circumstances in my life have contributed to excite in my bosom an indignant contempt for the forms of a world I should have bade a long good night to, had I not been a mother. (409)

Finally, Wollstonecraft expresses a clearer, calmer credo about her autonomous judgment, in a letter to Mary Hays: "Those who are bold enough to advance before the age they live in, and to throw off, by the force of their own minds, the prejudices which the maturing reason of the world will in time disavow, must learn to brave censure. We ought not to be too anxious respecting the opinion of others."[17]

While Siddons followed what Wollstonecraft called the "forms" of the world, she herself was often at the mercy of them, and in fact her own biography offers reasons to believe Godwin's defense that Siddons "regretted the necessity" to play by the social rules. A figure of strong contradictions, Siddons was no stranger to slander and calumny. Certainly, by the time she came to write her *Reminiscences* (in 1831, the last year of her life, at the age of 75), she acknowledged a contempt of social ceremonies she herself followed. One event in particular pitted her against the same kind of fashionable females that Wollstonecraft decries against. During her early career, when she was honored with Garrick's flattery and attention, she became what she called "the object of spite and malevolence" from the ladies who began using the "malicious appellation of *Garrick's Venus*" when referring to her. These accounts of her early years (the *Reminiscences* only covers the years of 1773–1785) also allude to the fickle audiences whose rejection of her gave her much pain. As early as the age of 19, she worried that the "fashionables" in the audience were judging her harshly; she relates that during one performance she

---

[16]   Wardle, *Collected Letters*, 408 n.865.

[17]   Wardle, 410. There is some speculation about this letter since it exists only as an excerpt but Wardle's inclusion of it validates it to most critics.

heard noises and concluded that "the fashionables were now in the full enjoyment of their anticipated amusement, tittering and laughing as I thought most cruelly and without mercy."[18] Although she, in her head, greatly exaggerated the nature of that specific event, her behavior through the years culminated in a series of public attacks, focused on her avarice. The "Divine Sarah" also came to be called "Lady Save-All" who was parodied in Gillray's 1784 caricature entitled *Melpomene*; emphasizing her avaricious nature, the image, unlike Reynolds's influential painting, very definitely illustrates a human being masquerading as the Tragic Muse as it depicts Siddons reaching upward for suspended bags of gold (see Fig. 6.1).[19] She also characterizes the worst public denunciation she ever experienced, her being booed by the Drury Lane audience (an event I talk about further below) as a "gathering Storm" and a poison (30).

Another way Siddons's public persona was damaged—and a material link between the biographies of Siddons and Wollstonecraft—is the fact that Siddons was not without her own sexual scandal, the Galindo affair. Five years after her rejection of Wollstonecraft, Siddons spent a great deal of time in Ireland with a married couple, both actors, to whose child she became godmother. During this tour she played Hamlet to Mr. Galindo's Laertes, and Galindo tutored her in fencing to prepare for the final swordplay in the last scene. This play with swords was fodder for the public imagination as evident in the caricature "A Palpable Hit!" published in *The Dublin Satirist* in 1810 (note that Laertes's foil is pointedly placed at Siddons's crotch in Fig. 6.2). While no tangible evidence of an affair became public, the fact that Siddons attempted to procure Galindo an acting job at Covent Garden caused a swell of outcry against its impropriety, as did her loan to him of 1,000 pounds, which he lost in an unprofitable theatrical effort. These public facts coalesced in 1809 with the publication of a scandalous attack by Catherine Galindo, *Mrs. Galindo's Letters to Mrs. Siddons*, which charged Siddons with hypocrisy and adultery. Addressed to Mrs. Siddons as one "long eminent" for public talents "and *supposed private virtues*" (quoted in McDonald 19), the narrative's frontispiece includes an epigraph from Congreve ominously announcing that the text will "draw the veil and leave / Thee bare, the naked mark of public view."[20]

Being left bare, naked, for public view—this rhetoric pinpoints a central link between Siddons and Wollstonecraft: both strong intellectual women whose cultural currency ultimately included being judged as female bodies. One of

---

[18] Siddons goes on to explain that in this case she found out later that the women were uncontrollably crying due to her emotional performance. See *Reminiscences*, 3.

[19] McDonald discusses the details of Siddons's apparent greed, including especially the engagement in Edinburgh which was incredibly lucrative and which spawned numerous attacks in the London press and her worst experience on stage, being hissed at and booed for some 40 minutes in her return to Drury Lane. See Russ McDonald, *Look to the Lady: Sarah Siddons, Ellen Terry, and Judi Dench on the Shakespearean Stage* (Athens: University of Georgia Press, 2005).

[20] Quoted in McDonald, 19.

Fig. 6.1   *Melpomene*, James Gillray. © Trustees of the British Museum.

Fig. 6.2   *A Palpable Hit, Dublin Satirist*, 1810. Thr 489.3.29, Harvard
Theatre Collection, Houghton Library, Harvard University.

Polwhele's original "unsex'd females," most known today for the nonfictional
Vindications, both works of rational philosophy, Wollstonecraft and her scandalous
life of passion, popularized by Godwin's *Memoirs*, was what overwhelmed the
public imagination, thus the cultural epithets applied to her like Walpole's famous
"hyena in petticoats." A similar paradoxical obsession with body informs the
reactions to Siddons, although she was often described as something of a cosmic
spirit. Hazlitt perhaps most strikingly invokes this apparitional identity. Almost
hyperventilating over her, he writes

> … she was regarded less with admiration than with wonder, as if a being of
> a superior order had dropped from a higher sphere, to awe the world with
> the majesty of her appearance. … She was not less than a goddess, or than
> a prophetess inspired by the gods. Power was seated on her brow, passion
> emanated from her breast as from a shrine. She was Tragedy personified.[21]

This abstract and cosmic description, however, refers to the same woman
referenced in this quote often attributed to Byron: "I'd sooner make love to the

---

[21]   William Hazlitt, *Characters of Shakespeare's Plays*, *The Complete Works of
William Hazlitt*, ed. P.P. Howe, 21 vols. (London: J.M. Dent and Sons, 1930), 4: 189.

Archbishop of Canterbury than that appalling creature Mrs. Siddons." An exposure of them as bodies informs the one visual caricature that links the two women. Rowlandson's *Melpomene in the Dumps* offers Siddons as a slobby Melpomene tainted by a relationship with Mary Wollstonecraft in a caricature showing a fat Siddons in laurel wreath by a table of books, most visibly *Rights of Woman* (see Fig. 6.3). While the satire suggests that a Wollstonecraft influence is a negative one on the formerly beautiful Siddons, the visual comparison calls attention to the vulnerability of all women to images of their bodies.

The attention to both Siddons and Wollstonecraft as bodies—the appalling creature, the hyena in petticoats—is crucial in a second parallel between them: their representations of tragic female victims. I argue in Chapter 2 that Siddons's interpretation of Rowe's penitent heroine Calista is an important source of Wollstonecraft's Maria in *Maria, or The Wrongs of Woman* (the novel in which Siddons is cited directly), but more interesting theoretically is the performance of female victimhood. The excessive emotional responses Siddons inspired were commonly satirized, as in this account of a Dublin performance:

> One hundred and nine ladies fainted! Forty-six went into fits! And ninety-five had strong hysterics! The world will scarcely credit the truth when told that fourteen children, five old women, a one-handed sailor, and six common council-men were actually drowned in the inundation of tears that flowed from the galleries ... ." (McDonald 18)

It is similarly easy to catalogue Wollstonecraft's fiction as a series of unfortunate events for all of its female characters, yet the continuing critical question about the effect of Wollstonecraft's manipulation of sentimental and gothic fictional conventions belies such one-dimensional summaries. The fact that Wollstonecraft manipulates genre so sharply means that readers have to negotiate subtle intonations of popular conventions. While using the frame of the gothic, for instance, or reproducing the plot and rhetoric of sentimental novels, Wollstonecraft's *Maria, or The Wrongs of Woman* boldly defies expectations of those genres by offering a performative female whose speech becomes her authority. While critics disagree to what extent this text succeeds—Mary Poovey, for example, arguing that Wollstonecraft's "repeated lapses back into sentimental jargon" undercut the radical agenda of the novel—the novel's constant trope of theatricality challenges and ultimately expands' readers sympathies for tragic female heroines. My primary thesis then depends on how the Romantic stage served as a central paradigmatic source for Wollstonecraft's performances, Siddons in particular offering compelling, gender-destabilizing performances and in essence an acting theory that transformed the coercive nature of theatrical illusion into subversive actions.

That Siddons perceived the spectatorial paradigm off-stage as well as on is clear from her *Reminiscences*, and before turning to Siddons's approach to dramatic roles, most notably Lady Macbeth and Hamlet, I take a thorough look at this frequently

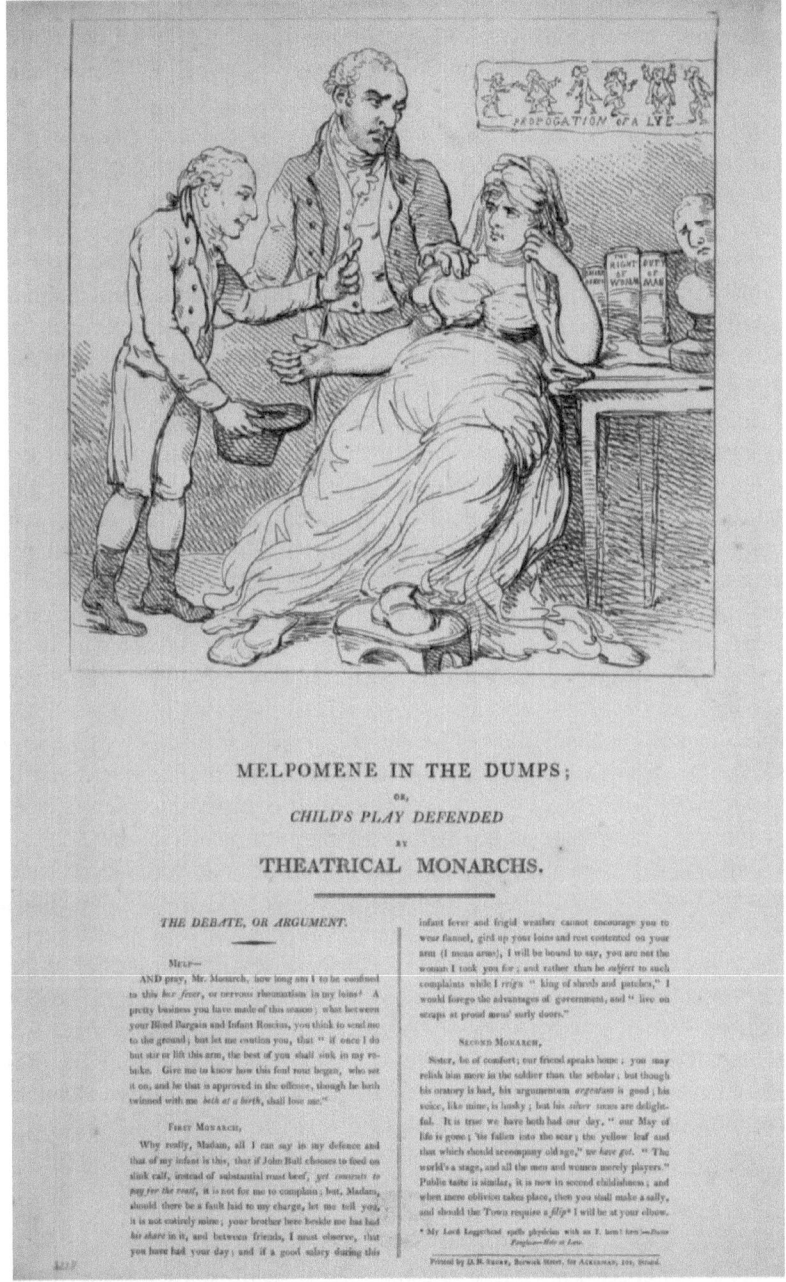

Fig. 6.3   *Melpomene in the Dumps*, Thomas Rowlandson. Photo © Victoria
and Albert Museum, London.

underestimated text.[22] Interesting for the incomplete biographical information they offer (only covering the years 1773–1785) and especially to art historians for the account Siddons gives of sitting for Reynolds's painting, the *Reminiscences* offer three significant perspectives on performance and theatricality: a critique of social performances by "fashionable" women, as we have seen in comparison with Wollstonecraft above, a consistent use of gothic imagery to represent her anxieties before and during stage appearances, and an exposure of the mechanisms of alternating between being the object of the gaze and a subject, whether on a social or theatrical stage. Appropriating the language of gothic to represent the experience of pre-performance anxieties is not surprising; Wollstonecraft's manipulations of the genre, as we have seen, emphasize the multiple ways in which gothic can offer representations of female powerlessness. "Abodes of horror have frequently been described, and castles, filled with specters and chimeras," Wollstonecraft writes in the opening line of *Maria, or The Wrongs of Woman*, "… But formed of such stuff as dreams are made of, what were they to the mansion of despair, in one corner of which Maria sat … ."[23] This broad invocation of gothic imagery, used here to suggest the discrepancy between fictional horrors and very real ones, extends throughout Wollstonecraft's work, especially in representing the terrors attendant to the powerlessness of females, both in marital and economic realms. Describing her husband Venables, who pursues and imprisons her, Maria says, "Sometimes a wild cat, a roaring bull, or hideous assassin, whom I vainly attempted to fly at; at other [times] he was a demon, hurrying me to the brink of a precipice, plunging me into dark waves." Allaying such horrid anxiety attacks are Maria's deliberate, conscious mental contemplations of tranquility, of "Italian vales" or "some august ruins," the thought of which produces some calm. Quite similar in terms of both the gothic rendition of anxiety and her response is Siddons's account of several of her most anxious moments before and during performances, where she fears not a pursuing husband but a hostile audience. Of her return to Drury Lane in the character of Isabella in Southern's tragedy, she writes, "Who can imagine my terror? I fear'd to utter a sound above an audible whisper. …" Like Wollstonecraft's heroine, however, Siddons gets through such psychological "fiery trial[s]" through an act of mental will, which she describes as "one of what I call my desperate tranquilities (which usually possess me under terrific circumstances) … to the astonishment of my attendants" (10). This kind of manipulation of gothic proves Claudia Johnson's shrewd summary of female gothic in this period as documenting the coercion of powerless females in situations where the drawing room is just

---

[22]   Viv Gardner's study of actresses' autobiographies, for example, considers it as an "act of self-effacement" and says that it offers primarily retellings of well-known events. See Viv Gardner, "By Herself: The Actress and Autobiography, 1775–1939," *The Cambridge Companion to the Actress*, ed. Maggie B. Gale and John Stokes (Cambridge: Cambridge University Press, 2007), 173–92. The quotation is from 177.

[23]   Wollstonecraft, *Maria, or The Wrongs of Woman* (New York: Norton, 1975), 7.

as frightening as a gothic precipice.[24] In her narratives of basic encounters with fans and stage managers, Siddons accentuates the dynamics of being the object of the gaze, the anxiety such meetings engender, and her increasingly aggressive response to them. Siddons vividly describes her first awareness of becoming a spectacle for others in an account of a social invitation by a Miss Monckton (later Lady Cork), an invitation she labels in retrospect a "Snare." The lady having promised Siddons that only a few close friends would be in attendance, Siddons narrates in detail her going to the house very casually, "very much in undress," in the presence of her son, whom she realizes was invited for "*effect*." After a short time, she continues, there were "successive and repeated thundering at the door, and the sudden influx of a throng of people as I had never seen collected in a public room," and the fact that she is the public exhibition becomes clear. Simply sitting down in the middle of the room, Siddons records that "people actually stood upon the chairs round the walls, that they might look over their neighbor's heads to stare at me" (15–16). Similar events occur in her dressing room, again perpetrated by fashionable ladies whom Siddons speculates to be of high rank but whose "curiosity [became] too powerful for [their] good breeding." One of these ladies confesses their sole reason for coming is to *look*:

> "You must think it strange," said she, "to see a person entirely unknown to you intrude in this manner on your privacy; but you must know I am in a very delicate state of health, and my Physician won't let me go to the Theatre to see you, so I am come to look at you here." So she sat down to *look*, and *I* to be looked at. (21)

While these examples of being objectified as spectacle demonstrate the coercive and oppressive force of the theatricality of the social mechanism of celebrity, Siddons's *Reminiscences* also document potentially subversive moments of acting, or mimicry, both offstage and on, moments in which the objectified actress turns the tables, once through a tangible object, a mirror, once in the presence of the royal family to whom she is obviously a "subject" which means paradoxically occupying the object position, and once on stage with a hostile audience. Siddons's narrative of her being assigned Garrick's dressing room at Drury Lane highlights a moment of spectacle, particularly resonant since she herself is the scene:

> It is impossible to imagine my gratification when I saw my own figure in the self same Glass which had so often reflected the face and form of that unequalled Genius, not perhaps without some vague, fanciful hope of a little degree of inspiration from it. (12)

Like the moment when the "I" of Siddons walks up the stairs, assumes a pose for Reynolds, and becomes the "She," this transfiguration of sorts melds "[her] own figure" with the "face and form of that unequalled Genius." Not a conscious

---

[24] See Claudia Johnson, *Jane Austen: Women, Politics, and the Novel* (Chicago: University of Chicago Press, 1988).

momentary assumption of Garrick's identity nor a pose of him, the epiphany of the spectacle is, nonetheless, that she becomes in the mirror an embodiment of the "form" that previously stood on that spot. That she is aware of this as a potential moment of empowerment is suggested in her "vague, fanciful hope" of gaining inspiration from it. It is this kind of awareness of acting, of becoming an Other through an intellectual and creative effort, that characterizes Siddons's accounts of spectatorship. Her description of the experience of reading to the royals at Buckingham Palace similarly casts the event as pure theater and herself as strangely subject and object. She first has to wear, in order to appear in the presence of the queen, a special costume, a "Saque" dress or contouche with "hoops, treble ruffles and Lappets [and] in which costume [she] felt not at all [her] ease" (21). While costumed, Siddons is clearly the spectator or audience here at first, having the little three-year-old Princess Amelia come up to her and "[hold] her little Royal *hand* to my mouth to be kissed; so early had she learnd this lesson of Royalty" (22). Siddons also comically narrates her fear of leaving the room to take refreshments or rest because in observing "a ceremony not to be dispensed with," she would be required to walk backwards out of the room, never turning her back on the royals; given her costume, and the fact that the floors were slippery (having just been "rubbed bright"), she stays in the same room "til [she] was ready to drop." Upon hearing afterwards that the Queen was impressed and amazed to see her so collected and to have "conducted [herself] as if [she] had been used to a Court," Siddons wryly and flippantly remarks, "At any rate I had frequently personated Queens" (22). The juxtaposition of and distinction between the "I" here who confidently comments on her impersonation of queens and the nervous, uncomfortable woman in the stiff dress afraid of falling reveals a mind that knows full well the power that acting can confer, even if the power is not from the inside.

A final example of Siddons's awareness and manipulation of the spectatorial dynamic is her worst night on the stage, the night of 5 October 5 1784, her return to the stage after her summer season in Dublin (and the scandal that followed her home) and the subject of much historical discussion. In "Mrs. Siddons Looks Back in Anger: Feminist Historiography for Eighteenth-Century British Theater," Ellen Donkin interprets the events onstage through a feminist spectatorial lens, arguing that it further expands our understanding of how "the playhouse ... functioned as a luminal space in which gender roles were negotiated and renegotiated" and in which "the audience was a wild card."[25] Drawing on three different accounts of the evening (from Wally Oulten, contemporary theater critic; James Boaden, a Siddons biographer; and Siddons herself), Donkin sketches out the most important facts of what happened: upon her entrance, she was greeted with hostile cries of "Off! Off!"; her brother Kemble came onstage and led her off by the hand; after

[25]   Ellen Donkin, "Mrs. Siddons Looks Back in Anger: Feminist Historiography for Eighteenth-Century British Theater," *Critical Theory and Performance*, ed. Janelle G. Reinelt and Joseph R. Roach (Ann Arbor: University of Michigan Press, 1992), 276–90. The quotation is from 279.

a six-minute hiatus, she returned to the stage and made a brief statement about how she had been unfairly accused; she left the stage again and forty minutes or more later, the curtain rose and she played the role with great success. While the contemporary writer Oulten simply summarizes her statement, Boaden, who was also present, reconstructs her statement as including the firm avowal that she did not deserve such:

> Ladies and Gentleman the kind and flattering partiality which I have uniformly experienced in this place would make the present interruption distressing to me indeed, were I in the slightest degree conscious of having deserved your censure. I feel no such consciousness.[26]

Both Boaden and Oulton characterize Siddons's composure as masculine, Oulton saying that she played the role with "astonishing firmness" and Boaden praising the "male dignity" of her speech to the audience. When we turn to her own account in the *Reminiscences*, prefaced by gothic rhetoric again as "the horrors of this dreadful night" and a "scene of savage persecution" (30), Siddons significantly makes no reference to perhaps the most significant fact of the night, her speech to the audience. According to her, she went offstage, fainted, and was begged by her husband, brother, and Sheridan to go back onstage, which she decides to do only "in consideration of my children." Her account then describes a magical moment of return: "But what was my astonishment to find [myself], on the rising of the curtain, received with a *silence* so profound that I was absolutely awe-struck and never yet have been able to account for this surprising contrast, for I really think the falling of a pin might have been heard on stage" (31). Her omission of the address to the audience, which both Boaden and Olten recount, prompts Donkin's consideration of her performance that night. Playing Mrs. Beverley in Edward Moore's *The Gamester*, Siddons would have had several strong scenes including one where she indignantly refuses to give in to a seduction even for money she desperately needs. Donkin invokes the moment on stage when Siddons would have spoken strong, indignant rhetoric while looking at the audience that had just wronged her:

> It was one of those moments in which the performance of the text gave the actress an opportunity to *hint* at a powerful subjectivity within the confines of a recuperative plot. ... In that moment she registered what she thought of [the audience]. She forced her audience to deal with her, not as object but as speaking subject. ... In other words, she reversed the direction of the gaze. (285)

Embodying both the hegemonic and the oppositional voice at the same time, Siddons in this moment of acting boldly claims the enabling theatricality that I argue for in the sense of Cixous's "mimicry" and Koestenbaum's "retaliatory self-invention."

---

[26] Quoted in Donkin 282.

The Romantic stage is, of course, a rich cultural site of gender destabilization (I outline the scholarly context in Chapter 1). It is important to see Siddons's stage performances in the context of this site where women on stage offered a spectacle of female beauty but had the potential to disrupt proper social codes; as Cox argues, "Siddons' *power* as a woman on stage, ironically arose from depicting women as *lacking the power to act*, and the sign of that power was her ability to overwhelm—to render passive—her audience and particularly the women in it" (38). While Cox's assertion pinpoints the paradox of Siddons's portrayals of powerless women, the word "passive" is misleading. Certainly, Siddons did overwhelm some audience members—stories of people fainting and weeping uncontrollably were reported in the popular press—but I agree with Donkin's assessment of the dynamic: "Although audiences demanded from the text the comfort and familiarity of the norms of Womanhood, what in fact they responded to in performance was something that potentially ruptured that comfort and familiarity" (278). The question underlying these paradoxical representations of powerlessnesss by the powerful is to what extent performance itself can be subversive even if the role is coercive. In other words, just as the theatricality of social praxis and custom is more often coercive, manipulating individual desires into collective values, an individual performance can dispel and disrupt those norms. I now turn to how Siddons's provocative interpretations of Shakespearean roles and her acting theory compare to Wollstonecraft's belief that authenticity can come from performing a wide number of roles, especially through the conflation of maternity, sexuality, and masculinity.

The complicated nexus of maternal and sexual roles for women pervades both women's lives in a very public way. Wollstonecraft's scandalous sexual behavior is visibly manifest in the figure of her daughter Fanny Imlay, a scandal made public by the announcement of her being pregnant by Godwin with the child who will become Mary Shelley; her most well-known fictional heroine Maria is wrenched from her still nursing daughter and tells her tale as a memoir of sorts written to the child; and her *VRW* celebrates motherhood as the highest purpose a woman can live for and, strikingly, the most important reason for women's education and autonomy from men. Siddons's celebrity is clear from her many various appellations—The Divine Sarah, the Siddons, and then the variants "Siddonian" and "Siddonsmania"—yet the most frequent label is Mrs. Siddons, a title which stakes out a conventional domestic identity. Partially as a means of countering the dubious moral reputations of actresses, perhaps especially the outcry following actress Mary Robinson's public scandal with the Prince of Wales, Siddons worked hard to maintain a reputation of moral rectitude, of conventional domestic and maternal roles. Her private life was, indeed, known to the public through her maternal identity. Offstage, mothering six children (a seventh died in infancy), Siddons balanced her professional career in a very modern sense, by actively communicating her childcare issues with her audiences. Her London debut had to be postponed to accommodate the birth of her second child, and a performance in Gloucester was shortened by her going into labor and delivering a daughter that very night. Finally, as many critics have analyzed, her ceremonial farewell to the stage for a leave of absence from Drury Lane starred her three offspring on stage, introduced as the three reasons why she must leave the stage for a while. Siddons's constant concern, in the *Reminiscences*, is for her children, whom she refers to as "poor babies," telling stories of long hard days of rehearsing in a theater at Bath until noon, acting on stage at Bristol in the same evening, driving the 12 miles back to Bath and arriving at midnight, only to represent some other "fatiguing part" on stage there the next evening, all of which "involved the subsistence of two helpless infants" (7). This complicated nexus of independent and collaborative roles, of autonomous female versus mother, makes Siddons an intriguing counterpart to Wollstonecraft; the fact that both were characterized as and at times castigated for being masculine further allies them.

Despite Siddons's foregrounding of her maternal identity, she was frequently portrayed as masculine, even in rumors about her domestic life. Gossips alluded to an emasculation of her husband, whose stage career was eclipsed by his wife and who devoted most of his time to managing family concerns. Ten years into her career, a satirist identifying himself as "Stage Trick" published theatrical gossip pamphlets and dropped this suggestion about Siddons's cross-dressing personality: "I shall just hint, that it has been *whispered* by others, she wears the *breeches* every day of her life."[27] Referring to Siddons's own performances of breeches parts and cross-dressing, the comment indicates a public obsession with undermining the official moral role Siddons played. To what extent this desire to challenge her moral authority stemmed from the destabilizing gender performances on stage is a fascinating question, especially with Shakespearean roles.

Siddons played 18 Shakespeare parts in her lifetime, including Hamlet, and as Celestine Woo documents, Siddons "played Hamlet repeatedly, if sporadically, for three decades."[28] Yet few scholars have critically discussed the roles, partly due to lack of information, but partly due to the assumption that these performances were oddities, always played in the provinces and not the London playhouses. Even notable performance scholar Laurence Senelick, in his discussion of female performances of male Shakespearean roles, contributes to this assumption, saying that "most of these were 'freak' performances, offered once or twice as sensational attractions, and usually not at the main metropolitan playhouses (Mrs. Siddons confined her Hamlet to Worcester)."[29]

Her 1805 production with herself as Hamlet and her reputed lover Galindo as Laertes gets comment from critics, but usually only in reference to the caricature in *The Dublin Satirist* in 1810. Woo's important study reads Siddons's choice of costume as an encapsulation of how she foregrounds and complicates gender

---

[27]   Quoted in McDonald 12.

[28]   Woo, "Sarah Siddons's Performances as Hamlet: Breaching the Breeches Part," *European Romantic Review* 18.5 (2007): 573–95, 575.

[29]   Laurence Senelick, *The Changing Room: Sex, Drag, and Theatre* (London and New York: Routledge, 2000), 270.

(a costume neither conventionally masculine nor feminine) and elucidates another factor in the historical elision of these performances, a critical lack of distinction between the ideologies of traditional breeches parts and cross-gendered roles:

> A "breeches part" refers to a female character who during the course of the dramatic narrative, dresses as a boy or a man, and almost always returns to her normative feminine garb by the end. The appeal of breeches parts lay partially for the (heterosexual male) viewer in the titillating opportunity to leer at women's legs, ordinarily invisible … . By contrast, the decision by a player of whatever gender to portray a character of the opposite gender is a choice exterior to the narrative and plot … a cross-gendered role invites reflection on the part of the spectator as to why an actor would portray the opposite gender, to a greater extent than a breeches part, which at best prompts reflection on why the *character* crossdresses—a question with a ready answer provided by the plot. (576)

In her work on actresses and drag, Bratton claims that a woman's dressing up as a man is more transgressive than the reverse and repeats Butler's assertion of it as a "monstrous ascent into phallicism."[30] The appeal of the "breeches part" was, of course, to expose parts of the body that were hidden in the drapery of female dress, but more interesting than that kind of straightforward "hypersexuality," to use Pullen's label, is the matrix of gender performance that it elicits.[31] Siddons's cross-dressed performance did more than titillate with sexy legs: she made the audience question the gender, as opposed to the irrefutably clear biological sex, of a character. Sarah Bernhardt similarly conceived Hamlet as a woman and remarked in fact that he should *only* be played by a woman: "I cannot see Hamlet as a man. The things Hamlet says, his impulses, his actions, all indicate to me that he was a woman."[32]

As Bernhardt's sensational comment suggests, and as theoretical work by Bratton, Senelick, Garber, and Dollimore attests, the scholarly appeal of cross-dressing is related to its status as a sign of the constructedness of gender categories; once sexual identity is shifted into the domain of custom, it can be contested. Garber's insistence on seeing the cross-dressed character "as it is" instead of a sign of something else is pertinent here. Of Greenblatt's point that

---

[30]   See Jacky Bratton, "Mirroring Men: The Actress in Drag," *The Cambridge Companion to the Actress*, ed. Maggie B. Gale and John Stokes (Cambridge: Cambridge University Press, 2007), 235–52, 235. See also Leslie Ferris's helpful collection *Crossing the Stage: Controversies on Cross-Dressing* (London and New York: Routledge, 1993). The Butler quote is from *Bodies That Matter: On the Discursive Limits of Sex* (London and New York: Routledge, 1993), 103.

[31]   See Kirsten Pullen, *Actresses and Whores On Stage and In Society* (Cambridge: Cambridge University Press, 2005), 120.

[32]   Woo references this statement as an untitled article, January 21, 1923 (stamped January 21, 1923. Harvard Theatre Collection: "Hamlet—Productions—Women as Hamlet"). The article reports that Bernhardt made the above remarks after her performance as Hamlet on May 20, 1899.

characters in Shakespeare's play who cross-dress pass through states of men to become women, Garber cautions against "the underestimation of the object, the transvestite itself.[33] Her argument that we see this figure as neither hermaphrodite nor androgyne but rather a "mode of articulation" or a "way of describing a space of possibility" encourages us to see Siddons's performances through this lens; however, I take a much more positive view of its effect. Garber contends that the figure of the transvestite marks a "kind of displacement, substitution, or slippage ... [and is] both a signifier and that which signifies the undecidability of signification" (36–7). Undecidability, though, is not the same as (im)possibility, making a possibility where there was none through embodying an abstract (a role, a character, a principle) through the physical. In this sense, my reading parallels Dollimore's argument about the "transgressive aesthetic" in Oscar Wilde. In *Sexual Dissidence*, Dollimore allies cross-dressing in early Modern England with Wilde's transgression. Labeling cross-dressing a kind of "mimicry" that "has the power not just to deceive but to subvert social differentiation and identity itself," Dollimore then compares it to what he argues is the Wildean transgressive aesthetic:

> ... a transgression which finds expression through inversion and perversion of those pre-existing categories and structures which its humanist counterpart seeks to transcend, a mode of transgression which seeks not an escape from existing structures but rather a subversive reinscription within them, and in the process their dislocation or displacement.[34]

The distinction between a "humanist" concept of a transgression that transcends its order and a "subversive reinscription within" an existing order is at the heart of the kind of mimicry I argue for Siddons and Wollstonecraft. It can be likened to Cixous' theory of feminine mimicry and to Lacan's image of mimicry as camouflage:

> Mimicry reveals something in so far as it is distinct from what might be called an itself that is behind. The effect of mimicry is camouflage. ... It is not a question of harmonizing with the background, but against a mottled background, of becoming mottled—exactly like the technique of camouflage practised in human warfare.[35]

Siddons had already evinced a desire to experiment with the connotations evoked by the trappings of gender; an early costume adopted for the part of

---

[33] Marjorie Garber, *Vested Interests: Cross-Dressing and Cultural Anxiety* (New York: Routledge, 1997), 10.

[34] Jonathon Dollimore, *Sexual Dissidence: Augustine to Wilde, Freud to Foucault* (Oxford: Oxford University Press, 1991), 285. The quotation on mimicry is from 291.

[35] This quotation from Lacan's *Of the Gaze* is used as the opening of Homi Bhabha's essay on mimicry although Bhabha reads mimicry very differently in the postcolonial political context. See my discussion in Chapter 1. Homi Bhabha, *The Location of Culture* (New York: Routledge, 1994).

Rosalind/Ganymede was derided in *The Morning Chronicle* as "most absurdly perverse" and in *The Morning Herald* thus: "The dress of Mrs. Siddons was demi-feminine, demi-masculine, and therefore we may properly call it the *habit neuter*. She appeared in half a petticoat and half a pair of breeches that seemed to disagree like an ill-matched man and wife."[36] Woo convincingly argues that Siddons adopts an inherently critical and theoretical stance and invites an androgynous consideration of the qualities of her character and of human nature. The costume she wore, a black toga-like garment, ensured that the audience would interpret her performance through gender since only a woman would play Hamlet *without* breeches; thus, Siddons manages to avoid sexualization but retain the physicality of her body on stage.

Yet it is not the cross-dressed role of Hamlet but that of Lady Macbeth in which she is most often visually depicted and that is the occasion for both controversy and a significant parallel to Wollstonecraft. The public controversy which perhaps occasioned Gillray's satire of her an avaricious Melpomene was her appearance of Lady Macbeth while pregnant in 1794. As Mrs. Piozzi writes, "Mrs. Siddons is going to act Lady Macbeth on the new Theatry Drury Lane next Easter Monday; She is big with Child, & I fear will for that reason scarce be well received for people have a notion She is covetous, and this unnecessary Exertion to gain Money will confirm it."[37] The comment reveals a public unable to conceive of a woman's decision to follow her career despite physical demands of the female body, seeing the only possible reason for her to act while pregnant as a greed for money. Siddons's portrayals of Lady Macbeth, in fact, offer rich questions about performing bodies.

She first played the role at 20, to little success, but her comments on that performance underscore why the role of Lady Macbeth had such a palpable hold on both her and Wollstonecraft. She remarks that fear characterized her first performance:

> On the night preceding that in which I was to appear in this part for the first time, I shut myself up, as usual, when all the family was retired, and commenced my study. ... But to proceed, I went on with tolerable composure in the silence of the night, (a night I can never forget), till I came to the assassination scene, when the horrors of the scene rose to a degree that made it impossible for me to get farther. I snatched up my candle and hurried out of the room, in a paroxysm of terror. My dress was of silk, and the rustling of it, as I ascended the stairs to go to bed, seemed to my panic-struck fancy like the movement of a spectre pursuing me.[38]

The gothic rhetoric and imagery is very similar to Wollstonecraft's account, in her *HMV*, of her empathetic identification with the French king and queen whose politics she loathes but whose terrorized humanity she sees as her own.

---

[36]   Reviews from *The Morning Herald* and *The Morning Chronicle* are quoted in Pearce's *The Jolly Duchess*, a miscellany of theatrical anecdotes, according to Woo, 590 n.11.

[37]   Quoted in McDonald, 15.

[38]   Quoted in McDonald, 37.

Quite simply, the shifting allegiances and competing agendas of the Parisian market women and the French queen intersect with the vulnerability of all women, herself among them, as she concludes her "history" of events in France by staging a dramatic scene. Writing alone in a Paris hotel room, after having seen Louis XVI being taken to his death, she recounts that she imagined "eyes glar[ing] through a glass door opposite my chair and bloody hands shak[ing] at me" (324). This striking narration of herself as threatened by "bloody hands" juxtaposes her alongside the royals; when compared to her earlier narrative apostrophe to Versailles, where as we have seen in Chapter 5, she stages herself walking alone through empty corridors, haunted by her reflection in mirrors, this gothic fantasy aligns her with the those who are ultimately no more and no less than she, a body implicated in competing dramatic roles. Her invocation of bloody hands also significantly brings Lady Macbeth's guilty hand-wringing into the scene, in a nexus of French Revolutionary violence and Shakespearean tropes. As Jacobus has demonstrated, *Macbeth* became particularly charged for Romantic writers because of the ways in which it mirrored theatrical and political concerns being enacted in the Revolution, the play becoming for Romantic writers a "paradigm of their own unease about the power of the imagination" (37). For Wollstonecraft and for Siddons, I believe, it is less unease about the power of imagination than the frightening but empowering potential available in such imaginative identifications with characters whom the culture or one's politics deem as monstrous.

The power of such imaginative identifications and, I argue, performances of Otherness comes from intense intellectual preparation. Siddons's preparations for her dramatic roles were both scholarly and creative. Siddons's notes and the reviews of her work all underscore a work ethic, a seriousness to her approach to all roles, more commensurate with twentieth-century than eighteenth-century acting. Exponents of what we know as the Stanislavkian "method acting" may see this seriousness of purpose as mandatory, but the eighteenth century did not see any such consistency; as strange as it may sound, some actresses routinely greeted their late-comer friends in the audience from the stage, so Siddons's sustained characterizations were legendary. Her study of the text itself as an essential first step was not common procedure, certainly not to those actresses who came before her, as a conversation with Dr. Johnson evidences. Responding to Siddons's request to hear his opinion of Mrs. Pritchard's acting, Johnson said, "Madam, she was a vulgar idiot. She never read any part of the play except her own part" to which Siddons thinks to herself, "Is it possible … [that] the greatest of all Lady Macbeths should never have read the play? … . I cannot believe it."[39] Siddons's private rehearsals apparently consisted of her reading and memorizing the script silently, never out loud. Boaden relates in the *Memoirs*, "As to her mode of study, in her apartment it was silent. She conceived there certainly all that she meant to do; but it was only at rehearsal that she knew the effect of her voice upon the conception" (218).

---

[39] *Reminiscences*, 14.

Her silent preparation for the role in which voicing was so important suggests the extent to which she embodied the character on stage. Pascoe's work on Siddons's vocal powers and early sound recordings suggests that one of the reasons why *Macbeth* provided such a showcase for Siddons's voice is that it takes the female voice as subject of fascination from the very first scene with a gathering of witches. Her many permutations of the role, from playing Lady Macbeth with a kind of masculine authority to playing the part pregnant in 1794 (a spectacle surely difficult to reconcile with the line "Unsex me here"), foreground her innovations in the character, for rather than seeing her as monstrous, Siddons empathizes with her. As Burroughs suggests, Siddons enacts a kind of cultural critique by envisioning the Lady as a supportively agonized eighteenth-century wife and saw a potential to learn how to live a more enlightened life off stage by playing her in this way:

> Schooling herself to tolerate negative characters in order to make herself more capable of empathizing with the strange, the threatening, and the despicable, she confessed that she had for some years "perceived the difficulty of assuming a personage [Lady Macbeth] with whom no one feeling of general nature as congenial or assistant. One's own heart could prompt one to express, with some degree of truth, the sentiments of a mother, a daughter, a wife, a lover, a sister & etc. ... but to adopt this character must be an effort of the judgment alone."[40]

Siddons's remarks ultimately posit the Lady as a fascinating, potent women who has a rare "combination of energy and strength of mind," and Siddons warns her audience that they will probably object to her performance initially due to an inability to let go of accustomed views of the character. Burroughs concludes, "Siddons' system of acting ... implies that the performance of complicated characterizations on stage can educate spectators in a mode of observing that is more conducive to tolerating the strange, the alarming, and the traditionally ostracized" (57). Thus from performing powerless female victims with an empowering, disruptive force to, conversely, performing powerful females with empathetic force, Siddons provides Wollstonecraft with provocative models. The idea that a "mode of observing" a complicated performance can itself transform the observer informs the complex power dynamics in Wollstonecraft's persistent appropriations of theatricality in almost every genre she undertakes. I contend that the key to answering Wollstonecraft's unfinished thought in her letter to Godwin—"when shall I tell you what I think of her?"—lies in seeing the strong intellectual and creative parallels between them, especially the transgressive potential in theatricality.

---

[40]   Catherine Burroughs, *Closet Stages: Joanna Baillie and the Theater Theory of British Romantic Women Writers* (Philadelphia: University of Pennsylvania Press, 1997), 57. The Siddons quotation embedded in Burroughs's quotation is from her "Remarks of the Character of Lady Macbeth," included on 134 of Thomas Campbell's *Life of Mrs. Siddons* (New York: Harper and Brothers, 1834), 123–35.

While she did once supposedly write a play that Godwin destroyed, Wollstonecraft, unlike many of her female friends, never acted on stage, and yet she consciously adopted a number of roles. As Taylor asserts,

> The experimental drive was never more evident than in Wollstonecraft's diverse, often highly dramatized self-presentations as a writer. Over the years she ran through an extraordinary range of literary personae, from the prissy moralist of her earliest *Thoughts on the Education of Daughters* (1787), to the bluntspoken philosophical radical of the two *Vindications* (1790, 1792), to the lyrical romantic of her letters from Sweden (1796), with many other postures—satirist, teacher, melancholy solitaire—tried out along the way. (31)[41]

As a translator, Wollstonecraft found herself and her voice through other voices and roles, making an actress of sorts, and her stint as a reviewer of fiction reveals, as Mitzi Myers's work asserts, a disdain of the formulaic jargon of women's fiction, a "hardening of the emotional arteries so that women feel and act as by rote, casting themselves as sentimental heroines and losing touch with cultural realities."[42] Moreover, her *Letters Written During a Short Residence* includes a conscious awareness and classification of women as playing their parts by rote,

> All the world's a stage, thought I; and few are there in it who do not play the part they have learnt by rote; and those who do not seem marks to be pelted at by fortune; or rather as sign-posts, which point out the road to others.[43]

The common thread, paradoxically, throughout all these literary personae was her deep preoccupation with personal authenticity, a desire which signals, as Taylor puts it, her commitment to "a personal authenticity sharply at odds with the masquerade of femininity" (33). But how is authenticity registered? If it is in constant binary opposition to masquerade, does that make it necessarily at odds with forms of theatricality? Consider that one of Wollstonecraft's most forceful, independent actions, where her agency is most on view, helping her sister Eliza escape her abusive husband, she recounts in theatrical terms: "I knew I should be the Mrs. Brown, the *shameful incendiary* in this shocking affair of a woman's leaving her bedfellow."[44] (Wardle glosses this a possible allusion to Robert Lloyd's *Chit-Chat* [1762] in which a Mrs. Brown mocks husbands.) Although she refers here to the ways in which the public will label her actions, her words evoke a kind of celebration, if not pride, in *being* the Mrs. Brown, in adopting consciously the role

---

[41] Barbara Taylor, *Wollstonecraft and the Radical Imagination* (Cambridge: Cambridge University Press, 2002).

[42] Mitzi Myers, "Mary Wollstonecraft's Literary Reviews," *Cambridge Companion to Mary Wollstonecraft*, ed. Claudia L. Johnson (Cambridge: Cambridge University Press, 2002), 82–98. The quote is from 92.

[43] *Letters Written During a Short Residence in Sweden, Norway, and Denmark*, ed. Carol H. Poston (Lincoln: University of Nebraska Press, 1976), 181.

[44] "Letter to Everina Wollstonecraft," *Collected Letters*, 47.

of the shameful incendiary. Claiming the performance, neither hollow nor artificial, wrests it from the public, judgmental interpretation and, defying expectations of the role, thwarts it. It is in this way that Wollstonecraft's appropriation of theatrical tropes stems from conscious reflections about the potentially empowering nature of acting, what I call a fully embodied performance.

In the advertisement to her play *A Day in Turkey; or the Russian Slaves* (1792), playwright Hannah Cowley, as she takes pains to distinguish herself from Wollstonecraft, offers a provocative phrase about her. Asserting that her play is not "tainted" with politics, she writes: "I protest I know nothing about politics;—will Miss Wollstonecraft forgive me—whose book contains such a body of mind as I hardly ever met with—if I say that politics are unfeminine? I never in my life could attend to their discussion."[45] In quoting this line, Bolton says that Cowley has apparently read Wollstonecraft's *A Vindication of the Rights of Woman* enough to remark somewhat ambiguously on its "body of mind." Yet, unwittingly perhaps, the phrase "body of mind" is a felicitous one, a paradox articulating a kind of meshing of materiality/character and a phrase which could just as easily have been directed at Siddons.

Charles Lambs's assertion—"We speak of Lady Macbeth while in reality we are thinking of Mrs. S"—returns us to questions raised in the beginning of this chapter with regard to Manckiewicz's film, to Reynolds's painting, and my study's premises about the coercive/subversive powers of performance. "I walked up the steps," Siddons writes of sitting for Reynolds, "and seated myself instantly in the attitude in which She now appears." As Weinsheimer concludes about the painting, using Merleau-Ponty's ideas about community, "Siddons is herself as others see her because she incarnates herself into the historical situation. She takes a role in the world, presents herself to the public, appears to the artist. It is she herself that she enacts. More precisely, her role is both similar to and different from herself" (324). In *All About Eve*, Margo discovers the void behind the public persona that had, with her connivance, usurped her personal identity. Acknowledging that she does not know how to recreate herself, she says, "After all these years of exile what will my Self turn out to be?" The famous monologue with which I started the chapter as an epigraph concludes with Karen's asking a simple question to Margo's troubling ruminations: "I want [Bill] to want me. But me, not Margo Channing. And if I can't tell them apart, how can he?" "But why should he? Why should you?" Siddons's performances suggest that Margo has it all wrong; in a review of one of her Lady Macbeth performances, a critic marvels that she "combines **more than ever existed** at once in the same person." Siddons and Wollstonecraft offer the startling proposition that performance can be, as Koestenbaum has said of gay opera divas, a "retaliatory self-invention."[46]

---

45   Hannah Cowley, *A Day in Turkey; or the Russian Slaves* (London: G.G.J. and J. Robinson, 1792), n.p.

46   Wayne Koestenbaum, *The Queen's Throat: Opera, Homosexuality, and the Mystery of Desire* (New York: Poseidon Press, 1993), 133.

Works Cited

Andrew, Donna. "'Adultery a-la-Mode': Privilege, the Law, and Attitudes to Adultery, 1770–1809." *History* 82 (1997): 5–23.

Austin, J.L. *How To Do Things With Words*. Oxford: Oxford University Press, 1976.

Backscheider, Paula R. *Spectacular Politics: Theatrical Power and Mass Culture in Early Modern England*. Baltimore: Johns Hopkins University Press, 1993.

Baer, Marc. *Theater and Disorder in Late Georgian London*. Oxford: Clarendon, 1992.

Bahar, Saba. *Mary Wollstonecraft's Social and Aesthetic Philosophy*. New York: Palgrave, 2002.

Barish, John. *The Antitheatrical Prejudice*. Berkeley: University of California Press, 1981.

Barrell, John. "Imaginary Treason, Imaginary Law: The State Trials of 1794." *The Birth of Pandora and the Division of Knowledge*. Philadelphia: University of Pennsylvania Press, 1992.

Bennett, Shelley. "New Light on British Paintings at the Huntingdon." *Burlington Magazine* 137 (1995): 512–13.

Bhabha, Homi. *The Location of Culture*. New York: Routledge, 1994.

Boaden, James. *Memoirs of Mrs. Siddons*. Philadelphia: J.P. Lippincott Company, 1893.

Bolton, Betsy. *Women, Nationalism, and the Romantic Stage: Theatre and Politics in Britain, 1780–1800*. Cambridge: Cambridge University Press, 2001.

Bromwich, David. *Politics by Other Means*. New Haven: Yale University Press, 1992.

Brown, Phillip Anthony. *The French Revolution in English History*. London: Crosby, Lockwood, and Son, 1918.

Bruhm, Steven. *Gothic Bodies: The Politics of Pain in Romantic Fiction*. Philadelphia: University of Pennsylvania Press, 1994.

Burke, Edmund. *Correspondence of Edmund Burke*. Ed. Thomas Copeland et al. 10 vols. Chicago: University of Chicago Press, 1958–1978.

———. *Reflections on the Revolution in France*. Ed. Conor Cruise O'Brien. New York: Penguin, 1968.

Burroughs, Catherine. *Closet Stages: Joanna Baillie and the Theater Theory of British Romantic Women Writers*. Philadelphia: University of Pennsylvania Press, 1997.

———, ed. *Women in British Romantic Theatre: Drama, Performance, and Society, 1790–1840*. Cambridge: Cambridge University Press, 2000.

Butler, Judith. *Bodies That Matter: On the Discursive Limits of Sex*. London and New York: Routledge, 1993.

————. "Critically Queer." *GLQ* 1.1 (1993): 21–4.

————. *Excitable Speech: A Politics of the Performative*. London and New York: Routledge, 1997.

————. *Gender Trouble: Feminism and the Subversion of Identity*. New York: Routledge, 1999.

————. *Psychic Life of Power: Theories in Subjection*. Stanford: Stanford University Press, 1997.

Carlson, Julie. *In The Theatre of Romanticism: Coleridge, Nationalism, Women*. Cambridge: Cambridge University Press, 1994.

————. "A New Stage for Romantic Drama." *Studies in Romanticism* 27.3 (1988): 419–27.

Castle, Terry. *Masquerade and Civilization: The Carnivalesque in Eighteenth Century English Culture and Fiction*. Stanford, CA: Stanford University Press, 1986.

Chaveau-Lagarde, M. *Note historique sur les process de Marie-Antoinette d'Autriche, Reine de France, et de Madame Elisabeth de France, au Tribunal Revolutionnaire*. Paris, 1816.

Coleridge, Samuel Taylor. *Collected Letters of Samuel Taylor Coleridge*. Ed. E.L. Griggs. 6 vols. Oxford: Clarendon, 1956.

Colwill, Elizabeth. "Just Another *Citoyenne*? Marie-Antoinette on Trial, 1790–1793." *History Workshop Journal* 28 (1989): 63–87.

Cone, Carl B. The *English Jacobins: Reformers in Late Eighteenth-Century England*. New York: Charles Scribner's Sons, 1968.

Conger, Syndy McMillen. *Mary Wollstonecraft and the Language of Sensibility*. Rutherford, NJ: Fairleigh Dickinson University Press, 1994.

————."The Power of the Unnamed You in Mary Wollstonecraft's *Letters*." *Mary Wollstonecraft and Mary Shelley: Writing Lives*. Ed. Helen Buss, D.L. Macdonald, and Anne McWhir. Waterloo, Ontario: Wilfred Laurier University Press, 2001. 43–53.

Costelloe, Timothy M. "The Theater of Morals: Culture and Community in Rousseau's *Lettre a M. d'Alembert*." *Eighteenth-Century Life* 27.1 (2003): 52–71.

Cox, Jeffrey N. "Baillie, Siddons, Larpent: Gender, Power, and Politics." *Women in British Romantic Theatre: Drama, Performance, and Society, 1790–1840*. Ed. Catherine Burroughs. Cambridge: Cambridge University Press, 2000. 23–47.

Craft-Fairchild, Elizabeth. *Masquerade as Gender: Disguise and Female Identity in Eighteenth-Century Fictions by Women*. University Park: Pennsylvania State University Press, 1993.

Crafton, Lisa. "'Ancient Voices': The New Language of Blake's *The French Revolution*." *The French Revolution Debate in English Literature and Culture*. Ed. Lisa Plummer Crafton. Westport, CT: Greenwood Press, 1997.

————. "'Insipid Decency': Modesty and Female Sexuality in Wollstonecraft." *European Romantic Review* 31.1 (Summer 2000): 55–88.

————. "'A Shameful Tale to Tell for Public Sport': Wollstonecraft's Revision of Rowe's *The Fair Penitent*." *New Perspectives on the Eighteenth Century* 4.1 (2007): 28–37.

————. "'Stage Effect': Transgressive Theatricality in Wollstonecraft's *Maria, or The Wrongs of Woman*." *Women's Writing* 14.3 (2007): 367–81.

Culler, Jonathan. "The Fortunes of the Performative In Literary and Cultural Theory." *Literature and Psychology* 45.1–2 (1999): 7–28.

Dart, Gregory. *Rousseau, Robespierre, and English Romanticism*. Cambridge: Cambridge University Press, 1999.

Diamond, Elin, ed. *Performance and Cultural Politics*. New York: Routledge, 1996.

Dolan, Jill. *Geographies of Learning: Theory and Practice, Activism and Performance*. Middletown, CT: Wesleyan University Press, 2001.

Dollimore, Jonathon. *Sexual Dissidence: Augustine to Wilde, Freud to Foucault*. Oxford: Oxford University Press, 1991.

Donkin, Ellen. "Mrs. Siddons Looks Back in Anger: Feminist Historiography for Eighteenth-Century British Theater." *Critical Theory and Performance*. Ed. Janelle G. Reinelt and Joseph R. Roach. Ann Arbor: University of Michigan Press, 1992. 317–33.

Franklin, Caroline. *Mary Wollstonecraft: A Literary Life*. New York: Palgrave, 2006.

Furniss, Tom. "Mary Wollstonecraft's French Revolution." *Cambridge Companion to Mary Wollstonecraft*. Ed. Claudia L. Johnson. Cambridge: Cambridge University Press, 2002. 59–81.

Galperin, William. *The Return of the Visible in British Romanticism*. Baltimore and London: Johns Hopkins University Press, 1993.

Garber, Marjorie. *Vested Interests: Cross-Dressing and Cultural Anxiety*. New York: Routledge, 1997.

Gardner, Viv. "By Herself: The Actress and Autobiography, 1775–1939." *The Cambridge Companion to the Actress*. Ed. Maggie B. Gale and John Stokes. Cambridge: Cambridge University Press, 2007. 173–92.

Gibbons, Luke. *Edmund Burke and Ireland: Aesthetics, Politics, and the Colonial Sublime*. Cambridge: Cambridge University Press, 2003.

Godwin, William. *Memoirs of the Author of A Vindication of the Rights of Woman* in *The Wrongs of Woman and Godwin's Memoirs*. Ed. Cynthia Richards. Glen Allen, VA: College Publishing, 2004.

————. *William Godwin: His Friends and Contemporaries*. Ed. C. Kegan Paul. London: Henry S. King & Co., 1876.

Goodman, Dena, ed. *Marie-Antoinette: Writings on the Body of a Queen*. New York: Routledge, 2003.

Graham, Ruth. "Loaves and Liberty: Women in the French Revolution." *Becoming Visible: Women in European History*. Ed. Renate Bridenthal and Claudia Koonz. New York: Houghton Mifflin, 1977. 236–54.

Greenberg, Mitchell. *Subjectivity and Subjugation in Seventeenth-Century Drama and Prose: The Family Romance in French Classicism*. Cambridge: Cambridge University Press, 2006.

Gutwirth, Madelyn. *The Twilight of the Goddesses: Women and Representation in the French Revolutionary Era.* New Brunswick, NJ: Rutgers University Press, 1992.

Hadley, Elaine. *Melodramatic Tactics: Theatricalized Dissent in the English Marketplace.* Stanford: Stanford University Press, 1995.

Harris, Susan Cannon. "Outside the Box: The Female Spectator, *The Fair Penitent*, and the Kelly Riots of 1747." *Theatre Journal* 57.1 (2005): 33–55.

Henstra, Sarah. "Looking the Part: Performative Narration in Djuna Barnes's *Nightwood* and Katherine Mansfield's 'Je Ne Parle Pas Français.'" *Twentieth-Century Literature* 46.2 (Summer 2000): 125–49.

Hoeveler, Diane. *Gothic Feminism: The Professionalization of Gender from Charlotte Smith to the Brontës.* University Park: Pennsylvania State University Press, 1998.

Howe, Elizabeth. *The First English Actresses: Women and Drama 1660–1700.* Cambridge: Cambridge University Press, 1992.

Hunt, Lynn, ed. *Eroticism and the Body Politic.* Baltimore: Johns Hopkins University Press, 1991.

———. "The Many Bodies of Marie Antoinette: Political Pornography and the Problem of the Feminine in the French Revolution." *Eroticism and the Body Politic.* Ed. Lynn Hunt. Baltimore: Johns Hopkins University Press, 1991. 108–30.

Irigary, Luce. *This Sex Which Is Not One.* Ithaca: Cornell University Press, 1985.

Jacobus, Mary. "'That Great Stage Where Senators Perform': *Macbeth* and the Politics of Romantic Theatre." *Romanticism, Writing, and Sexual Difference.* Oxford: Clarendon Press, 1989. 33–68.

Jenkins, Annabel. *Nicholas Rowe.* Boston: Twayne, 1977.

Johnson, Claudia. *Jane Austen: Women, Politics, and the Novel.* Chicago: University of Chicago Press, 1988.

Jones, Vivien. "Women Writing Revolution: Narratives of History and Sexuality in Wollstonecraft and Williams." *Beyond Romanticism: New Approaches to Texts and Contexts, 1780–1832.* Ed. Stephen Copley and John Whale. London and New York: Routledge, 1992. 178–99.

Jordan, Elaine. "Criminal Conversation: Mary Wollstonecraft's *The Wrongs of Woman.*" *Women's Writing* 4.2 (1997): 221–34.

Karr, David. "'Thoughts that Flash Like Lightning': Thomas Holcroft, Radical Theater, and the Production of Meaning in 1790s London." *Journal of British Studies* 40 (2001): 324–56.

Keane, Angela. "Mary Wollstonecraft's Imperious Sympathies: Population, Maternity, and Romantic Individualism." *Body Matters: Feminism, Textuality, Corporeality.* Ed. Avril Horner and Angela Keane. Manchester: Manchester University Press, 2000. 29–42.

Kelly, Gary, ed. *Mary and the Wrongs of Woman,* by Mary Wollstonecraft. Oxford: Oxford University Press, 1976.

———. *Revolutionary Feminism: The Mind and Career of Mary Wollstonecraft.* New York: Macmillan, 1992.

Koestenbaum, Wayne. *The Queen's Throat: Opera, Homosexuality, and the Mystery of Desire*. New York: Poseidon Press, 1993.

Komisaruk, Adam. "The Privatization of Pleasure: 'Crim.Con' in Wollstonecraft's *Maria*." *Law and Literature* 16.1 (2004): 33–40.

Kramnick, Isaac. *The Rage of Edmund Burke*. New York: Basic Books, 1977.

Litvak, Joseph. *Caught in the Act: Theatricality in the Nineteenth-Century English Novel*. Berkeley: University of California Press, 1992.

Lloyd, Sarah. "Amour in the Shrubbery: Reading the Detail of English Adultery Trial Publications of the 1780s." *Eighteenth-Century Studies* 39.4 (2006): 421–42.

Mankiewicz, Joseph. "All About the Women in *All About Eve*." *New Yorker* 16 Oct. 1972.

Marin, Louis. *Portrait of the King*. Trans. Martha M. Houle. Minneapolis: University of Minnesota Press, 1988.

Marsden, Jean. "Sex, Politics, and the She-Tragedy: Reconfiguring *Lady Jane Grey*," *Studies in English Literature* 42.3 (2002): 501–22.

Marshall, David. *The Surprising Effects of Sympathy*. Chicago: University of Chicago Press, 1988.

Maza, Sara. "The Diamond Necklace Affair: The Case of the Missing Queen." *Eroticism and the Body Politic*. Ed. Lynn Hunt. Baltimore: Johns Hopkins University Press, 1991. 63–89.

McDonald, Russ. *Look to the Lady: Sarah Siddons, Ellen Terry, and Judi Dench on the Shakespearean Stage*. Athens: University of Georgia Press, 2005.

McPherson, Heather. "Picturing Tragedy: *Mrs. Siddons as the Tragic Muse* Revisited." *Eighteenth-Century Studies* 33.3 (2000): 401–30.

———. "Siddons Rediviva: Death, Memory, and Theatrical Afterlife," in Tom Mole, *Romanticism and Celebrity Culture 1750–1850*. Cambridge: Cambridge University Press, 1009. 120–40.

McWhir, Anne. "Revising Rowe's *The Fair Penitent*: Goldsmith, Holcroft, and Wollstonecraft." *Women's Studies* 304 (1992): 827–30.

Mellor, Anne K. "Preface." *Maria or the Wrongs of Woman*. By Mary Wollstonecraft. New York: Norton, 1975. 5–18.

Mole, Tom. *Romanticism and Celebrity Culture, 1750–1850*. Cambridge: Cambridge University Press, 2009.

Myers, Mitzi. "Mary Wollstonecraft's Literary Reviews." *Cambridge Companion to Mary Wollstonecraft*. Ed. Claudia L. Johnson. Cambridge: Cambridge University Press, 2002. 82–98.

O'Neill, Daniel I. *The Burke-Wollstonecraft Debate: Savagery, Civilization, and Democracy*. University Park: Pennsylvania State University Press, 2007.

Opie, Amelia. *Memorials of the Life of Amelia Opie*. Ed. Cecilia Lucy Bridewell. London: Longman, Brown, and Company, 1854.

Outram, Dorinda. *The Body and the French Revolution: Sex, Class, and Political Culture*. New Haven: Yale University Press, 1989.

Ozouf, Mona. *La Fete Revolutionnaire 1789–1799*. Paris: Editions Gallimard, 1976.

Paine, Thomas. *Rights of Man*. Ed. Henry Collins. New York: Penguin, 1984.

Parker, Andrew, and Eve Kosofsky Sedgwick, eds. *Performativity and Performance*. New York and London: Routledge, 1995.

Pascoe, Judith. *Romantic Theatricality: Gender, Poetry, and Spectatorship*. Ithaca: Cornell University Press, 1977.

———. "Siddons Speaks: Theatre Voices and Recorded Memory." *Shakespeare Survey* 61 (2008): 1–12.

Paulson, Ronald. *Emblem and Expression: Meaning in English Art of the Eighteenth Century*. London: Thames and Hudson, 1975.

Pocock, J.G.A. *Virtue, Commerce, and History: Essays in Political Thought and History*. Cambridge: Cambridge University Press, 1985.

Poovey, Mary. *The Proper Lady and the Woman Writer: Ideology as Style in the Works of Mary Wollstonecraft, Mary Shelley, and Jane Austen*. Chicago: University of Chicago Press, 1984.

Rajan, Tillotama. "Wollstonecraft and Godwin: Reading the Secrets of the Political Novel." *Studies in Romanticism* 27 (1988): 221–51.

Reinelt, Janelle G., and Joseph R. Roach, eds. *Critical Theory and Performance*. Ann Arbor: University of Michigan Press, 1992.

Richards, Cynthia, ed. *Memoirs of the Author of A Vindication of the Rights of Woman*. By William Godwin. Glen Allen, VA: College Publishing, 2004.

Rowe, Nicolas. *The Fair Penitent*. Ed. Malcolm Goldstein. Lincoln: University of Nebraska Press, 1969.

Russell, Gillian. *The Theatres of War: Performance, Politics, and Society, 1793–1815*. Oxford: Oxford University Press, 1995.

Saint-Amand, Pierre. "Terrorizing Marie Antoinette." Trans. Jennifer Curtiss Gage. *Critical Inquiry* 2.3 (1994): 379–400.

Samet, Elizabeth D. "Spectacular History and the Politics of Theater: Sympathetic Arts in the Shadow of the Bastille." *PMLA* 118.5 (2003): 1305–19.

Sapiro, Virginia. *A Vindication of Political Virtue: The Political Theory of Mary Wollstonecraft*. Chicago: University of Chicago Press, 1992.

Schulman, Alex. "Gothic Piles and Endless Forests: Wollstonecraft Between Burke and Rousseau." *Eighteenth-Century Studies* 41.1 (2007): 41–54.

Scott, Joan. *Only Paradoxes to Offer: French Feminists and the Rights of Man*. Cambridge: Harvard University Press, 1996.

Senelick, Laurence. *The Changing Room: Sex, Drag, and Theatre*. London and New York: Routledge, 2000.

Siddons, Sarah. *The Reminiscences of Sarah Kemble Siddons, 1773–1785*. Ed. William Van Lennep. Cambridge: Cambridge University Press, 1942.

Stone, Lawrence. *Broken Lives: Separation and Divorce in England, 1660–1857*. Oxford: Oxford University Press, 1993.

———. *Road to Divorce: England 1530–1987*. Oxford: Oxford University Press, 1990.

Straub, Kristina. *Sexual Suspects: Eighteenth-Century Players and Sexual Ideology*. Princeton: Princeton University Press, 1992.

Taylor, Barbara. *Wollstonecraft and the Radical Imagination*. Cambridge: Cambridge University Press, 2002.

Todd, Janet. "Introduction." *A Vindication of the Rights of Men, A Vindication of the Rights of Woman, An Historical and Moral View of the French Revolution*. By Mary Wollstonecraft. Oxford: Oxford University Press, 1993. vii–xxx.

———. *Mary Wollstonecraft: A Revolutionary Life*. London: Weidenfeld and Nicolson, 2000.

Tomalin, Claire. *The Life and Death of Mary Wollstonecraft*. London: Weidenfeld and Nicolson, 1974.

Trials for Adultery; Or, the The History of Divorces. Clark, NJ: Lawbook Exchange, 2006.

Trumbach, Randolph. *Sex and the Gender Revolution*. Chicago and London: University of Chicago Press, 1998.

Tumir, Vaska. "She-Tragedy and Its Men: Conflict and Form in *The Orphan* and *The Fair Penitent*." *Studies in English Literature* 30.0 (1990): 411–29.

Turner, David M. *Fashioning Adultery: Gender, Sex, and Civility in England, 1660–1740*. Cambridge: Cambridge University Press, 2002.

Wardle, Ralph, ed., *Collected Letters of Mary Wollstonecraft*. Ithaca: Cornell University Press, 1979.

———. *Mary Wollstonecraft: A Critical Biography*. Lawrence: University of Kansas Press, 1951.

Weinsheimer, Joel. "Mrs. Siddons, The Tragic Muse, and the Problem of 'As.'" *The Journal of Aesthetics and Art Criticism* 36.3 (1978): 317–28.

Wendorf, Richard. *Sir Joshua Reynolds: The Painter in Society*. Cambridge: Harvard University Press, 1996.

Wharam, Alan. *The Treason Trials, 1794*. Leicester: Leicester University Press, 1991.

Wilson, Anna. *Persuasive Fictions: Feminist Narrative and Critical Myth*. Lewisburg, PA: Bucknell University Press, 2001.

Wilson, Brett. "Jane Shore and the Jacobites: Nicholas Rowe, The Pretender, and the National She-Tragedy." *ELH* 72.4 (2005): 823–42.

Wollstonecraft, Mary. *The Collected Letters of Mary Wollstonecraft*. Ed. Janet Todd. London: Penguin, 2003.

———. *An Historical and Moral View of the French Revolution. The Works of Mary Wollstonecraft*. Ed. Janet Todd and Marilyn Butler. 7 vols. Volume 6. New York: New York University Press, 1989.

———. *Letters Written During a Short Residence in Sweden, Norway, and Denmark*. Ed. Carol H. Poston. Lincoln: University of Nebraska Press, 1976.

———. *Maria, or the Wrongs of Woman*. Ed. Ann K. Mellor. New York: Norton, 1975.

———. *Thoughts on the Education of Daughters. The Works of Mary Wollstonecraft*. Ed. Janet Todd and Marilyn Butler. 7 vols. Volume 4. New York: New York University Press, 1989.

————. *A Vindication of the Rights of Men and A Vindication of the Rights of Woman*. Ed. D.L. Macdonald and Kathleen Scherf. Orchard Park, New York: Broadview Press, 1997.

————. *A Vindication of the Rights of Woman*. 2nd ed. Ed. Carol Poston. New York: Norton, 1985.

Woo, Celestine. "Sarah Siddons as Hamlet: Three Decades, Five Towns, Absent Breeches, and Rife Critical Confusion." *ANQ* 20.1 (2007): 37–43.

Wordsworth, William. *Lyrical Ballads*. Ed. W.J.B. Owen. 2nd edition. Oxford: Oxford University Press, 1970.

————. *The Prelude: 1799, 1805, 1850*. Ed. M.H. Abrams, Stephen Gill, and Jonathon Wordsworth. New York: Norton, 1979.

Worthen, W.B. "Drama, Performativity, and Performance." *PMLA* 113.5 (Oct. 1998): 1093–107.

Zerilli, Linda. "'The Furies of Hell': Women in Burke's 'French Revolution.'" *Signifying Woman: Culture and Chaos in Rousseau, Burke, and Mill*. Ithaca: Cornell University Press, 1994. 60–94.

Index